The Essentials of Special Education Research

SPECIAL EDUCATION LAW, POLICY, AND PRACTICE

Series Editors

Mitchell L. Yell, PhD, University of South Carolina, and David F. Bateman, PhD, American Institutes for Research

The Special Education Law, Policy, and Practice series highlights current trends and legal issues in the education of students with disabilities. The books in this series link legal requirements, evidence-based instruction, and practical applications for working with students with disabilities. The titles are designed to be textbooks for general education and special education preservice education programs and also for practicing teachers, administrators, principals, school counselors, school psychologists, parents, and others interested in improving the lives of students. The series is committed to research-based practices to provide appropriate and meaningful educational programming for students with disabilities and their families.

Titles in Series

Dispute Resolution Under the IDEA: Understanding, Avoiding, and Managing Special Education Disputes by D. F. Bateman, M. L. Yell, and J. S. Dorego

Advocating for the Common Good: People, Politics, Process, and Policy on Capitol Hill by J. E. West

Related Services in Special Education: Working Together as a Team by L. Goran and D. F. Bateman

The Essentials of Special Education Advocacy by A. M. Markelz, S. A. Nagro, K. Monnin, and D. F. Bateman

Disability and Motor Behavior: A Handbook of Research by A. S. Brian and P. S. Haibach-Beach

Supporting and Accommodating Students with Special Health Care Needs by A. D. S. Angelov and M. Rattermann

You're Hired! Practical Strategies for Guiding Individuals with Autism Spectrum Disorder to Competitive Employment by P. S. Arter, T. B. H. Brown, and J. Barna

Unraveling Dyslexia: A Guide for Teachers and Families by K. L. Sayeski

Disability, Intersectionality, and Belonging in Special Education: Socioculturally Sustaining Practices by E. A. Harkins Monaco, L. L. Stansberry Brusnahan, M. C. Fuller, and M. Odima Jr.

The Educator's Guide to Action Research: Practical Connections for Implementation of Data-Driven Decision-Making by M. E. Little, D. D. Slanda, and E. Cramer

The Essentials of Special Education Research by A. M. Markelz and B. Riden

For a full list of books in this series, visit https://rowman.com/Action/SERIES/_/RLSELPP/Special-Education-Law,-Policy,-and-Practice

The Essentials of Special Education Research

Andrew M. Markelz and Benjamin S. Riden

ROWMAN & LITTLEFIELD
Lanham • Boulder • New York • London

Published by Rowman & Littlefield
An imprint of The Rowman & Littlefield Publishing Group, Inc.
4501 Forbes Boulevard, Suite 200, Lanham, Maryland 20706
www.rowman.com
86-90 Paul Street, London EC2A 4NE

Copyright © 2024 by Andrew M. Markelz and Benjamin S. Riden

All rights reserved. No part of this book may be reproduced in any form or by any electronic or mechanical means, including information storage and retrieval systems, without written permission from the publisher, except by a reviewer who may quote passages in a review.

British Library Cataloguing in Publication Information available

Library of Congress Cataloging-in-Publication Data

Names: Markelz, Andrew M., 1980- author. | Riden, Benjamin S., author.
Title: The essentials of special education research / Andrew M. Markelz and Benjamin S. Riden.
Description: Lanham, Maryland : Rowman & Littlefield, 2024. | Series: Special education law, policy, and practice | Includes bibliographical references and index.
Identifiers: LCCN 2024027343 (print) | LCCN 2024027344 (ebook) | ISBN 9781538193341 (cloth) | ISBN 9781538193358 (paperback) | ISBN 9781538193365 (epub)
Subjects: LCSH: Special education--Research--Methodology.
Classification: LCC LC3969 .M338 2024 (print) | LCC LC3969 (ebook) | DDC 371.9072/1--dc23/eng/20240718
LC record available at https://lccn.loc.gov/2024027343
LC ebook record available at https://lccn.loc.gov/2024027344

Contents

PART I: INTRODUCTION TO RESEARCH   1

Chapter 1: History of Research   3

    What Is Educational Research?   4

    Why Are Ethics Important When Conducting Educational Research?   9

    How Has Research Affected the Field of Special Education?   10

    Where Can I Find More Information About Educational Research?   16

    Discussion Questions | Key Terms   17

Chapter 2: Finding and Reading Educational Research   21

    Why Read Educational Research Articles?   22

    How Do I Access Educational Research Articles?   25

    How Do I Read Educational Research Articles?   34

    Where Can I Find More Information About Finding and Reading Educational Research Articles?   37

    Discussion Questions | Key Terms   39

PART II: METHODOLOGIES IN SPECIAL EDUCATION RESEARCH   43

Chapter 3: Systematic Literature Reviews   45

    What Are Systematic Literature Reviews?   46

What Are the Critical Components of Systematic Literature Reviews?	47
What Are the Limitations of Systematic Literature Reviews?	52
How Do I Interpret Systematic Literature Reviews?	55
Where Can I Find More Information About Systematic Literature Reviews?	58
Discussion Questions | Key Terms	59
Chapter 4: Group Research Designs	**61**
What Are Group Research Designs?	62
What Are the Critical Components of Group Research Designs?	70
What Are the Limitations of Group Research Designs?	75
How Do I Interpret Group Research Designs?	79
Where Can I Find More Information About Group Research Designs?	80
Discussion Questions | Key Terms	81
Chapter 5: Single-Case Research Designs	**85**
What Are Single-Case Research Designs?	86
What Are the Critical Components of Single-Case Research Designs?	87
What Are the Limitations of Single-Case Research Designs?	96
How Do I Interpret Single-Case Research Designs?	99
Where Can I Find More Information About Single-Case Research Designs?	103
Discussion Questions | Key Terms	105
Chapter 6: Qualitative Research Designs	**109**
What Are Qualitative Research Designs?	110
What Are the Critical Components of Qualitative Research Designs?	115
What Are the Limitations of Qualitative Research Designs?	118
How Do I Interpret Qualitative Research Designs?	121

Where Can I Find More Information About Qualitative Research Designs?	123
Discussion Questions | Key Terms	124
Chapter 7: Additional Research Methods	**129**
What, Why, and How Are Some Additional Research Methods Used in Special Education Research?	130
Where Can I Find More Information About These Research Methods?	141
Discussion Questions | Key Terms	142
PART III: READING AND IMPLEMENTING RESEARCH IN PRACTICE	**145**
Chapter 8: Classroom Management	**147**
What Are Some of the Issues Concerning Classroom Management?	148
What Are Some of the Best Practices in Classroom Management?	149
How Do I Use Research to Address Classroom Management Issues?	156
Where Can I Find More Information About Classroom Management?	187
Discussion Questions | Key Terms	188
Chapter 9: Math Instruction	**191**
What Are Some of the Issues Concerning Math Instruction?	192
What Are Some of the Best Practices in Math Instruction?	193
How Do I Use Research to Address Math Instruction Issues?	196
Where Can I Find More Information About Math Instruction?	223
Discussion Questions | Key Terms	224
Chapter 10: Product and Curriculum Reviews	**227**
What Are Some of the Issues Concerning Product and Curriculum Reviews?	228
How Do I Assess the Validity of Products and Curricula?	231

How Do I Advocate for the Adoption of a Product or
    Curriculum in My School? 236

Where Can I Find More Information About Product and
    Curriculum Reviews? 239

Discussion Questions | Key Terms 240

Index 243

PART I

Introduction to Research

Chapter 1

History of Research

The evolution of science has been a long and winding road. In fact, even today, there is not one completely agreed-upon definition of the term *science*. In general, though, science is the search for understanding of the world around us. Intense debate has occurred for centuries on how best to view and understand the world and find lawful relations. Although ancient Egyptian and Babylonian records indicate investigations into nature and medical conditions with empirical methods—that is, observation, diagnosis, treatment, and scrutiny of outcomes—it was not until Aristotle and the Greek empire that modern science was born (O'Leary, 1949). Aristotle established the inductive–deductive method of inquiry. Induction is when an observation occurs, a pattern is recognized, and then a theory is made. For example, the flamingos here are pink, and all flamingos I have ever seen are pink; therefore, all flamingos must be pink. Deduction is idea first, followed by observation and then a conclusion. For example, all birds have feathers, and all cardinals are birds; therefore, all cardinals have feathers. Both deduction and induction are types of inference, which means reaching a conclusion based on evidence and reasoning. Aristotle established that cycles of the induction–deduction method of inquiry could be used to continue the advancement of knowledge (Gauch, 2003).

During the Middle Ages (400–1400 AD), scientists started combining theory with practice. Many Islamic scientists began using experimentation to obtain results and support theories, yet religion and faith still remained huge components to event interpretation and human understanding. It was not until 1623 in a book titled *The Assayer* that Galileo first detailed the scientific method as we know it today. The 15th century is often called the Age of Science because, while not replacing religious explanation, scientific reasoning began to have an equal footing among leaders and scholars. Figure 1.1 outlines the iterative steps of the scientific method. With a process in place for observing and understanding the world around us, research was established as a systematic way to create new knowledge and/or use existing knowledge in

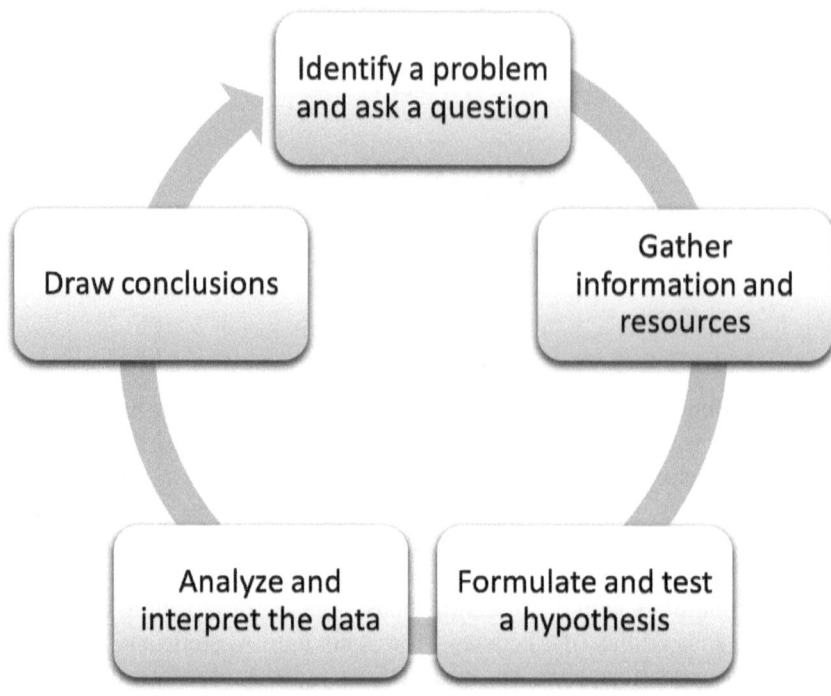

Figure 1.1 Steps in the Scientific Method.

new and creative ways to generate new concepts and understandings. Based in the scientific method, researchers across all domains of science have generated new knowledge and practices, propelling society toward greater understanding of the world around us. Educational researchers were no different. In this chapter, we discuss the foundations of educational research and answer these essential questions:

1. What is educational research?
2. Why are ethics important when conducting educational research?
3. How has research affected the field of special education?
4. Where can I find more information about educational research?

WHAT IS EDUCATIONAL RESEARCH?

The purpose of science is to describe and explain phenomena, predict events or outcomes, and improve practice (Gall et al., 2007). As an educator in the field of special education, it is quite easy to think of phenomena, events, and practices that would benefit from explanation or improvements. Educational research is a systematic way of examining issues related to education to generate new understanding. Although scientific inquiry and systematic research practices began centuries ago, educational research has a more recent history.

A Brief History of Educational Research

When people think of "science," they may think of fields such as chemistry, biology, and physics. These fields of science that explore the natural world are often referred to as **hard science**, where mathematical models are explicitly used to produce testable predictions. Hard sciences allow researchers to perform controlled experiments with quantifiable data to high degrees of accuracy and objectivity. Educational research is known as a **soft science**, where human behaviors are investigated and establishing measurable criteria, such as thoughts, feelings, and learning, may be difficult. Other fields of soft science include psychology, sociology, political science, and other social sciences.

The hard sciences may have been the first fields to develop rigorous methods of scientific inquiry; however, soft sciences are equally important in understanding the world around us. It is, after all, humans who are interacting with each other and trying to understand the world!

Educational research in the United States can be traced back to the late 1830s as schoolhouses, as we know them today, were established. It was during these fundamental years that society began to realize the importance of education to the functioning of a constitutional republic. Political leaders understood that an educated electorate was better for the country. In response to this progression of ideas, state governments passed compulsory education laws that required children to attend a certain amount of education. Even though every state within the United States had a compulsory education law by 1918, it is well documented that many minority and disabled children were excluded (Markelz & Bateman, 2021). Yet the formalization of public education created school supervision, planning, and data collection, all of which established a whole new field of inquiry based on human interactions in school settings.

The founding of John Hopkins University as the first research university in 1876 set the stage for the founding of additional elite research universities such as the University of Chicago and Stanford University. As more public K–12 schools were started across the country, more teachers needed to be trained to fill those roles. During the 1900s, there was exponential growth in universities, which created departments of education to offer bachelor's-, master's-, and doctoral-level degrees in education. Education was growing as a field within universities, yet pioneers of educational research were scorned by their faculty peers in other fields. In 1890, Harvard faculty were reported to say that the very idea of "educational science was bogus" (Powell, 1980, p. 78). A Stanford faculty member was quoted as saying, "Education is hardly considered to be up to the dignity of [either] a Science or an Art" (Sears & Henderson, 1957, p. 57).

Even though the hard science community rejected the promise of educational research, educational researchers found intellectual comradery with one another and formed national organizations, such as the American Educational Research Association (AERA) and the National Society of College Teachers of Education. These professional organizations helped define problems of the field and fostered professional self-consciousness among educationists and gave them visibility and validity as a professional group (Lagemann, 1997).

During the early 1900s, educational researchers at universities were small in number and privileged in character—mostly white, male, and Protestant. Yet they were responsible for some powerful insights concerning the process of learning. For example, Thorndike (1905) introduced the concept of **reinforcement** and was the first to apply psychological principles to the area of learning. Unfortunately, at that time, some members of the educational research community also gave authority to harmful theories about race and the nature of intelligence. But despite these deviations, which in hindsight are easy to see, the authority and expertise of educational research seemed secure as a legitimate field of inquiry.

During the 1920s, societal debates around the purpose of education put school curricula at the forefront of educational researchers' attention. Schools increasingly became responsible for preparing children to become contributing members of society. Priorities arose, such as providing vocational training to meet manufacturing workforce demands, preparing students for higher education to accelerate an expanding economy, and teaching moral and ethical character. While content-specific university departments (e.g., Math, Physics, Chemistry) still spurned the validity of education departments, educational researchers partnered with colleagues in public schools to develop and assess appropriate curricula (Freeman, 1924). By the 1930s, educational researchers and teachers in the field had curriculum development projects underway in most cities and states.

A fractioning of priorities occurred around this time between educational researchers. Some valued child-centered goals for education, which emphasized active, project-based curricula focused on the growth of the child. Others valued society-centered goals, which emphasized the preparation for life after school and the skills needed to contribute to society. Labaree (1997) suggested that three philosophical goals for education have been at the root of educational conflicts over the years: democratic equality, social efficiency, and social mobility. Those with a *democratic equality* approach to education believe democratic societies cannot exist without preparing children to take on the responsibilities of citizenship. Public schooling is seen as a public good, designed to prepare members of society for political roles (i.e., political participants and informed constituents). The *social efficiency* approach to schooling suggests society's economic well-being depends on the ability to prepare children to grow up and become contributing workers to fill necessary economic roles (e.g., teachers, doctors, entrepreneurs, engineers, and laborers). The foundation of this belief is that society benefits from a healthy economydriven by the productivity of its citizens. The *social mobility* philosophy of education is that schooling is a commodity that provides individuals with competitive advantages over other individuals who are struggling for desirable social positions. Education is a private good, consumed by individuals in their quest to compete against others for a limited number of privileged positions. According to Labaree (1997), these three philosophies have waxed and waned over time yet continue to affect society's prioritization of and resource allocation to education.

After the passage of the G.I. Bill in 1944 and the report of the Truman Commission on Higher Education (1947), more people began to think of college as a necessary postsecondary school path. The rise of the Cold War heightened parental and public worries about the competence of the next generation and the quality of schools. The public became critical of educators' move away from academics, and scholars among the hard science fields readily amplified these critiques. Discipline-based scholars saw their opportunity to restore their place within curriculum-making decisions.

Discipline-based scholars' involvement in curriculum research swung the pendulum in the opposite direction as academic content became the focus on "course-improvement" projects rather than assessing full curriculum. Scholars took a centralist approach to developing the basic outlines of school courses, then disseminated them outward to schools and teacher colleges. The aim of this approach was to anchor school subjects in the structures of individual disciplines (e.g., reading, math, and science) rather than a variety of theories across the states (Lagemann, 1997). Also, during the 1950s and 1960s, new lines of research in psychology, school administration, and the behavioral sciences developed, mostly due to philanthropic dollars from organizations such as the Ford Foundation.

At the height of the Cold War and Civil Rights Movement in the 1960s, there were substantial increases in federal funding for educational research. Universities developed research centers under the Cooperative Research Act of 1954, with millions of dollars aimed at areas of federal interest, such as urban education and school administration. The federal government's major move into public education with the Elementary and Secondary Education Act of 1965 (Markelz & Bateman, 2021) also established educational laboratories under Title IV to improve the links between research and school practice. In 1975, the Education for All Handicapped Children Act (EAHCA) further solidified the federal government's role in public education because states were no longer able to deny education to students with disabilities. Although research pertaining to children and people with disabilities started gaining momentum in the 1950s, the federal government's movement into special education was a catalyst for special education research.

Special Education Research

Traditional psychological research in the early 1900s had difficulty making predictions that could be tested experimentally because introspective methods relied on the measurement of thoughts and feelings. But in 1924, John B. Watson devised methods of **behaviorism**, which sought to understand behavior by measuring observable behaviors and events. These methods relied on earlier work by Edward Thorndike, who pioneered the "law of effect," which states that "responses that produce a satisfying effect in a particular situation become more likely to occur again in that situation, and responses that produce a discomforting effect become less likely to occur again in that situation" (Gray, 2011, pp. 108–109). These principles of behavior are called reinforcement and punishment. B. F. Skinner was also a major researcher in the area of behaviorism as he systematically examined the manner in which environmental variables control behavior. He identified two kinds of behavior that are controlled in different ways. **Respondent behaviors** are actions an organism takes in response to an antecedent stimuli in the environment (Cooper et al., 2020). These behaviors are involuntary, or reflexive, and generally help species survive over generations (e.g., the need to sleep, eat, and reproduce). **Operant behaviors** are voluntary actions an organism takes because they produce some type of consequence (Cooper et al., 2020). For example, a student works hard on their math test to get a good grade. These behaviors are learned over time, and the scientific inquiry into the antecedent–behavior–consequence contingency led to the establishment of **applied behavior analysis** (ABA).

ABA is a science devoted to developing procedures that produce observable changes in behavior (Baer et al., 1968). Ivar Lovaas was one of the first researchers in the 1960s to use ABA principles to teach children with autism and a founding member of the Autism Society of America in 1965. While more and more students with disabilities were being included in public education during the 1960s and 1970s, special education researchers heavily relied on behaviorism as the guiding theory of human learning.

Although ABA is often associated with autism intervention, its applications are far reaching into classroom instruction, schoolwide positive behavior support, and organizational behavior and management. The principles of behaviorism and procedures developed by ABA scientists are still dominant in the field of special education research today.

WHY ARE ETHICS IMPORTANT WHEN CONDUCTING EDUCATIONAL RESEARCH?

When people think of the term *ethics*, they often think of a distinction between right and wrong. In fact, the most common way of defining ethics is norms for conduct that distinguish between acceptable and unacceptable behavior (Resnik, 2020). Societies have legal rules to govern behavior, yet ethical norms tend to be broader and more informal than laws. An action may be legal but unethical or illegal but ethical. Simply look at the efforts of special education advocates to combat federal and state laws allowing the exclusion of children with disabilities from public education (Markelz et al., 2023). These advocates took an ethical stance against unethical laws.

Ethics in research establish standards and norms for researchers. There are several reasons why ethical norms in research are important. First, norms promote the overall purpose of research, such as seeking knowledge and truth and avoiding error. Second, research is often a collaborative endeavor; therefore, ethical standards promote the values that are needed for collaborative work, such as trust, accountability, and fairness. Third, ethical norms help ensure researchers can be held accountable to the public for their actions, which helps build public support to trust the quality and integrity of research. Finally, many ethical norms in research promote social responsibility, human rights, compliance with the law, and public health and safety. Table 1.1 is a list of common ethical principles of educational research.

Ethics in special education research are particularly important because researchers are often working with vulnerable populations, that is, children. One particular area of ethical concern regarding ABA is the use of aversives (i.e., punishment) to reduce undesirable behaviors. Although decades of research support the effectiveness of punishment procedures to reduce behaviors (Lydon et al., 2015), specific punishment aversives, such as electric shock and physical restraint, present heightened risks of illness or injury to participants. As such, these types of punishment procedures have significantly declined in use over the decades by educational researchers and are considered by many as unethical practices. Furthermore, the use of reinforcement, rather than punishment, procedures to teach and encourage appropriate behaviors has been established as being more effective and socially beneficial (Scott et al., 2022).

Another ethical concern in educational research is focusing on socially valid behaviors. **Social validity** is the idea that there is value in treatment

Table 1.1 Ethical Principles of Educational Research

Honesty	Honestly report data, results, methods, and procedures. Do not fabricate, falsify, or misrepresent data.
Objectivity	Strive to avoid bias in experimental design, data analysis, data interpretation, peer review, grant writing, and other aspects of research where objectivity is expected.
Integrity	Act with sincerity and strive for consistency of thought and action.
Carefulness	Avoid careless errors and negligence. Critically examine your work and your colleagues' work. Keep good records of research activity, data collection, and research design.
Openness	Share data, results, ideas, tools, and resources.
Transparency	Disclose methods, materials, assumptions, analyses, and other information needed to evaluate your research.
Intellectual property	Give proper acknowledgment or credit for all contributions to research. Do not plagiarize.
Confidentiality	Protect confidential communications and personnel records.
Human subjects	When conducting research on human subjects, minimize harms and risks and maximize benefits; respect human dignity, privacy, and autonomy; and take special precautions with vulnerable populations.
Nondiscrimination	Avoid discrimination against colleagues, students, and research participants.

Adapted from Shamoo, A., & Resnik, D. (2015). *Responsible conduct of research* (3rd ed.). Oxford University Press.

goals, procedures, and outcomes. For example, do participants of a treatment consider the procedures acceptable? Are outcomes of the treatment important, and do participants and their caregivers value the changes in behavior? Social validity has become an important aspect of educational research as scientists have become more conscientious to ethical practices and have developed standardized measures for social validity assessments.

HOW HAS RESEARCH AFFECTED THE FIELD OF SPECIAL EDUCATION?

Prior to societal acknowledgment that people with disabilities have civil rights, the reality of disability history was mass disenfranchisement, marginalization, and physical and cognitive oppression (Martin & Rodriguez, 2022). With the passage of the EAHCA (1975), now known as the Individuals with Disabilities Education Act (IDEA, 2004), the inclusion of students with disabilities in public schools expedited the progression of special education research.

Early research methods employed in the field of special education were derived from medicine. In fact, many of the pioneers of services for individuals with disabilities were physicians. Yet as psychology and sociology developed into academic disciplines, they provided additional methodological tools for research in special education. By the early 2000s, the U.S. Department of Education sought to improve the quality of research in the field of education (Whitehurst, 2003) with the rationale that improved research would lead to improved practice, which would improve student outcomes.

There are issues in special education as a field that makes conducting scientific inquiry challenging. Odom and colleagues (2005) stated, "Special education research, because of its complexity, may be the hardest of the hardest-to-do science" (p. 139). The default setup for educational research is that there is a classroom, led by a teacher using a curriculum to guide instruction, and ongoing assessments of student learning. Based on these conditions, educational research in general attempts to answer questions such as the following:

- What do students need to learn?
- How can we improve the learning process?
- How can we help teachers teach better?

These questions are also very important in special education research; however, there are additional complexities to special education research that general education researchers do not encounter.

One intricate aspect of special education research is the variability of student participants. The IDEA (2004) identifies 13 disability categories that children can qualify under for services; however, within those categories are vast spectrums of individual conditions. One student may have a mild intellectual disability requiring minimal supports and services in the general education setting. Another student may also have an intellectual disability but require extensive one-to-one supports and services to be successful in the general education setting. The field examines children and students from birth through age 22. The setting of instruction varies from general education classrooms down a continuum of restrictiveness to hospitals or homebound placements. Finally, the breadth of academic and functional skills targeted for instruction spans the entirety of human functioning, for example, from intensive supports for basic living skills, such as eating and toileting, to minimal supports for success at institutions of higher education. Furthermore, adult interactions (e.g., teachers, therapists, and service providers) are necessary components of special education service delivery, and, therefore, these participants must also be considered in research procedures.

The extensiveness of special education has one main implication for research. That is, researchers cannot simply ask whether a practice is effective. They must clarify for whom the practice is effective and in what context. Unlike controlled environments with hard science laboratories, classrooms and human interactions are unpredictable and multifaceted. Special education researchers must approach scientific inquiry with a variety of methods. In Part II of this book, we will unpack the various methodologies used by special education researchers to answer questions and generate new knowledge. But for now, we will introduce the main categories of educational research approaches.

Types of Educational Research

There are three approaches to educational research that scientists use to answer questions and understand the world around them. Often, the approach a researcher uses is influenced by their perspective about research and how best to produce new knowledge. These three approaches are called quantitative, qualitative, and mixed methods.

Quantitative Approach

The quantitative approach to inquiry follows the steps of the scientific method previously introduced and, generally, gathers data in the form of numbers that can be analyzed. Quantitative researchers use a confirmatory process where a **hypothesis** is stated, and then a test (i.e., intervention) is done to gather empirical data to see if that hypothesis is confirmed. Quantitative researchers generally assume cognition and human behavior are explainable and try to identify cause-and-effect relationships that enable them to make predictions and **generalizations** (Johnson & Christensen, 2019). Quantitative researchers attempt to remain objective. They assume there is a reality to be observed and that rational observers who see the same phenomenon will agree on its characteristics. Because quantitative research methods developed from the hard sciences, quantitative educational researchers try to hold constant variables not being studied. By manipulating only one factor, the researcher can then attribute changes in an outcome to that manipulated variable.

Qualitative Approach

Qualitative researchers follow an exploratory process of inquiry and gather words, narratives, and descriptions of experiences to describe phenomenon. Qualitative researchers view human behavior as dynamic, fluid, and changing over time. Unlike quantitative researchers, qualitative researchers do not want to intervene in the natural flow of behavior. They try to understand dimensions of behavior to explain what and why a phenomenon is occurring. Qualitative researchers generally believe reality is **socially constructed** and that the researchers themselves bring bias and subjectivity into the research process as an instrument of data collection (Johnson & Christensen, 2019).

Mixed-Methods Approach

As you could have guessed, the mixed-methods approach is a combination of quantitative and qualitative confirmatory and exploratory processes. Mixed-methods researchers see value in both the quantitative and qualitative views on human behavior and adjust methodologies based on the research questions asked. According to mixed-method researchers, it is important to understand the subjective (individuals), the intersubjective (e.g., language and culture), and the objective (environmental and causal) realities in the world (Johnson & Christensen, 2019). Mixed-method researchers attempt to limit influence or bias; however, they recognize the undeniable presence one has when conducting research. Table 1.2 outlines the three research approaches and their particular emphasis on various aspects of the research process.

Benefits of Special Education Research

Without question, the introduction of special education in public schools and advancements in special education research have greatly benefited children with disabilities. From validating assessment procedures to identify children more accurately to integration of assistive technology for instructional purposes, across the spectrum of educational practices, the field has gained new knowledge and refined techniques. At its core, special education is about providing a child with a disability an individualized education program (IEP) that is reasonably calculated for that child to make appropriate progress in light of that child's circumstances (*Endrew F. v. Douglas County School*, 2017).

According to IDEA (2004), educators must use **specially designed instruction** to provide special education services. For students with disabilities to succeed in school, specially designed instruction should be used to change instructional content, methods, or delivery to meet a student's unique needs as a result of their disability. Special education researchers have been studying effective and appropriate specially designed instruction methods.

Evidence-based practices (EBPs) are skills, techniques, and strategies that have been consistently supported through experimental research studies or large-scale research field studies (IRIS Center, 2014). These practices consistently demonstrate positive outcomes on student academic and behavioral achievement and, therefore, should be prioritized by educators.

Table 1.2 Perspectives of Quantitative, Qualitative, and Mixed-Methods Research

	Quantitative	Qualitative	Mixed-Methods
Scientific method	Confirmatory	Exploratory	Confirmatory and exploratory
Nature of reality	Objective, observable	Subjective, socially constructed	Pluralistic, both objective and subjective
Human thought and behavior	Predictable, generalizable	Situational, social, personal, unpredictable	Dynamic, complex, partially predictable
Research objectives	Numerical description, causal explanation, prediction	Subjective description, empathetic understanding, and exploration	Provide complex and fuller understanding, multiple perspectives
Interest	Identify general scientific laws	Understand particular groups and individuals	Connect theory and practice
Nature of observation	Study behavior under controlled conditions; isolate the causal effect of single variables	Study behavior in natural settings; attempt to understand insiders' views and perspectives	Study multiple contexts, perspectives, and conditions as they operate together
Nature of data	Numerical variables	Words, images, categories	Mixture of variables, including numbers and words
Data analysis	Identify statistical/causal relationships among variables	Identify patterns, themes, and holistic features	Quantitative and qualitative analysis used separately and in combination
Results	Generalizable findings representing objective outsider viewpoints	Particularistic findings representing insider viewpoints	Subjective insider and objective outsider findings represent multiple dimensions of viewpoints

Adapted from Johnson, R. B., & Christensen, L. (2019). *Educational research: Quantitative, qualitative, and mixed approaches* (7th ed.). Sage.

In addition to EBPs, the Council for Exceptional Children (CEC), in collaboration with a team of special education researchers, has identified 22 **high-leverage practices** (HLPs) that every special education teacher should master and be able to demonstrate (McLeskey et al., 2017). The practices are used frequently in classrooms and have been shown through research to improve student outcomes if successfully implemented. Figure 1.2 lists the 22 HLPs by their four domains: collaboration, assessment, social/emotional/behavioral, and instruction.

One indicator of the benefits of special education is the graduation rates of students with disabilities. During the 2019–2020 school year, 70.6% of students with disabilities graduated from public high school (National Center for Education Statistics, 2023). For nearly 50 years, the IDEA (2004) has

High-Leverage Practices by Domain

Collaboration

HLP 1 - Collaborate with professionals to increase student success.
HLP 2 - Organize and facilitate effective meetings with professionals and families.

Assessment

HLP 4 - Use multiple sources of information to develop a comprehensive understanding of a student's strengths and needs.
HLP 5 - Interpret and communicate assessment information with stakeholders to collaboratively design and implement educational programs.
HLP 6 - Use student assessment data, analyze instructional practices, and make necessary adjustments that improve student outcomes.

Social / Emotional / Behavioral

HLP 7 - Establish a consistent, organized, and respectful learning environment.
HLP 8 - Provide positive and constructive feedback to guide students' learning and behavior.
HLP 9 - Teach social behaviors.
HLP 10 - Conduct functional behavioral assessments to develop individual student behavior support plans.

Instruction

HLP 11 - Identify and prioritize long- and short-term learning goals.
HLP 12 - Systematically design instruction toward a specific learning goal.
HLP 13 - Adapt curriculum tasks and materials for specific learning goals.
HLP 14 - Teach cognitive and metacognitive strategies to support learning and independence.
HLP 15 - Provide scaffolded support.
HLP 16 - Use explicit instruction.
HLP 17 - Use flexible grouping.
HLP 18 - Use strategies to promote active student engagement.
HLP 19 - Use assistive and instructional technologies.
HLP 20 - Provide intensive instruction.
HLP 21 - Teach students to maintain and generalize new learning across time and settings.
HLP 22 - Provide positive and constructive feedback to guide students' learning and behavior.

Figure 1.2 High-Leverage Practices by Domain

provided educational opportunity for students who previously were not even allowed access to school buildings. Students with disabilities today are now pursuing higher education in greater numbers and more meaningful employment opportunities and are living fuller lives with increased dignity.

It is important to note that even though significant progress has been made, work remains to be done regarding the equitable inclusion of people and students with disabilities in society and education. Disproportionality in special education remains a persistent problem. **Disproportionality** refers to the overrepresentation or underrepresentation of groups of students in contrast to their share of the general population (Kauffman et al., 2017). Special education stakeholders often note the overrepresentation of minority students receiving special education services due to their race or ethnicity. Similarly, disproportionality can refer to the overrepresentation of minority students in a more restrictive environment or disproportionate punishment for minority students (National Center for Learning Disabilities, 2017). Special education researchers must continue to advance the field by exploring factors that contribute to disproportionality. Conscious and subconscious biases can be explored further, assessment procedures can be improved, preservice and in-service training can be enhanced. By no means has the field of special education reached its pinnacle of progression; however, the positive trends of the past should encourage the field to continually purse new knowledge into the future for the betterment of students with disabilities.

WHERE CAN I FIND MORE INFORMATION ABOUT EDUCATIONAL RESEARCH?

American Educational Research Association: Educational researchers are guided by the American Educational Research Association. The stated ethical principles and code of conduct of this international organization can be found at https://www.aera.net/About-AERA/AERA-Rules-Policies/Professional-Ethics.

Applied Behavior Analysis: The following resource is provided by the Behavior Analyst Certification Board, which describes what behavior analysis is, subspecialties of ABA, and multiple videos of professionals in the field discussing the uses of ABA. You can find these resources at https://www.bacb.com/about-behavior-analysis/.

Educational Research: Quantitative, Qualitative, and Mixed Approaches: Johnson and Christensen (2019) wrote a textbook that comprehensively explores aspects of educational research. This book is written for graduate students and provides extensive detail into the various methodologies of quantitative, qualitative, and mixed-methods approaches to research.

Introduction to Educational Research: In this YouTube video, a brief overview is provided of what educational research is and why educational research is conducted. Watch the video at https://www.youtube.com/watch?v=PcEU3a2u3-w.

What Works Clearinghouse: The U.S. Department of Education established the What Works Clearinghouse (WWC), which has been a central and trusted source of scientific evidence on education programs, products, practices, and policies. The WWC reviews research, determines which studies meet rigorous standards, and summarizes the findings. It focuses on high-quality research to answer the question "What works in education?" Visit the WWC to search for evidence-based practices at https://ies.ed.gov/ncee/wwc/FWW.

DISCUSSION QUESTIONS

1. Discuss the roll ethical decision-making plays in educational research.
2. How has educational research changed over time? What have been some of the big questions scientists have tried to answer?
3. Thorndike introduced the "law of effect." What is the law of effect, and how did it influence behavioral scientists, such as B. F. Skinner? How does the law of effect continue to affect researchers in the behavioral sciences?
4. How has special education research benefited students with disabilities?
5. If the purpose of science is to explain phenomena, predict events or outcomes, and improve practices, what educational phenomena would you like explained or questions answered?

KEY TERMS

applied behavior analysis: A science devoted to developing procedures to produce observable changes in behavior.
behaviorism: A systematic approach to understanding behavior by examining environmental conditioning factors.
disproportionality: The overrepresentation or underrepresentation of groups of students in comparison to their share of the general population.
evidence-based practices: Specific teaching techniques that are supported by high-quality research to positively affect student outcomes.
generalization: Taking something specific and applying it more broadly.
hard science: Disciplines that use mathematical models and controlled experiments to produce quantifiable data and testable predictions.

high-leverage practices: Frequently used practices by special educators that have been shown to improve student outcomes if successfully implemented.

hypothesis: An idea that can be tested by observations or experiments about the natural world.

operant behavior: An action taken because it produces some type of consequence.

reinforcement: A consequence applied that will strengthen future behavior.

respondent behavior: An action taken in response to a stimulus in the environment.

socially constructed: Exists not in objective reality but as a result of human creation and agreement.

social validity: The social importance and acceptability of treatment goals, procedures, and outcomes.

soft science: Disciplines that examine human behavior in less controlled environments given the nature of living beings.

specially designed instruction: Changing instructional content, methods, or delivery to meet a student's unique needs as a result of their disability.

REFERENCES

Baer, D. M., Wolf, M. M., & Risley, T. R. (1968). Some current dimensions of applied behavior analysis. *Journal of Applied Behavior Analysis*, *1*(1), 91–97. https://doi.org/10.1901/jaba.1968.1-91

Cooper, J. O., Heron, T. E., & Heward, W. L. (2020). *Applied behavior analysis* (3rd ed.). Pearson.

Cooperative Research Act. Pub. L. No. 83–531 (1954).

Education for All Handicapped Children Act of 1975, 20 U.S.C. § 1401.

Elementary and Secondary Education Act. Pub. L. No. 89–10 (1965).

Endrew F. v. Douglas County School District, 137 S. Ct. 988 (2017).

Freeman, F. N. (1924). Review of Superintendent Wilson's paper. In *2nd yearbook of the NEA Department of Superintendence* (pp. 45–47). NEA.

Gall, M. D., Gall, J. P., & Borg, W. R. (2007). *Educational research: An introduction* (8th ed.). Pearson.

Gauch, H. G. (2003). *Scientific method in practice*. Cambridge University Press.

G.I. Bill. Pub. L. No. 78–346 (1944).

Gray, P. (2011). *Psychology* (6th ed.). Worth Publishers.

Individuals with Disabilities Education Act of 2004, 20 U.S.C. § 1400.

IRIS Center. (2014). *Evidence-based practices (part 1): Identifying and selecting a practice or program.* https://iris.peabody.vanderbilt.edu/module/ebp_01/

Johnson, R. B., & Christensen, L. (2019). *Educational research: Quantitative, qualitative, and mixed approaches* (7th ed.). Sage.

Kauffman, J. M., Nelson, C. M., Simpson, R. L., & Mock Ward, D. (2017). Contemporary issues. In J. M. Kauffman, D. P. Hallahan, & P. C. Pullen (Eds.), *Handbook of special education* (2nd ed., pp. 16–28). Routledge. https://doi.org/10.4324/9781315517698

Labaree, D. F. (1997). Public goods, private goods: The American struggle over educational goals. *American Educational Research Journal, 34*(1), 39–81. https://doi.org/10.2307/1163342

Lagemann, E. C. (1997). Contested terrain: A history of education research in the United States, 1890–1990. *Educational Researcher, 26*(9), 5–17.

Lydon, S., Healy, O., Moran, L., & Foody, C. (2015). A quantitative examination of punishment research. *Research in Developmental Disabilities, 36*, 470–484. https://doi.org/10.1016/j.ridd.2014.10.036

Markelz, A. M., & Bateman, D. F. (2021). *The essentials of special education law.* Rowman & Littlefield.

Markelz, A. M., Nagro, S. A., Monnin, K., & Bateman, D. F. (2023). *The essentials special education advocacy.* Rowman & Littlefield.

Martin, E., & Rodriquez, J. A. (2022) Historical foundations of special education law: A civil rights movement. In W. Murkowski & J. Rodriguez (Eds.), *Special education law and policy: From foundation to application* (pp. 37–72). Plural Publishing.

McLeskey, J., Barringer, M.-D., Billingsly, B., Brownell, M., Jackson, D., Kennedy, M., Lewis, T., Maheady, L., Rodriguez, J., Scheeler, M. C., Winn, J., & Ziegler, D. (2017). *High-leverage practices in special education.* Council for Exceptional Children & CEEDAR Center.

National Center for Education Statistics. (2023). *Public high school 4-year adjusted cohort graduation rate (ACGR), by race/ethnicity and selected demographic characteristics for the United States, the 50 states, the District of Columbia, and Puerto Rico: School year 2019–2020.* https://nces.ed.gov/ccd/tables/ACGR_RE_and_characteristics_2019-20.asp

National Center for Learning Disabilities. (2017). *Significant disproportionality in special education: Current trends and actions for impact.* https://web.archive.org/web/20230715172029/https://www.ncld.org/wp-content/uploads/2020/10/2020-NCLD-Disproportionality_Trends-and-Actions-for-Impact_FINAL-1.pdf

Odom, S. L., Brantlinger, E., Gersten, R., Horner, R. H., Thompson, B., & Harris, K. R. (2005). Research in special education: Scientific methods and evidence-based practices. *Exceptional Children, 71*(2), 137–148. https://doi.org/10.1177/001440290507100201

O'Leary, D. (1949). *How Greek science passed to the Arabs.* Routledge & Kegan Paul Ltd.

Powell, A. G. (1980). *The uncertain profession: Harvard and the search for educational authority.* Harvard University Press.

Resnik, D. B. (2020). *What is ethics in research and why is it important?* National Institute of Environmental Health Sciences. https://www.niehs.nih.gov/research/resources/bioethics/whatis/index.cfm

Scott, H. K., Jain, A., & Cogburn, M. (2022). *Behavior modification.* StatPearls Publishing.
Sears, J. B., & Henderson, A. D. (1957). *Cubberley of Stanford and his contribution to American education.* Stanford University Press.
Shamoo, A., & Resnik, D. (2015). *Responsible conduct of research* (3rd ed.). Oxford University Press.
Thorndike, E. L. (1905). *The elements of psychology.* A. G. Seiler.
Truman's Commission on Higher Education. (1947). *Higher education for American democracy.* Harper & Brothers Publishers.
Whitehurst, G. J. (2003). *The Institute of Education Sciences: New wine, new bottles.* Paper presented at the annual conference of the American Educational Research Association, Los Angeles. https://eric.ed.gov/?id=ED478983

Chapter 2

Finding and Reading Educational Research

Every day as a special education teacher is an opportunity to learn about your students, implement instructional strategies, collaborate with colleagues, and grow as a professional. Whether you are a preservice teacher with emerging experience or a veteran teacher with years of practice, the classroom is filled with new challenges and successes for you and your students. Even though one's formal education may end upon graduation and receiving a teaching license, informal education never ends. It is believed that Albert Einstein once said, "Commit yourself to lifelong learning. The most valuable asset you will ever have is your mind and what you put into it." To be a successful special education teacher, continuous learning is critical. You will get new students on your caseload. Individual student needs will change based on instruction and progress. Special education laws will change. New regulatory guidance will be provided. Educational research has and will continue to identify new best instructional practices. These are just a few examples of why a teacher's education never ends. Clearly, the profession of special education is not stagnant.

After reading Chapter 1, we know educational research is a systematic way of examining issues related to education to generate new understanding. Putting the historical progression of educational research into perspective indicates that knowledge and practices about teaching students with disabilities will continue to advance. Special education teachers must be capable and motivated to access and implement these new understandings. In Chapter 2, we will discuss how you can find and read educational research, and we will answer these essential questions:

1. Why read educational research articles?
2. How do I access educational research articles?

3. How do I read educational research articles?
4. Where can I find more information about finding and reading educational research articles?

WHY READ EDUCATIONAL RESEARCH ARTICLES?

Education is a unique field of study and practice because of a difference between educational scholars (i.e., researchers) and teachers in the field (i.e., practitioners). This distinction leads to a persistent problem called the **research-to-practice gap**, which has been identified and discussed in detail for decades (Cook & Odom, 2013). Although faculty at universities conduct scientific experiments and explore new knowledge about education, those findings are essentially meaningless if they are not consumed and implemented by administrators in schools and teachers in classrooms. Researchers communicating between themselves about what works best has no practical implication on student outcomes unless that new knowledge is transferred into the field and implemented with **fidelity**.

In contrast, consider medical research. Scientists developing medication conduct their research in controlled laboratory settings. Discoveries in one laboratory are easy to replicate and build upon in a different laboratory by other researchers. Once a breakthrough has been achieved, that medication is mass-produced, distributed to professionals in the field, and prescribed to patients. Doctors are not required to re-create the medication themselves under similarly controlled conditions; they simply learn about the utility of the medication and potential side effects, then use their professional judgment on when to prescribe it.

Teachers, on the other hand, do not have the luxury of simply prescribing interventions. They need to understand the environmental conditions in which the intervention was researched, the population and specific characteristics of the students researched, the exact procedures of the intervention, and how to monitor progress to ensure the intervention is effective. Teachers are required to do all these components while using their professional judgment because no two students nor classrooms are alike. Contextual factors will always play a role in the implementation of any teaching practice.

Given all these complexities when integrating research and practice, we contend that special education teachers are called to be **scientific practitioners**. The term developed from a training model in the field of psychology in the 1940s (Committee on Training in Clinical Psychology, 1947). The goal of the model was to train psychologists in research and practice so that each aspect could continually inform the other. Psychologists would be capable of applying psychological knowledge to their work with patients as well as possessing the ability to move the field forward and generate fresh knowledge in the form of new empirical findings, new theories, or new treatment programs.

Our interpretation of a scientific practitioner is slightly different than the one used in the traditional sense. Rather than conducting research in classroom settings, often referred to as **action research** (Lohmann, 2023), we believe scientific practitioners must know how to find, read, and implement researched practices in their classrooms to positively affect the outcomes of their students (Figure 2.1). Special education scholars continue to generate new knowledge about the field of special education, but it is up to special education teachers to consume that knowledge and implement current best strategies.

And thus, we have reached the purpose of this book. Bridging the research-to-practice gap requires scholars to conduct research and present their findings in practitioner-friendly ways, but at the same time, practitioners (i.e., you) must be able to do the following:

1. Identify and understand a problem in the classroom.
2. Know where to look for potential researched solutions.
3. Read and understand a variety of research articles to gather information.
4. Use professional judgment to implement researched strategies across individual contexts.

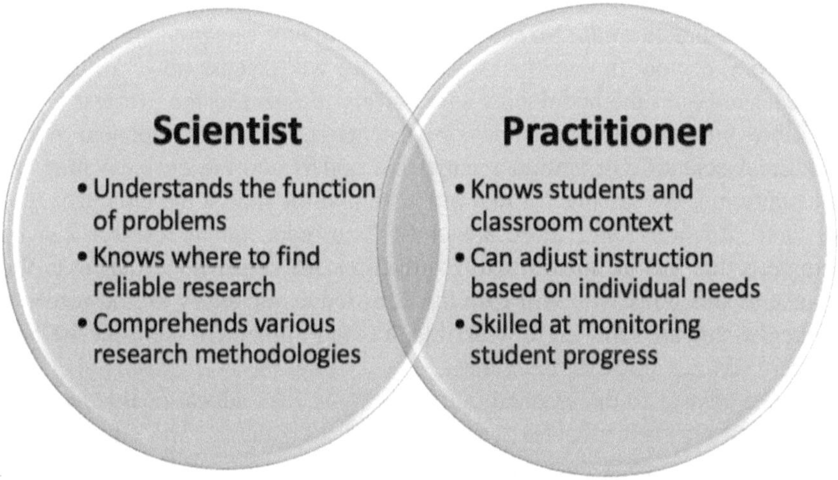

Scientist
- Understands the function of problems
- Knows where to find reliable research
- Comprehends various research methodologies

Practitioner
- Knows students and classroom context
- Can adjust instruction based on individual needs
- Skilled at monitoring student progress

Figure 2.1 Special Education Scientific Practitioner

Identify and Understand a Problem

It is not too challenging to identify when a persistent problem is occurring in your classroom. Scientific practitioners, however, go beyond just identifying a problem. They examine why a problem is occurring. In special education we call this determining the **function of behavior**. Although the first question might be to ask, "What is the problem?" the more important question to ask is, "Why is this problem occurring?"

Understanding the cause of a problem requires scientific practitioners to be proactive and investigative. Environmental factors should be observed. Data collection might be required to better understand how frequently or how long a problem has been occurring. Most importantly, the antecedent–behavior–consequence (ABC) contingency of the problem should be considered.

The **ABC contingency** is a foundational concept in special education. It refers to the relationship between environmental events and behaviors. The "antecedent" is the event or situation that precedes the behavior, the "behavior" is the observable action, and the "consequence" is the outcome or event that follows the behavior. The ABC contingency is used to identify patterns of behavior and their causes. By analyzing the ABC contingency, scientific practitioners can identify triggers for problems and/or reinforcing consequences that maintain the behavior. Antecedents or consequences can then be modified to affect the problem behavior.

In Part III of this book, we will identify several examples of common classroom problems. More importantly, we will investigate common reasons for these problems. Yet as we previously discussed, every student, teacher, and classroom is different. Individual contexts will contribute to the reasons a specific problem is occurring. This is part of the challenge of bridging the research-to-practice gap. No scientific study can re-create your students, your classroom, or you. In Part II of this book, we will discuss how various educational research methodologies address this problem to the greatest extent possible, but at the end of the day, the teacher is a critical component of that bridge. A scientific practitioner must first understand the problem they are encountering, the reasons for that problem, and the individual circumstances of their situation. Once those are understood, educational research can be explored that has examined similar situations. It is our hope that over the course of this book, you will gain the knowledge and skills to find research strategies that are relevant to your situation and implement them for the betterment of your students' outcomes.

So the answer to the essential question "Why read educational research?" is because classroom contexts are continually changing. The education of a teacher never ends because laws, policies, standards, and best practices evolve. Problems arise that may not have an obvious or easy solution.

Educational research can provide new knowledge and skills to help you do your job better and have greater job satisfaction. Educational research can provide answers to problems that have been tested and verified through a scientific process.

HOW DO I ACCESS EDUCATIONAL RESEARCH ARTICLES?

An incomprehensible amount of information is available at our fingertips. In fact, we are bombarded by information daily with social media and 24-hour news cycles. Wading through information that is **reliable** and accurate is a daunting task. Clicking on the first search result in a search engine may not be the best practice when searching for the best answer. In this section, we will discuss the different types of educational research publications and how to find them.

Types of Publications

Nonacademic Publications

The beauty of the internet is that anyone can present their ideas in a public forum. The problem with the internet is that anyone can present their ideas in a public forum. Blogs, websites, Pinterest pages, and TikTok are just a few examples of outlets for people to post content. There are no validation processes to determine whether the content posted is accurate or credible. Take, for example, a teacher who posted a TikTok video about a new math game she played with her students to learn fractions. The teacher swears that all of her students loved the game and mastered fractions in one lesson. That sounds great! Maybe you should try playing this math game in your classroom. You try it the next day during math class, and it goes horribly wrong. Your students get frustrated. They start arguing with each other and shut down. Very little learning takes place, and they definitely did not love the game nor did they master fractions. This example is not to say that all nonacademic publications should be ignored. Nor does it mean they cannot be based in sound pedagogical principles. The problem is that nonacademic publications are the "wild west" in terms of **validity**. There are few guardrails to steer teachers in the right direction of what practices are science based and reliable.

When non-science–based teaching practices get into the mainstream, it is very difficult to reverse the trends. The concept of learningstyles is a perfect example. Many teachers believe students have individual learning styles (e.g., visual, auditory, and kinesthetic) and that they should alter content presentation to match students' preferred learning style to increase engagement and comprehension. Although this is a deeply ingrained belief among teachers, there is no scientific evidence to support this belief (Khazan, 2018; Pashler et al., 2008). Countless hours and dollars have been spent conforming instruction based on a belief that holds no merit. Rather than spending significant resources on fads and invalid teaching practices, wouldn't it be best to dedicate those resources to teaching practices with a proven record of success?

Academic Publications

The best way to ensure educational research has gone through rigorous expert validation is by the **peer-review** process. All research submitted for publication in academic journals is sent for peer review to experts in the field to maintain high-quality standards of scientific research. The first stage of peer review is conducted by the journal editor, who will assess whether the article meets the minimum standards for review. For example, is it well written? Does it conform to the journal's requirements? Does the article discuss topics (e.g., student populations) that the journal is designed for? Once an article passes this stage, it is sent to two or more "double-anonymous" reviewers. This means the reviewers do not know who authored the article, nor do the article authors know who the reviewers are. The reviewers are expected to provide a report to the journal editor and authors with their suggestions on how to revise the article, improve it, and address any concerns the reviewers may have. In addition, the reviewers typically suggest whether the editor should do the following:

- Accept the article for publication with no changes (very rarely happens)
- Accept the article with minor changes (sometimes used)
- After the changes have been made, the article does not go for another round of reviews.
- Accept the article with major changes (often used)
- After the changes have been made, the article goes back to the reviewers to determine if the changes are satisfactory. This back-and-forth between authors and reviewers can happen multiple times.
- Reject the article

The peer-review process is often timely and not without criticism. On average, it can take between one to two years for an article to go through the peer-review process and be published. The inefficient lag in publication means published research is already dated and may not reflect current contexts. The COVID-19 pandemic is a great example. Even though the pandemic massively disrupted schools during the 2020 and 2021 school years, educational research on the impacts of school closures was not published until several years after. It takes time to conduct research and for that research to go through the peer-review process.

Another criticism of the peer-review process is that it may lead to **publication bias**. Editors of academic journals and reviewers want to publish studies that demonstrate some sort of positive effect. They want to publish articles that bring new knowledge to the field. In other words, they do not want to publish educational studies that did not work. But sometimes, finding out what *does not* work might be as useful as finding out what *does* work. Nevertheless, this overrepresentation of positive or confirmatory results and exclusion of negative results in research is known as publication bias (Franco et al., 2014).

To combat publication bias, some scholars are advocating for **open science** reforms to increase transparency, accessibility, and credibility in the research and publication process (Cook et al., 2018). Transparent processes, such as preregistration of studies, open data and materials, nonanonymous peer review, and open access to publications, would increase the validity, credibility, application, and impact of scientific special education research (Cook et al., 2021).

Although the peer-review process may have some drawbacks, it is the most reliable way of ensuring published research has undergone examination for quality. Unlike non-peer-reviewed outlets, such as blogs or Facebook posts, educators can have confidence that turning to peer-reviewed articles for solutions meets a high bar for scientific rigor. For special education teachers to be deemed scientific practitioners, you must be able to find, read, and implement peer-reviewed research from academic journals. The next sections of this chapter will explain how to do so, but first, a distinction needs to be drawn between two types of peer-reviewed academic journals.

Practitioner Journals Practitioner journals are designed for practitioners in the field (i.e., teachers and administrators). Practitioner journals are an excellent bridge to combat the research-to-practice gap. Rather than presenting **empirical studies**, practitioner journals publish articles that describe how to implement researched practices. They are written in user-friendly language with minimal technical jargon. The purpose of practitioner journals is to condense the scientific technicalities of research studies and present the content in a way that teachers in the field can read and implement. One example of a practitioner journal that every special educator must read is ***TEACHING Exceptional Children*** (https://journals.sagepub.com/home/tcx).

According to the Council for Exceptional Children (CEC), *TEACHING Exceptional Children* features research-to-practice information and materials for classroom use as well as current issues in special education teaching and learning. The journal is published six times a year on instructional technologies, strategies, procedures, and techniques with applications to students with exceptionalities.

Practitioner journals are excellent resources for special education teachers. Previously in this chapter, we identified the purpose of this book. Part two of that purpose was to "know where to look for potential researched solutions." Without question, we suggest special education teachers turn to practitioner journals/articles for researched solutions. These articles distill the complexities of research and focus on how to implement best practices. We wish more practitioner journals existed to help bridge the research-to-practice gap. Unfortunately, only a few practitioner journals are available and often require subscription fees to access the content. Under the "Where can I find more information about finding and reading educational research articles?" section at the end of this chapter, we list other practitioner journals that special education teachers should be aware of. But because practitioner journals are limited and not all answers can be found in the few available, we will now focus on the second type of academic journal that every scientific practitioner must be able to find and read. The remainder of this book will focus on research journals and research articles because it is critical that special education teachers be capable of finding, reading, and implementing practices from the research literature.

Research Journals Research journals are academic publications that disseminate scholarly research and scientific knowledge to academic communities. They are a place for researchers to share their findings, methodologies, and insights with fellow experts and the wider scientific community. All research journals have a specific discipline of focus. For example, *The Journal of Special Education* publishes research on improving education and services for individuals with disabilities. Sometimes a journal's focus is more targeted, such as the journal *Behavioral Disorders*, which exclusively publishes articles related to individuals with behavioral challenges, or the journal *Autism*, which publishes research to help improve the quality of life for individuals with autism or autism-related disorders. In the "Where can I find more information about finding and reading educational research articles?" at the end of this chapter, we list other prominent research journals that special education teachers should know about.

Unlike practitioner journals, research journals are written for other scholars in the field. The technical structure and writing styles used in research articles make them less accessible to practitioners who typically do not have PhD levels of scientific training. Nevertheless, research articles are where various aspects of special education are rigorously examined, such as instructional strategies, assessment methods, curriculum development, inclusion practices, classroom management, and interventions for specific disabilities. Research articles are where **evidence-based practices** are identified and scrutinized.

It is important to mention here that not all research journals are created equal. In fact, there is a spectrum of quality and reputation. On one end, there are well-established journals with high **impact factors**. On the other end of the spectrum are predatory journals. Predatory journals prioritize profit over academic integrity. They engage in unethical practices, such as charging exploitive author publication fees without providing proper peer review or editorial oversight. These journals often masquerade as legitimate scholarly outlets, making it challenging for researchers to identify them. They prey on researchers, particularly those under pressure to publish, by promising quick publication and wide dissemination of their work. Articles published in predatory journals, however, lack the rigorous review process and scholarly standards upheld by reputable academic journals. As a result, predatory journals contribute to the proliferation of low-quality, unreliable research, undermining the credibility of scientific literature as a whole.

High-quality research journals in the field of special education do not require researchers to pay a publication fee. Checking a journal's "author guidelines" online to see if there is a publication fee is a quick way to determine whether a journal may be publishing low-quality research. Any journal with an impact factor is also a quick way to determine whether it is reputable or not, although just because a journal does not have an impact factor does not mean it is not reputable or publishes poor research. Becoming familiar with common research journals within your areas of interest takes time and practice.

Because there are far more special education research journals than there are special education practitioner journals, much of the conversation about instructional best practices is taking place among scholars. Sometimes that information trickles down into classrooms, but with a lack of practitioner journals to assist in the transferring of knowledge or a lack of implementation training, the research-to-practice gap remains. We believe there is a plethora of valuable information being discussed by scholars within research journals. Providing the knowledge and skills for special education teachers to access that information would benefit them greatly as scientific practitioners. When special education teachers have a problem, they should be able to utilize research articles to find solutions. The first step in doing so is to know where and how to find research articles.

Finding Educational Research Articles

Finding educational research that answers your questions or provides insight into your specific circumstance is not a simple task. There is a lot of research taking place and being published in many academic journals. Knowing how to search for relevant research and quickly assess the quality is a necessary skill to help avoid wasting time on irrelevant literature.

What to Search

The first place to start is to identify what you want to search for. This is determined by the problem you are trying to solve or the information you are seeking. An easy way to begin is to formulate your initial search as a question. This question will generate several **keywords** that will be used to search for and find research articles. Figure 2.2 outlines an example of the process of taking a classroom problem, asking a question, and then identifying search keywords. It is important that your keywords ultimately fall into at least three buckets to narrow your search criteria.

Identifying the population of students you teach will help narrow search results to interventions that have been examined with similar populations. If you are a kindergarten teacher, for example, interventions that have been studied with high school students may not be age or developmentally appropriate for your students. Similarly, type and severity of disability may also be important considerations.

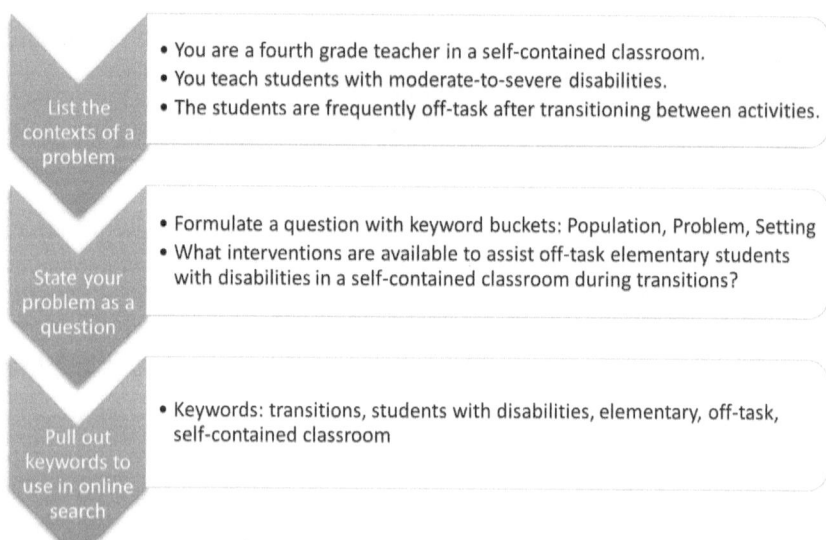

Figure 2.2   Process for Identifying Search Keywords

The second bucket that your keywords should identify is the specific problem, or behavior, you are examining. In the example in Figure 2.2, student off-task behavior is the problem. Research interventions are studied under strict conditions and observe changes in specific student behaviors. Explicitly identifying those behaviors will help narrow search results and find more relevant articles to your circumstances.

Lastly, the setting or conditions in which the behaviors occur will also provide additional details to narrow search results. In the example, students are having a difficult time during and after transitions between activities. Transition-targeted solutions for off-task behavior may be significantly different than solutions for off-task behaviors during silent reading time. Identifying these contextual factors with an ABC contingency mindset will help when searching for solutions.

There are many ways to ask a question based on a problem you are having in the classroom. Likewise, there are synonymous terms that could be used to describe your students, their behaviors, and the context. Part of the initial process in determining what to search for involves thinking about as many keywords as you can that may be relevant. Sometimes those keywords may be too broad, and sometimes they may be too narrow. Just like any internet search, there is a trial-and-error process to refine search keywords for the best results.

Where to Search

Once a list of keywords has been identified, it is time to start searching for articles. There are a number of databases and search engines that specialize in locating scholarly and academic work. Unfortunately, these databases often require university institutional access or have limited access without subscription fees. Therefore, we will focus on a publicly available database and one with much notoriety, Google Scholar.

Google Scholar The problem with a general online search is that using the keywords identified in Figure 2.2 could generate millions of hits with everything included on the internet, such as websites, videos, images, and nonacademic publications. To better target search results that are useful and credible, Google Scholar is a database that searches research articles, theses, and books from academic publishers.

Now that you have your keywords and Google Scholar ready, the next step is to plug in those words. Here is a list of basic search rules to be aware of when using Google Scholar that are relevant to other search engine databases as well:

1. Choose a range of descriptive words. Too few keywords will give overly broad results that are not applicable to your situation. Too many

keywords might overly narrow results and eliminate valuable articles. Trial and error is an expected part of the search process.
2. Use double quotation marks to search for precise phrases. Using quotation marks for the keyword "evidence-based practices" will guarantee results that include that specific phrase and not search for the three words individually, "evidence," "based," and "practices."
3. Use Boolean operators as needed. Boolean operators specify what words the results should or should not contain. There are three main Boolean operators to combine or exclude keywords: AND, OR, and NOT. Using the operator AND ensures both conditions are included in search results. For example, using the keywords and Boolean operator "elementary AND secondary" requires search results to include articles that mention "elementary" and "secondary." The operator OR broadens a search to include either keyword (e.g., "off-task OR disruptive"). The operator NOT is used to include the first term but not the second (e.g., "autism NOT intellectual disability").
4. The order in which you insert keywords matters. Google Scholar prioritizes search terms in the order of their appearance. "Math AND students with disabilities" will garner different results than "students with disabilities AND math."

Google Scholar also has an advanced search option as another way of narrowing search parameters (see Figure 2.3). Pay particular attention to the option in advanced search of "return articles published in." This option allows you to specify specific journals to search, such as practitioner journals (e.g., *TEACHING Exceptional Children*) or reputable research journals that you know publish research on specific populations (e.g., *Journal of Early Intervention* for early childhood populations).

Even with refined keywords and advanced search options, there is a possibility that many potential articles will appear. Examining the components of the Google Scholar search results page will help navigate those results. Figure 2.4 is an example of a search return using the keywords from our example.

University Institutional Access Although we recommend Google Scholar as the first database to use when searching for articles, all preservice teachers and many in-service teachers have access to their university's online library, which also has database search capabilities. Depending on the university's size and financial commitment to pay journal subscription fees, some libraries have extensive access to databases and articles, but some may be more limited. If an article is not publicly available on Google Scholar and you have institutional access to your university's library, it is

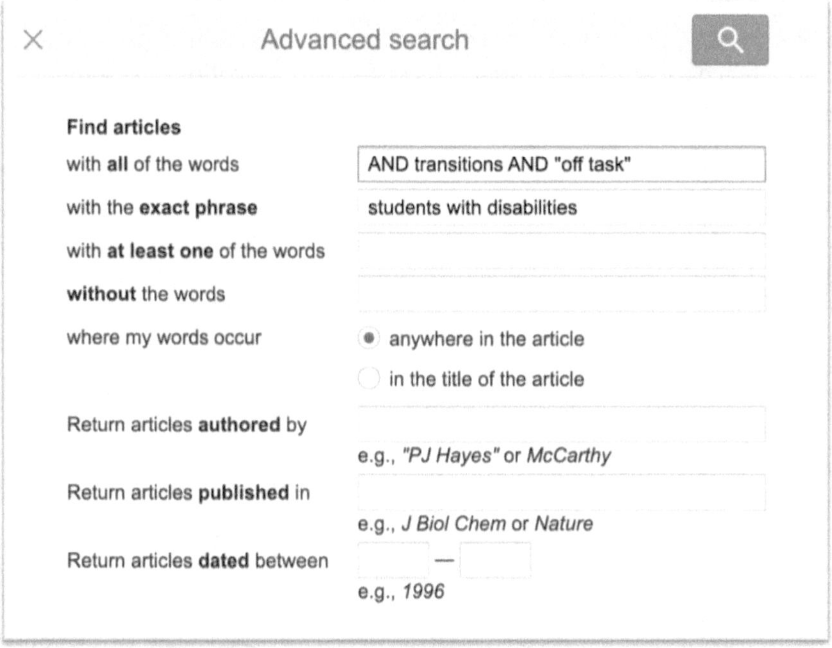

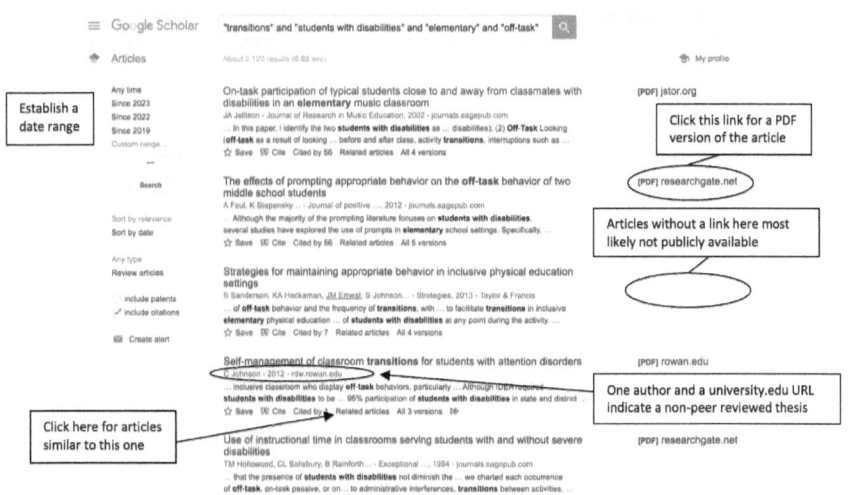

Figure 2.3 Google Scholar Advanced Search

Figure 2.4 Google Scholar Search Results Page

worth conducting a keyword search to see if additional access is available. Unfortunately, the cost structures associated with publishing peer-reviewed research (i.e., journal subscription fees) limits availability to practitioners, which is a contributor to the research-to-practice gap (Dew & Boydell, 2017).

Emailing Research Authors Most published research articles will have a "correspondence section" on the first page of the article where an author's contact information is listed. Simply emailing the corresponding author and asking for a PDF copy of the article is a great way to access research that may be inaccessible otherwise. Educational researchers conduct studies to discover new knowledge, and they publish those studies to disseminate the findings. We are confident that they would happily share a PDF of their study to assist practitioners in bettering their practice and affecting the outcomes of students.

HOW DO I READ EDUCATIONAL RESEARCH ARTICLES?

Once a potentially beneficial research article has been identified through database searching, the next step is to access whether the article is pertinent to your situation. Part II of this book will explore each component of a research article as it relates to a particular research methodology in greater detail; however, almost all research articles follow a similar structure. Knowing that structure will help you more quickly skim an article to determine if a more careful read is warranted.

The Title

Every research article has a title that should be clear and concise. The title will be the first component read during the search process and will almost always give some immediate sense of what the article is about. A good title should identify the three buckets of a research article (i.e., the population, the problem, and the setting) to give readers enough information to determine if further reading of the article is justified.

The Abstract

If the title has provided enough information to convince a reader to examine more of the article, the abstract is the next component worth reading. Abstracts are almost always publicly available. Abstracts are generally 100 to 250 words long and are designed to do the following: (a) provide an overview of the article, (b) address how and why the research was done, (c) describe research participants and setting, (d) specify the type of research design and analysis, and (e) summarize key findings. Abstracts are very important components of a research article because the decision to read further is greatly affected by its content.

The Introduction

Sometimes the introduction is labeled as such in an article, but often it is not. After the abstract and up to the methods section of an article is the introduction. The introduction comprises the rationale, the literature review, and the purpose of the research.

The rationale addresses the important reasons the researchers looked at their topic in the first place. The rationale answers the "So what?" question that readers may have about the topic being studied. Sometimes the researchers will explicitly state what their rationales are for conducting the research. Other times, the rationales will be implied as the researchers describe the context and connection to larger educational issues. An important part of the rationale section is for researchers to discuss previous literature on their topic.

The literature review of an introduction is an important part because previous research that is relevant to the study is discussed, critiqued, and analyzed. The literature review allows researchers to clearly state what is already known about the topic and to identify areas needing further exploration. Based on the researchers' rationales and literature review, the purpose of the research study should emerge.

The purpose is generally stated at the end of the introduction section to summarize the rationale and literature review and then state what the research study is attempting to accomplish. In many ways, the purpose is the concrete application of the rationale. The purpose is often structured like this: "Because of X, Y, and Z, the purpose of this research is to do A, B, and C." Having a clear understanding of the rationales and purposes of the research can help you decide whether those issues are important to you as well. If the introduction convinces you that the article is valuable to your situation, then continuing into the "heart" of the article is worthwhile.

The Research Question

As we know from the scientific process, the first step in conducting research is to ask a question. All research articles will have at least one research question that is clear and explicit. The research question is almost like the title of the method section. It specifically states what question the researchers are trying to answer. Most often, the research question will identify the **independent**

variable and the **dependent variable**. The independent variable (IV) is what the researcher manipulates to cause an effect. The dependent variable (DV) is what the researcher wants to see changed. When trying to determine whether X caused Y, X is the IV that produces change in Y, the DV. For example, a researcher wants to see if a particular reading program has effects on student reading scores. The researcher implements the reading program (i.e., the IV) and measures changes in student reading scores (i.e., the DV).

The Method

The method section details very clearly how researchers plan to answer their research question. A good method section will answer the following questions: who, what, how, when, and where. A method section should show that the researchers measured or described what they intended to; that they implemented research procedures in a precise and consistent manner; and that they interpreted their data in a strategic, unbiased way. In carefully doing so, the results of their research will be seen as valid, reliable, and trustworthy. Most method sections are organized chronologically starting with what happened first (e.g., the recruitment and selection of participants) and ending with what happened last (e.g., the coding and analysis of data) but may vary depending on research methodology. The method section is also where the IV and DV are meticulously described so that readers know exactly what the researchers were implementing and how they were measuring outcomes.

The Results

The results section of an article will report key findings from the study and (hopefully) answers to the research questions previously stated. Results are often presented in tables, graphs, or narrative descriptions of the data collected during the study. The results section of an article is strictly a fact-reporting section and is not a place for researchers to interpret their findings. Objective reporting of the data collected is essential.

The Discussion

The discussion section is where researchers explore what the results mean and how to contextualize them within other educational research issues and findings. Researchers will interpret their findings to answer the following: What happened? What was not expected? What do these results mean? What should other researchers interested in this topic do next? Oftentimes, researchers will connect their findings back to the rationales from the introduction section. This circular justification helps readers consider the importance of the research findings within the previous literature gaps.

The discussion section will also include a part where the researchers discuss limitations of the study. No study is without limitations. Given the challenges of conducting social science research where many variables are uncontrollable, there is bound to be characteristics of the study that affected the interpretation of results. Identifying study limitations helps readers understand the constraints of generalizing results and provides future researchers valuable information when designing similar studies.

Lastly, a discussion section will typically have an implications section where researchers attempt to reflect on the potential impact of their research study. Within educational research, this often translates into practical classroom application. What is the tangible takeaway from the study? What new knowledge has been generated from the study, and how does it affect practice? The implications of the discussion section are valuable for readers because they help move them from theoretical principles to applicable implementation.

The components of a research article that make up its structure can be visualized as an hourglass model. Figure 2.5 demonstrates the flow of concepts from broad in the beginning stages of the introduction to very narrow and controlled when detailing data collection and analysis procedures. The spectrum of concepts broadens out again as researchers analyze their findings and draw conclusions pertaining to the research questions, then even broader as they generalize those findings to the field at large. Almost all research articles will follow this hourglass model because it is an effective and time-tested structure of presenting and discussing research.

WHERE CAN I FIND MORE INFORMATION ABOUT FINDING AND READING EDUCATIONAL RESEARCH ARTICLES?

Accessing Open Peer-Reviewed Research: In this article by Cook and colleagues (2023), the authors described types of peer-reviewed articles and open-access publishing, provided guidance for searching open-access publications, and modeled how to email authors direction for articles that are not openly accessible. Read the article at https://doi.org/10.35542/osf.io/8sr9g.

Council for Exceptional Children (CEC): The CEC is the largest international professional organization dedicated to improving the success of children and youth with disabilities and/or gifts and talents. Resources are available for nonmembers; however, membership provides substantial access to professional development opportunities, including full access to

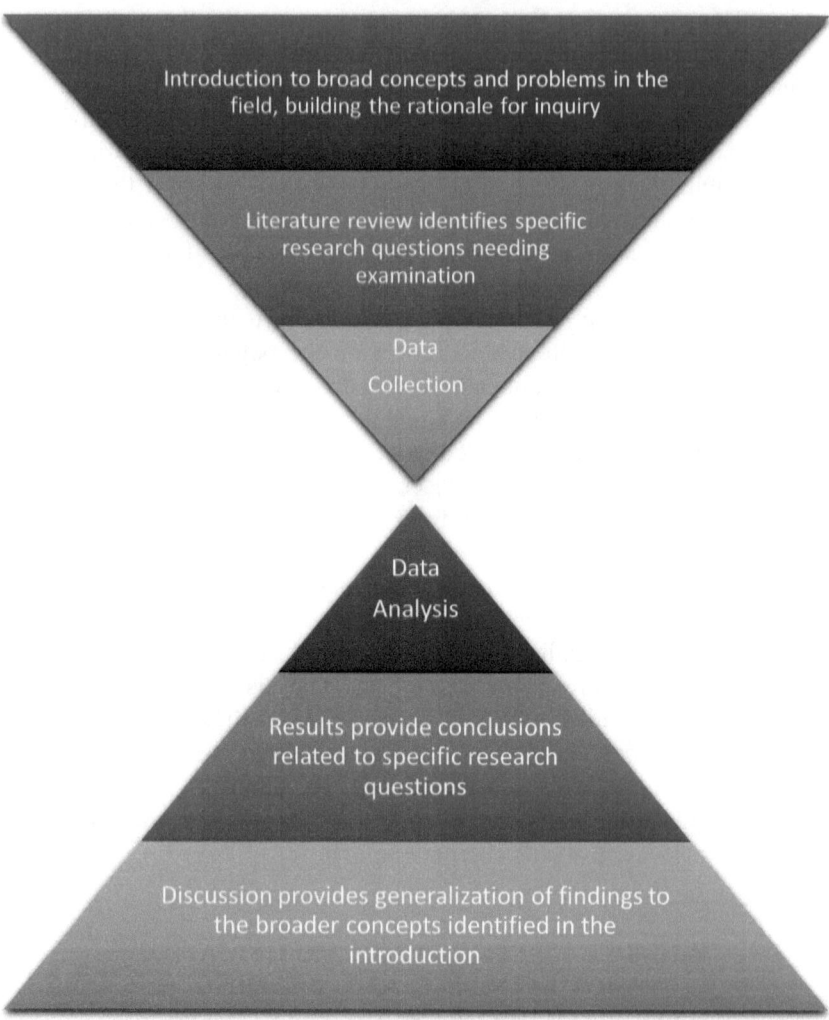

Figure 2.5 The Hourglass Flow of a Research Article

TEACHING Exceptional Children (the premier practitioner journal for special educators) and *Exceptional Children* (a highly regarded resource journal). The CEC website is at https://exceptionalchildren.org/.

Cult of Pedagogy: Committed to making you more awesome in the classroom, Cult of Pedagogy is a community of teachers supporting each other toward excellence. A podcast post, with supporting YouTube videos, about "How to Find, Read, and Use Academic Research" can be found at https://www.cultofpedagogy.com/academic-research/.

Institute of Education Sciences (IES): The IES is the statistics, research, and evaluation arm of the U.S. Department of Education. Their mission is to provide scientific evidence on which to ground education practice and policy and to share this information in formats that are useful and accessible to educators, parents, policymakers, researchers, and the public. Visit the IES website at https://ies.ed.gov/.

Practitioner Journals: Additional practitioner journals that special education teachers should consider subscribing to are *Beyond Behavior* (https://journals.sagepub.com/home/bbx), *Intervention in School and Clinic* (https://journals.sagepub.com/home/isc), and *Preventing School Failure: Alternative Education for Children and Youth* (https://www.tandfonline.com/journals/vpsf20).

YouTube: Several videos exist where content creators explain where to find research articles and how to read them. The University of Minnesota Library has a five-minute tutorial on how to read and comprehend scientific research articles. Watch the tutorial at https://www.youtube.com/watch?v=t2K6mJkSWoA.

DISCUSSION QUESTIONS

1. What experiences do you have regarding finding and reading research articles? What have you learned from those experiences?
2. Why should special education practitioners have the skill set to find and read educational research?
3. What is a scientific practitioner?
4. Which component of a research article do you feel is most important?
5. What are some drawbacks to using a search engine when searching for solutions as opposed to using Google Scholar?

KEY TERMS

ABC contingency: A three-term contingency that stands for antecedent, behavior, and consequence.

action research: A research method that aims to simultaneously investigate and solve an issue.

dependent variable: The variable that is affected by the independent variable.

empirical studies: Research that is based on observed and measured phenomena and derives knowledge from actual experience rather than from theory.

evidence-based practices: Skills, techniques, and strategies that have been consistently supported through experimental research.
fidelity: How closely prescribed procedures are followed.
function of behavior: The reason why a behavior is occurring.
impact factor: A metric commonly used to evaluate the importance of a journal in its field.
independent variable: The variable that produces changes in the dependent variable.
keywords: Terms that capture the essence of a topic.
open science: A movement to make scientific research accessible to all levels of society.
peer review: A process to evaluate scholarly work by one or more people with similar competencies.
publication bias: The failure to publish the results of a study on the basis of the direction or strength of the study findings.
reliable: Consistently good in quality; able to be trusted.
research-to-practice gap: A disconnect between what research scholars know to be best practices and what practitioners actually do in real-world settings.
scientific practitioners: Educators who know how to find, read, and implement researched practices in their classrooms to positively affect the outcomes of their students.
validity: The extent to which a concept, conclusion, or measurement is well founded and corresponds accurately to the real world.

REFERENCES

Committee on Training in Clinical Psychology. (1947). Recommended graduate training program in clinical psychology. *American Psychologist, 2*, 539–558.

Cook, B. G., Beahm, L. A., Myers, A. M., VanUitert, V. J., & Wilson, S. E. (2021). Open science and special education research. In B. G. Cook, M. Tankersley, & T. J. Landrum (Eds.), *The next big thing in learning and behavioral disabilities* (Vol. 31, pp. 61–74). Emerald Publishing Limited.

Cook, B. G., Lloyd, J. W., Mellor, D., Nosek, B. A., & Therrien, W. J. (2018). Promoting open science to increase the trustworthiness of evidence in special education. *Exceptional Children, 85*(1), 104–118. https://doi.org/10.1177/0014402918793138

Cook, B. G., & Odom, S. L. (2013). Evidence-based practices and implementation science in special education. *Exceptional Children, 79*(2), 135–144. https://doi.org/10.1177/001440291307900201

Cook, B. G., Spicer, S., Corr, F., Waterfield, D. A., Welker, N. P., Fleming, J. I., Wilson, S. E., & Therrien, W. (2023, August 9). Pushing past the paywall: Accessing open peer-reviewed research. https://doi.org/10.35542/osf.io/8sr9g

Dew, A., & Boydell, K. M. (2017). Knowledge translation: Bridging the disability research-to-practice gap. *Research and Practice in Intellectual and Developmental Disabilities, 4*(2), 142–157.

Franco, A., Malhotra, N., & Simonovits, G. (2014). Publication bias in the social sciences: Unlocking the file drawer. *Science, 345*(6203), 1502–1505. https://doi.org/10.1126/science.1255484

Khazan, O. (2018). The myth of 'learning styles.' *The Atlantic.* https://www.theatlantic.com/science/archive/2018/04/the-myth-of-learning-styles/557687/

Lohmann, M. J. (2023). *The teacher's guide to action research for special education in PK-12 classrooms.* Rowman & Littlefield.

Pashler, H., McDaniel, M., Rohrer, D., & Bjork, R. (2008). Learning styles: Concepts and evidence. *Psychological Science in the Public Interest, 9*(3), 105–119. http://dx.doi.org/10.1111/j.1539-6053.2009.01038.x

PART II

Methodologies in Special Education Research

Chapter 3

Systematic Literature Reviews

The field of educational research has grown at an impressive pace since the early 1900s. Today, there are educationalists and professional organizations across the world dedicated to improving practices for the benefit of students, families, educators, and administrators. As we have learned, scientific knowledge progresses as new knowledge is built upon existing knowledge. For researchers to explore and discover new knowledge, there are a variety of research methodologies available to use depending on a variety of factors. Although the basic structure of a research article remains consistent, the methods employed to conduct that research can vary greatly. There is no better research method compared to others because which research method to use depends on the research question being asked, the population being studied, and the setting in which the research is taking place. Part II of this book examines specific methodologies that every special educator should be familiar with when turning to research for answers. Understanding the methods employed to conduct research will assist in transferring that research to practice.

A quick Google Scholar search with broad keywords will result in thousands, if not millions, of hits, demonstrating the sheer quantity of research articles available. So how do researchers organize all this information? How can studies be grouped and classified to examine larger trends of evidence? In Chapter 2, we briefly discussed the role of literature reviews within an introduction to examine what has or has not been done as researchers develop their research question. Yet apart from an informal literature review within an introduction, there are formal literature review procedures that create a valuable type of research methodology. In this chapter, we will discuss systematic literature reviews and will answer these essential questions:

1. What are systematic literature reviews?
2. What are the critical components of systematic literature reviews?
3. What are the limitations of systematic literature reviews?

4. How do I interpret systematic literature reviews?
5. Where can I find more information about systematic literature reviews?

WHAT ARE SYSTEMATIC LITERATURE REVIEWS?

A literature review, sometimes called a research synthesis, involves assessing the facts and findings from a group of related studies. Cooper (2015) describes literature reviews as summarizing past research by drawing conclusions from separate investigations that address similar hypotheses. When researchers set out to conduct a literature review, they are attempting to synthesize empirical research for the purpose of creating **generalizations**. After bringing together collective knowledge on a subject, unresolved issues can be identified and new questions asked.

The underlying assumption of research is that new studies incorporate and improve on the findings of earlier work (Martella et al., 2013). This is what is meant by saying scientific knowledge is cumulative. New knowledge is built on old knowledge, and the progression of science continues. Literature reviews play a vital role in this scientific process. They ensure researchers are accumulating previous knowledge and designing new studies based on what is already known. For example, Thorndike (1905) and others in the early 1900s did a lot of research on the principles of reinforcement. It is well established that reinforcers, as a consequence contingency, maintain or increase behavior (Cooper et al., 2020). Rather than continuing to test this hypothesis, researchers apply this assumption in new and novel ways to study unresolved issues.

Literature reviews can be organized into two categories: unsystematic and systematic. Traditionally, literature reviews have been unsystematic and subjective in nature. No formal procedures or guidelines means researchers relied on their own judgments to conduct the review, which invited biases, haphazard procedures, inefficiency, and issues with **internal validity** and **external validity**.

In contrast, systematic literature reviews parallel the methodology used in empirical research with a set of standard procedures for guidance. Systematic literature reviews in educational research first started gaining notoriety in the 1970s when Glass (1976) introduced the term **meta-analysis**. Given the exponential growth of educational research at the time, scholars needed procedures to systematically find, synthesize, and analyze studies examining similar questions. Since that time, there have been several conceptualizations of how to conduct systematic literature reviews (e.g., Dunst & Trivette, 2009; Littell et al., 2008; Page et al., 2021).

In the next section of this chapter, we will examine the critical components of systematic literature reviews, but to answer our first essential question, a systematic literature review is a methodological procedure to comprehensively and accurately find and gather similar research, synthesize results in a replicable manner, and answer research questions based on the accumulation of knowledge. Cumming et al. (2023) suggested that high-quality systematic literature reviews provide a process for identifying, synthesizing, and critiquing multiple studies to inform theory, research, practice, and policy. Conducting systematic literature reviews is necessary for the scientific community to organize information and examine larger trends of evidence. Systematic literature reviews are essential in grouping similarly investigated phenomenon to see what researchers are or are not investigating and what is or is not working.

WHAT ARE THE CRITICAL COMPONENTS OF SYSTEMATIC LITERATURE REVIEWS?

Systematic literature reviews differ from unsystematic ones in that scholars use a set of agreed-upon procedures. Although the procedures may vary depending on the type of systematic review (e.g., qualitative versus quantitative), according to Martella and colleagues (2013), all systematic reviews will include (a) research questions; (b) description of the procedures used to select individual research articles; (c) details of study characteristics examined (e.g., participants, settings, independent variables, dependent variables, and research design); (d) explanation of the procedures to analyze results of individual studies; and (e) objective reporting of the findings.

Systematic literature reviews are published in peer-reviewed journals just like empirical studies. Some journals are exclusively dedicated to publishing literature reviews, such as *The Review of Educational Research*. Most journals, however, publish both empirical research and literature reviews based on the aims and scope of the journal. When searching through databases, such as Google Scholar, after entering keywords, systematic literature reviews may be integrated within the search results. It depends on whether the topic being searched has been investigated by many researchers. For researchers to conduct a literature review, there first needs to be enough individual studies with similar characteristics to be grouped and analyzed. There is no minimum number of studies required to conduct a literature review, yet around four or fewer studies is generally considered not enough to examine larger trends and infer generalizations. If a researcher started exploring the literature and did not find enough studies to conduct a literature review, that suggests the field could benefit from additional research on that topic. Most systematic literature reviews tend to include 10 to 20 studies, although many more could be included if the topic has been extensively researched or the scope of the review is very broad.

Title and Abstract

The title of a systematic literature review often explicitly states the article is a literature review. For example, "School Reentry Program Characteristics for Students With Chronic Illness: A Literature Review" by Wikel and Markelz (2023) examined the effects of school reentry programs as students with chronic illnesses transitioned from hospital settings back to their public school settings, and "The Effectiveness of Interventions to Increase Parent Involvement in Special Education: A Systematic Literature Review and Meta-Analysis" by Goldman and Burke (2017) compiled the literature on parent trainings to increase their involvement in school. Sometimes the title will not be as explicit as these two examples, which is why reading the abstract is important.

The abstract of systematic literature reviews should indicate that the research conducted was a literature review. The purpose of an abstract is to concisely describe the rationale for conducting the research, the methods employed, and a summary of the findings. Within literature review abstracts, researchers will use phrases such as "The purpose of this review was to" or "This article aims to systematically review the literature on." Reading systematic literature reviews on a topic you are exploring is very beneficial because the researchers have already completed the work of searching databases and compiling studies. In addition, it means the topic you are exploring has also been, to some degree, researched by scholars. The structure of a systematic literature review article follows the hourglass flow of all research articles.

Introduction

The purpose of a systematic literature review introduction is to provide a rationale as to why a literature review on a particular topic is needed. The reasoning can vary depending on what the researchers want to explore. Typically, though, systematic reviews are conducted when there are enough individual studies with similar characteristics. Sometimes a systematic review is warranted because there has not been a review in several years. The researchers might include the previous review in their introduction but then include only studies that have been published after the last review to analyze more recent research on the topic. When there have been several systematic reviews on a topic, researchers might want to conduct a meta-analysis to systematically review all the previous literature reviews. Whatever the rationale is, researchers must funnel their purpose down to specific research questions, which are the guiding questions of the systematic review.

Research Questions

Precise research questions that provide structure and guide the planning and execution of the review are essential. A poor research question can lead to unfocused attempts to search the literature. Following are some common research questions asked by scholars conducting literature reviews:

1. To what degree have independent and dependent variables been studied?
2. Under what conditions is the independent variable effective?
3. Are versions of the independent variable more effective?
4. How should the independent variable be implemented to ensure effectiveness in particular situations?
5. What is the relationship between study characteristics and intervention outcomes?
6. With whom is the independent variable effective?

The structure of the research question will indicate whether the goal of the review is **hypothesis** testing or exploratory (Cooper, 2015). A hypothesis-testing research question asserts a particular outcome, such as "Is there a positive relationship between teacher-delivered behavior-specific praise and student on-task behavior?" In this example, researchers would search for and include studies that have specifically investigated the independent variable (behavior-specific praise) and the dependent variable (on-task behavior) with the assumption that behavior-specific praise positively affects student on-task behavior. The researchers would then examine and code individual studies to draw conclusions as to whether their hypothesis is correct. In contrast, an exploratory research question based on the same independent and dependent variables would be worded as "What is the relationship between teacher-delivered behavior-specific praise and student on-task behavior?" Researchers would select and review the same studies as the hypothesis-testing research question but would synthesize and analyze to determine whether a relationship between the independent and dependent variables existed at all, without the assumption that behavior-specific praise positively affects student on-task behavior.

Method

Figure 3.1 outlines the basic steps researchers follow when conducting a systematic literature review. Once the research questions have been finalized,

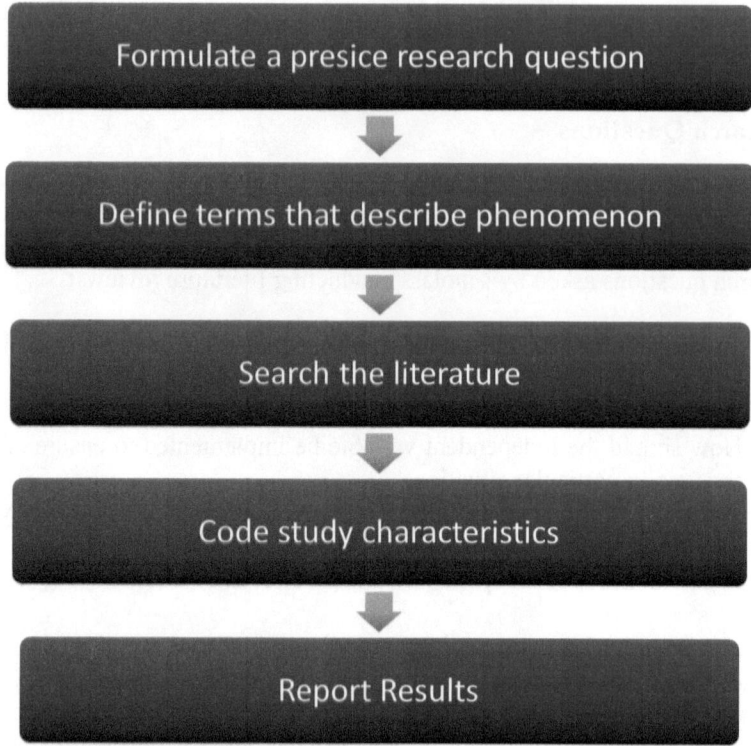

Figure 3.1 Steps in Conducting a Systematic Literature Review

the next step is to identify search term keywords. Similar to the process outlined in Chapter 2, the procedures of using keywords and Boolean operators to search the literature enables researchers to identify all relevant studies that target the phenomenon of interest. Researchers must precisely detail their search procedures to provide readers with confidence that their search accurately collected all studies available. Within this process, researchers should provide inclusion and exclusion criteria that explain how studies met certain standards to be included in the literature review and why other studies were excluded.

If researchers are using the Preferred Reporting Items for Systematic Reviews and Meta-Analyses (PRISMA) procedures (Page et al., 2021), a flowchart will often be included in the method section and described in the narrative to demonstrate the inclusion and exclusion of studies throughout the process until the final number of included studies is documented (see Figure 3.2 as an example).

After the final number of included studies have been collected, researchers must extract the important information from each study. This is called

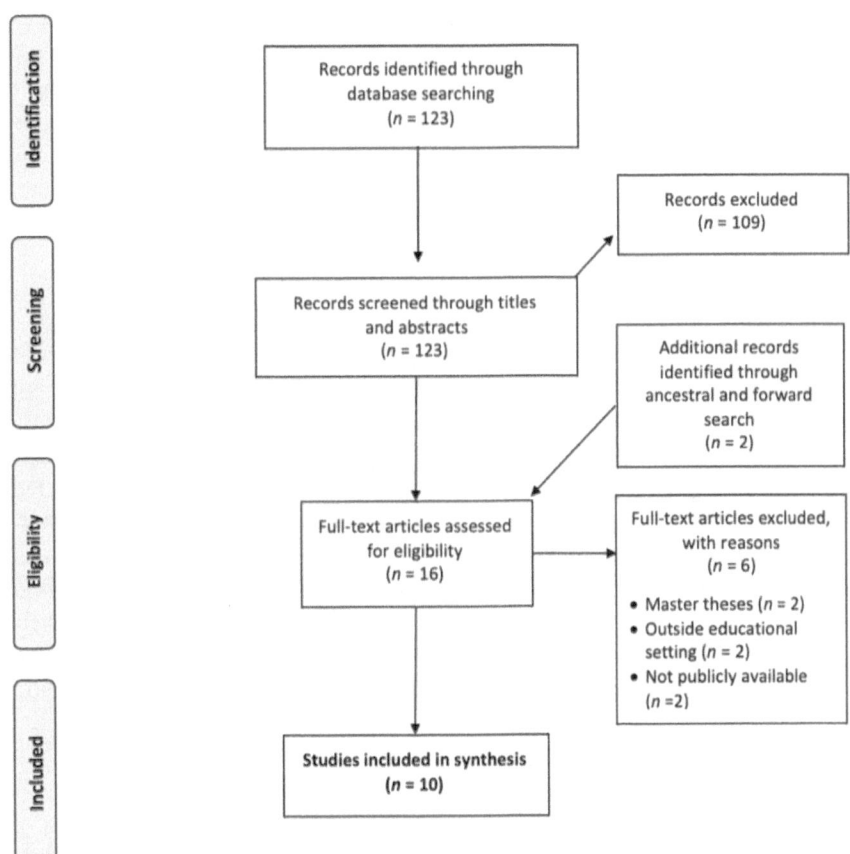

Figure 3.2 Example of a PRISMA Flow Diagram of Search Procedures. Flow diagram from Markelz et al. (2019).

coding study characteristics. A well-designed procedure for coding studies is an important step for increasing internal validity of the review. There are no prescribed guidelines for determining which study characteristics to code because it depends on what the researchers are investigating, but typically, researchers code key characteristics, such as (a) participants (e.g., age, gender, education, and disability), (b) setting (e.g., classroom characteristics, community characteristics, small-group instruction, and academic content), (c) methodology (e.g., research design and experiment procedures), (d) independent variable or intervention (e.g., description, duration, and intensity), (e) dependent variable (e.g., description and method of measurement), (f) research quality (e.g., threats to internal and external validity), and (g) outcomes (e.g., significant findings and author conclusions).

The process of identifying study characteristics is ongoing and may change during the coding procedure. Sometimes researchers may code for many characteristics but only report relevant findings within the article. If multiple researchers are coding studies, the article should include procedures for how those individuals were trained to use the coding forms and procedures. Some form of reliability calculation between coders is needed to demonstrate that each coder is extracting information from individual studies in an accurate and consistent manner.

Results

After the research team has coded individual studies, they must present results in an objective manner. Normally, the results section of a systematic literature review article will start with a table presenting the included studies and their coded characteristics (see Table 3.1 as an example). Each included article is identified by author and year of publication. Then, study characteristics are listed across columns. Identifying individual study characteristics is a start to the results section, but it is up to the research team to go beyond that and synthesize findings across the individual studies to answer their research questions. Findings can be described in narrative format but often include quantitative and graphical representations to best convey information to the reader.

Discussion

The discussion section should position the findings of the systematic review within the **contexts** of the field in general. The rationale of the review can be reexamined with the benefit of these new findings. The researchers should also discuss how their findings contribute to the progression of knowledge concerning the phenomenon they examined. In addition, suggestions for future research on the topic are often provided to assist future scholars.

The discussion section is an important component of systematic literature reviews because it guides readers to understanding the "So what?" of the findings. Why do the results matter? How do they affect the practices of teachers in classrooms? Often, there will be an **implications section** within the discussion where the research team is supposed to bridge the research-to-practice gap by explicitly identifying how their findings can affect practitioner practices. Of course, this is a valuable section for practitioners to read.

Table 3.1 Summary of Articles from Markelz et al. (2019) Systematic Literature Review

Studies	Participants	Setting	Design	Independent Variable	Dependent Variable	SV Measured	Mastery Measured	Maintenance Measured
Charlton (2016)	4 College students	Summer program	MB Participants	MotivAider +	BSP Gen. praise	Yes	No	No
Haydon & Musti-Rao (2011)	2 Gen. ed.	Middle	MB Participants	MotivAider	BSP Reprimands Gen. praise Student: Disruptions	Yes	No	No
LaBrot et al. (2016)	3 Early childhood	Head start	MB Participants	MotivAider +	BSP	No	No	No
Markelz et al. (2018)	1 SPED preservice	Elementary	MB Behaviors	Apple watch	BSP Active questioning Classroom scanning	Yes	Yes	Yes
Markelz et al. (2019)	3 SPED	Elementary	MB Participants	Apple watch	BSP Student: On-task	Yes	Yes	Yes
McDonald et al. (2014)	4 Gen. ed.	Elementary	MB Participants	Gentle reminder	BSP Token delivery Student: Stereotypic behavior	No	No	No
O'Handley et al. (2018)	3 Gen. ed.	Elementary	MB Participants	MotivAider	BSP Reprimands Student: Engaged and disruptive behavior	Yes	Yes	Yes
Petscher & Baily (2006)	3 Instructional assistants	Middle	MB Behaviors	Remote pager +	Managing disruptions Point delivery/BSP Prompting	No	Yes	Yes
Rivera et al. (2015)	2 SPED 2 Instructional assistants	Elementary	ABAB	Smartphone	BSP Student: On-task	Yes	No	No
Thompson et al. (2012)	3 Gen. ed.	Elementary	MB Participants	MotivAider +	BSP	Yes	Yes	No

Note. SPED = Special education; Gen ed. = General education; MB = Multiple baseline; "+" = Additional independent variables (e.g., performance feedback); BSP = Behavior-specific praise; SV = Social validity

WHAT ARE THE LIMITATIONS OF SYSTEMATIC LITERATURE REVIEWS?

Even though systematic literature reviews have a set standard of procedures and guidelines, there are still chances of error and bias. In fact, all educational research is susceptible to error and bias because it relies on the conceptual and interpretative skills of researchers. According to Martella et al. (2013), the validity of a systematic literature review is dependent on three points in time: (1) searching and selecting studies, (2) coding study characteristics, and (3) drawing conclusions.

Searching and Selecting

Researchers can make two types of errors when searching for and selecting studies to include in their review. First, studies that fall within the scope of the review may be unintentionally excluded from the review. Excluding studies that should be included means the entirety of the field of inquiry has not been examined. Therefore, conclusions made by the researchers may be missing important—even contradictory—information. In Chapter 2, we discussed how journal editorial teams may be biased toward publishing studies with significant findings. Research teams should consider publication bias during search procedures. One strategy to address publication bias is to include **gray literature** within searching procedures. Gray literature is considered research published outside traditional academic distribution channels, such as working papers, government reports, and white papers.

The second type of error involves researchers' abilities to discriminate between good and poor research. Some researchers may equally weight the findings from good and poor research. This error might mean their findings from the review do not accurately represent the phenomenon studied. Including studies from predatory journals that did not undergo a rigorous peer-review process may introduce a plethora of inaccuracies into the results, which will **skew** the researchers' conclusions. Appropriately weighting the findings from good research is important, as is excluding study results with too many threats to internal and external validity (i.e., poor research).

Coding

The procedures used to code study characteristics are part of the review process with the greatest chance of error and bias (Hunter & Schmidt, 2004). There are three types of errors that researchers can make at this part in the review process. The first type of error may result from inaccurate coding of the included studies. If researchers do not classify the studies accurately, they are unable to make comparisons across studies. For example, say researchers are studying the effects of a reading intervention during small-group instruction. If one of the included studies was actually a whole-group reading intervention, then comparing intervention effects would be invalid because that study was not similar in setting characteristics. Ensuring studies are comparable is essential in literature review research because one aspect is to examine relationships between study characteristics and intervention outcomes.

The second type of error centers on researchers' abilities to detect flawed conclusions of the included studies. Researchers of the included studies within the review may not accurately or fully report their findings. Researchers who are conducting the systematic review may unintentionally continue this misrepresentation if they do not critically examine the included study's findings.

The third type of error focuses on the inclusion of contrary findings. If research teams are approaching a systematic review with a hypothesis-testing framework, they may be subconsciously biased toward minimizing findings that contradict their hypothesis. Like weighting findings of good research versus poor research, researchers may be prejudiced to emphasize the findings that support a particular hypothesis rather than objective reporting.

Drawing Conclusions

The final point in the review process susceptible to error and bias is drawing conclusions. Any errors made in the previous two points in time will affect the ability of researchers to draw valid conclusions. The degree to which conclusions are invalid depends on the magnitude of inaccurate assessments or exclusion of findings. However, there is always potential for previous searching and coding mistakes to be compounded by the research team when analyzing results and making generalizations.

HOW DO I INTERPRET SYSTEMATIC LITERATURE REVIEWS?

In Part III of this book, we will examine specific research methodologies in a case study/application format. In particular, Chapter 9 presents a scenario where a special education teacher identifies a problem in their classroom, searches the literature, then reads a systematic literature review and implements researched best practice. In this section of the book, however, we will provide general guidelines for interpreting systematic literature reviews.

Searching the literature for solutions to classroom problems is likely to result in several potential articles. One type of article could be a systematic literature review. After ensuring the article was published in a reputable journal, the next step is to skim or read the article to evaluate whether it is of sufficient quality and relevancy. Table 3.2 presents a checklist for evaluating whether a systematic review has sufficient quality and relevancy to your specific situation.

Table 3.2 Checklist for Quality and Relevancy of a Systematic Literature Review

Introduction

Quality
- The research topic is specified at the outset of the article.
- The research problem or important issue is clearly identified.
- There is a sufficient (unsystematic) review of the relevant literature.
- The research questions are clearly stated.

Relevancy
- The context of the issue examined is similar to my situation.
- The stated research question is relevant to my situation and will provide answers to solving my problem.

Methods

Quality
- The search and selection procedures are described in detail, including inclusion and exclusion criteria.
- The coding procedures are descriptive and comprehensive.
- The characteristics of participants and settings are clearly described.
- The data analysis procedures are clear and appropriate.
- Reliability measures are reported to convey validity of methods.

Relevancy
- The participants' characteristics are similar enough to my students.'
- The setting characteristics are similar enough to my setting.
- Relevant key study characteristics have been coded, such as independent and dependent variables.
- Included studies are current and not outdated.

Results

Quality
- The findings of the review are presented clearly and objectively.
- Individual studies, as well as a synthesis of findings, are reported.
- No data are ignored or minimized.
- Researchers explicitly answer the research questions.

Relevancy
- Individual study and/or synthesized results provide solutions to my problem.
- The results present intervention effects.
- The results clearly identify best practices concerning intervention implementation.

Discussion

Quality
- Findings are interpreted within the context of other evidence.
- Limitations of the systematic review are discussed.

Relevancy
- The generalization of findings is applicable to my situation.
- Implications of the review provide concrete steps to implement best practices.

Use Professional Judgment

Unless a research team comes into your classroom and conducts a study with your students, no empirical investigation or systematic review is going to include participants and contexts that 100% match your situation. The important determination is whether the overall components of the review are examining a problem you have identified and include similar enough situations that you can generalize the findings to your specific circumstances. Just because a review examined intervention effects with 3rd graders does not mean the intervention will not be successful with 4th graders, or if the intervention was implemented for an average of 10 days does not mean it cannot work similarly if implemented for 8 days. Your **professional judgment** is needed to decide what is an acceptable level of variation between included study contexts and personal contexts.

One valuable tip to consider when reading a systematic literature review is that individual studies included in the review may be more relevant to your specific problem than others. Examining the articles in Table 3.1 can provide helpful information about the independent and dependent variables of those studies. If there is an indication that a particular study is more relevant than others, go to the reference section of the review to identify the study title and search for it in Google Scholar. Even if the research team is conducting a systematic review for reasons not helpful to finding intervention best practice, for example, they are assessing the quality of methodologies used, and the individual studies included in that review may be studying the effectiveness of an intervention you are interested in. As previously stated, systematic literature reviews are very helpful because a research team has already done the work of compiling literature on a specific topic.

Understand Magnitudes of Effect

Although not all systematic literature reviews are concerned with the magnitude of intervention outcomes (i.e., to what degree the independent variable affected the dependent variable), many systematic reviews are conducted to examine this relationship. For the betterment of educational practices, many researchers simply want to know what is working (e.g., improving student success), how well it is working, and how it can be done even better. The challenge with systematic literature reviews is quantifying the magnitude of intervention effect so that findings from individual studies can be compared and analyzed in a valid way.

Digging into all the techniques educational researchers have developed to compare magnitude of effects across individual studies is beyond the scope of this book. In fact, there are books upon books dedicated to the explanation of these statistical methods. Often, PhD-level training is required to grasp the pros, cons, and nuances of each procedure. In subsequent chapters, we will detail methods for measuring intervention outcomes as they relate to qualitative, quantitative, and single-case research methodologies. Yet when conducting systematic reviews, researchers might have to synthesize various magnitude-of-effect measures. If the measures are vastly different across individual studies, it might be like comparing apples to oranges.

As a scientific practitioner, it is not necessary to have a deep understanding of **statistical analysis**; however, it is important to identify how and where in the article researchers descriptively present intervention effects. Systematic review researchers should narratively describe intervention effects (and magnitude if available) in the results section after the presentation of statistics. Early in the discussion section is also a point where researchers sometimes summarize findings in a descriptive manner. If the purpose of the review was to examine intervention effects, then there will be a table in the article that will most likely have a column for this information.

WHERE CAN I FIND MORE INFORMATION ABOUT SYSTEMATIC LITERATURE REVIEWS?

Boston University Medical School: The Boston University Medical School provides a PowerPoint presentation that thoroughly describes what a systematic review is and provides overviews of each important component. Access the PowerPoint at https://www.bumc.bu.edu/medlib/files/2018/06/SystematicReviews.ppt.

Edanz: This company provides research support services, such as manuscript editing. A blog post on the differences between systematic reviews, scoping reviews, and narrative reviews is helpful in understanding their distinctions. Read it at https://www.edanz.com/excited-science/systematic-scoping-narrative.

PRISMA Statement: The Preferred Reporting Items for Systematic Reviews and Meta-Analyses (PRISMA) is an evidence-based minimum set of items for reporting in systematic reviews and meta-analyses. PRISMA primarily focuses on the reporting of reviews evaluating the effects of interventions and is becoming used by more and more educational researchers. You can learn about PRISMA at http://www.prisma-statement.org/.

Wikipedia: Often a first source to turn to when exploring novel concepts, Wikipedia provides a comprehensive overview of systematic reviews. A historical progression is outlined, and the various types of reviews are described. Access the Wikipedia page at https://en.wikipedia.org/wiki/Systematic_review.

DISCUSSION QUESTIONS

1. What are the advantages and disadvantages of a systematic literature review versus an unsystematic literature review?
2. What are important considerations when interpreting systematic literature reviews?
3. In your opinion, what is the most critical component of a systematic literature review?
4. What are some limitations of systematic literature reviews?
5. Search the literature and identify a systematic literature review that might be helpful in your special education instruction.

KEY TERMS

coding study characteristics: The process of extracting important information for analysis.
contexts: The interrelated conditions in which something exists or occurs.
external validity: The extent to which findings can be generalized to other people and contexts.
generalizations: Taking findings from a narrow scope and making broader, more universal claims.
gray literature: Research published outside traditional academic distribution channels.
hypothesis: A proposed explanation for a phenomenon.
implications section: A part of an article, typically in the discussion section, where researchers explain how their findings affect real-world practices.
internal validity: The extent to which findings accurately represent the truth.
meta-analysis: A statistical analysis of results from individual studies for the purpose of integrating the findings.

professional judgment: Decision-making based on knowledge, skills, and previous experiences.

skew: Alter, bias, or affect in one direction or another.

statistical analysis: The process of collecting and analyzing large volumes of data to identify trends and develop insights.

REFERENCES

Cooper, H. (2015). *Research synthesis and meta-analysis: A step-by-step approach* (Vol. 2). Sage.

Cooper, J. O., Heron, T. E., & Heward, W. L. (2020). *Applied behavior analysis* (3rd ed.). Pearson.

Cumming, M. M., Bettini, E., & Chow, J. C. (2023). High-quality systematic literature reviews in special education: Promoting coherence, contextualization, generativity, and transparency. *Exceptional Children, 89*(4), 412–431. https://doi.org/10.1177/00144029221146576

Dunst, C. J., & Trivette, C. M. (2009). Using research evidence to inform and evaluate early childhood intervention practices. *Topics in Early Childhood Special Education, 29*(1), 40–52. https://doi.org/10.1177/0271121408329227

Glass, G. V. (1976). Primary, secondary, and meta-analysis of research. *Educational Researcher, 5*(10), 3–8. https://doi.org/10.3102/0013189X005010003

Goldman, S. E., & Burke, M. M. (2017). The effectiveness of interventions to increase parent involvement in special education: A systematic literature review and meta-analysis. *Exceptionality, 25*(2), 97–115.

Hunter, J. E., & Schmidt, F. L. (2004). *Methods of meta-analysis: Correcting error and bias in research findings*. Sage.

Littell, J. H., Corcoran, J., & Pillai, C. (2008). *Systematic reviews and meta-analysis*. Sage.

Markelz, A. M., Scheeler, M. C., Riccomini, P. J., & Taylor, J. C. (2019). A systematic review of tactile prompting in teacher education. *Teacher Education and Special Education, 43*(4), 296–313. https://doi.org/10.1177/0888406419877500

Martella, R. C., Nelson, J. R., Morgan, R. L., & Marchand-Martella, N. E. (2013). *Understanding and interpreting educational research*. Guilford Press.

Page, M. J., McKenzie, J. E., Bossuyt, P. M., Boutron, I., Hoffmann, T. C., Mulrow, C. D., Shamseer, L., Tetzlaff, J. M., & Moher, D. (2021). Updating guidance for reporting systematic reviews: Development of the PRISMA 2020 statement. *Journal of Clinical Epidemiology, 134*, 103–112. https://doi.org/10.1016/j.jclinepi.2021.02.003

Thorndike, E. L. (1905). *The elements of psychology*. A. G. Seiler.

Wikel, K., & Markelz, A. M. (2023). School reentry program characteristics for students with chronic illness: A literature review. *Research, Advocacy, and Practice for Complex and Chronic Conditions, 41*(1), 22–44. https://doi.org/10.14434/rapcc.v41i1.31767

Chapter 4

Group Research Designs

In this chapter, we will focus on group research designs, often referred to as quantitative research. Quantitative research design is used in a variety of social sciences (e.g., education and psychology). The aim of quantitative research is to collect and analyze numerical data to answer research questions and test hypotheses. There are many advantages to using this research approach, including the ability to generalize findings to larger populations and the capacity to uncover patterns and relations among variables.

The application of statistics to identify effective and efficient strategies for addressing pressing issues humans face in their day-to-day lives has a long and sordid history. Statistical researchers generally agree the principles undergirding the design of experiments were chiefly developed by R. A. Fisher during his work at Rothamsted Experimental Station in the 1920s and 1930s. During that time, Fisher applied his statistical concepts in the field of agricultural research. We would be remiss if we did not mention Fisher was from an early age a supporter of certain eugenic ideas, and it is for this reason that he has been accused of being a racist and an advocate of forced sterilization, which has recently caused various organizations to remove his name from awards and dedications of buildings (Bodmer et al., 2021). Despite his abhorrent views, he is considered the father of statistics due to his development of statistical inference, experimental design, randomization, and analysis of variance (ANOVA), published in the first edition of his book *Statistical Methods for Research Workers* in 1925. In the years since, statistical analysis of group data has been applied to a wide variety of research areas, including special education.

As mentioned in Chapter 2, a quick search with broad keywords will result in thousands, if not millions, of results, demonstrating the volume of research articles available for consumption by practitioners in a plethora of scientific fields. In this chapter, we will discuss group research designs in the context of special education and answer these essential questions:

1. What are group research designs?
2. What are the critical components of group research designs?
3. What are the limitations of group research designs?
4. How do I interpret group research designs?
5. Where can I find more information about group research designs?

WHAT ARE GROUP RESEARCH DESIGNS?

To answer our first essential question of this chapter, group research designs often involve randomly assigning participants to two (or more) groups with at least one treatment group and one control group (Cooper et al., 2020). Random assignment is an aspect of group experimental design in which study participants are assigned to the treatment or control group using a random procedure. There are other methods for creating groups in this type of experimental research, including random selection, matched groups, and counterbalancing. Random selection refers to how participants are selected for inclusion in the study. Using a matched group approach involves assigning participants to various conditions that are matched based on the dependent variable or some other extraneous variables prior to manipulating the independent variables. Researchers can also employ counterbalancing, which entails testing different participants in different orders.

A **between-group design** has two or more groups of participants that are concurrently tested using different variables. The simplest between-group design occurs with two groups; one is generally regarded as the treatment group, which receives the **independent variable**, and the control group, which receives no treatment and is used as a comparison group. For example, if you wanted to compare two reading curricula (A and B) by looking at how school districts choose a reading curriculum, the study could be designed using a between-subjects design by having each participant test a single reading curriculum and examine the effects of the curriculum on student reading outcomes.

We could also test the reading curricula using a **within-subject design**. A within-subject design is a type of experimental design in which all participants are exposed to every treatment or condition. To analyze different reading curricula, we would have each participant test both curricula and examine the impact of each curriculum on reading outcomes. If we wanted to measure which of the two curricula, A or B, is better for teaching reading, we could choose *curriculum* (with two possible values—A and B) as the independent variable and the student reading outcomes as the **dependent variable**. The goal of the study would be to see whether the dependent variable (student reading outcomes) changes when teachers vary the curriculum or it stays the same. If the results are the same, we could say that neither curriculum is better than the other. But if student reading outcomes consistently improved using curriculum A, we could infer from the results that curriculum A is more effective than curriculum B. How those data are calculated involves **quantitative statistics**, which will subsequently be discussed.

Education, psychology, health sciences, and other disciplines have largely adopted the **randomized controlled trial** (RCT) as the methodological gold standard for providing evidence for evidence-based practice (Odom, 2021). Various components of RCTs had been used in medical research in the early 1900s, and numerous methodologists have attributed the introduction of RCTs to medical research (Bothwell et al., 2016). To identify evidence-based practice, researchers in educational science have adopted this medical model to enhance the evidence of the practices we presume to be effective. RCTs are prospective studies that measure the effectiveness of a new intervention or treatment. Although no study is likely on its own to prove causality, randomization reduces bias and provides a rigorous tool to examine cause-and-effect relationships between an intervention and outcome. This is because the act of randomization balances participant characteristics (both observed and unobserved) between the groups, allowing attribution of any differences in outcome to the study intervention. This is not possible with any other study design. Another important characteristic of RCTs is that they can ensure that there are no systematic differences between participant groups (i.e., participant variables) that could influence results based on particular participant characteristics and other variables. While expensive and time consuming, RCTs are the gold standard for studying causal relationships because randomization eliminates much of the bias inherent in other study designs (Hariton & Locascio, 2018). Although viewed as the gold standard, RCT is not always the correct endeavor. There are instances when this approach is not warranted, such as small sample size, feasibility, and ethics. If the sample size is too small, it is not possible to come to any conclusive results and certainly hurts the generalization of the findings. The resources that are required to run a proper RCT are difficult to come by; they include time, people, and other resources needed as well as finding the populations related to the area of study. Lastly, using an RCT is not always an ethical choice. For example, there can be ethical dilemmas surrounding participation and consent, the use of placebos and deception, and participant selection.

When we look at the field of special education (and other research fields), there is a variety of statistical tests that are used during experimental investigation based on what the researcher is exploring. It is important that practitioners can identify, understand, and interpret findings from group designed research studies to better inform their practice. Table 4.1 highlights the various statistical tests often associated with group designed research and examples for each. Later in this chapter, we will discuss the critical components of group designed research by discussing how to navigate and identify important information in a group design publication from title to discussion, including **effect sizes** commonly reported in group design studies and how to interpret them. Following that section, we will detail the limitations of group design studies and how governing bodies are working to mitigate those limitations as well as where you can find more information on group designed research.

Table 4.1 *Essentials of Statistical Tests*

Univariate		
Central Tendency		
Measure	*Definition*	*Example*
Mode	The commonly occurring value in a set.	If a set of numbers contained the following digits, 1, 2, 3, 5, 6, 6, 6, 6, 9, 9, the mode would be 6 because it appears more than any other number in the set.
Median	The center value is a set.	To find the median age of seven students with the ages of 11, 12, 10, 13, 9, 14, and 15, you would first line them up in numerical order from youngest to oldest, 9, 10, 11, 12, 13, 14, 15, and find the center number. In this example, the middle number, or the median, is 12.
Mean	The mathematical average of a set.	To find the mean of the previous set of ages (in the median row), you would add the age of person 1, person 2, person 3, and so on, then divide the total by the number of people in that set, which will give you the mean. In this case, the mean is 12.
Variance	Is a measure of how far each number in the set is from the mean.	Returns for stock in Company ABC are 10% in year 1, 20% in year 2, and −15% in year 3. The average of these three returns is 5%. The differences between each return and the average are 5%, 15%, and −20% for each consecutive year. Then, the average squared deviation of each number from its mean is computed, which gives us a variance of 3.25% (0.0325).
Standard deviation	How much scores deviate from the mean, which is the square root of the variance. It is the most used measure of spread.	Expanding on the above variance example, if we take the square root of the variance, it yields a standard deviation of 18% ($\sqrt{0.0325} = 0.180$) for the stock returns.

Bi- and Multivariate Inferential Statistical Tests

Differences of Groups

Measure	Definition	Example
Chi square	A statistical procedure for determining the difference between observed and expected data.	A meal delivery company in Virginia wants to investigate the link between gender, geography, and people's food preferences.
t-Test	Looks at differences between two groups on some variable of interest. The IV must have only two groups.	Do males and females differ in the number of hours they spend exercising in a given month?
ANOVA	Tests the significance of group differences between two or more groups. The IV has two or more categories and determines only that there is a difference between groups but doesn't tell us which is different.	The IV might be streaming service usage, and groups are assigned to low, medium, and high levels of streaming use to find out if there is a difference in hours of sleep per night.
ANCOVA	Same as ANOVA but adds control of one or more covariates that may influence the DV.	Do hours of sleep differ between low, medium, and high levels of streaming usage after controlling for siblings/no siblings?
MANOVA	Same as ANOVA, but two or more related DVs can be studied while controlling for the correlation between the DVs.	Does religious affiliation affect reading achievement, math achievement, and overall scholastic achievement among 11th graders?
MANCOVA	Same as MANOVA but adds control of one or more covariates that may influence the DV.	Does religious affiliation affect reading achievement, math achievement, and overall scholastic achievement among 11th graders after controlling for socioeconomic status?

Relationships

Correlation	Used with two variables to determine a relationship/ association.	Amount of damage to a house on fire and number of firefighters at the scene.
Multiple regression	Used with several IVs and one DV for prediction. Many IVs can be entered; by looking at all of them at the same time, the best predictors can be determined.	IVs—drug use, alcohol use, and traumatic event DV—suicidal tendencies
Path analysis	Looks at direct and indirect effects of predictor variables.	The traumatic event causes alcohol use, which leads to suicidal tendencies.

Group Membership

Logistic regression	Estimates the odds probability of the DV occurring as the values of the IVs change.	What are the odds of a car accident occurring at various levels of medical cannabis use?

Essentials of Statistical Testing

In the world of statistics, measures of central tendency are descriptive summaries of a particular set of data. Using a single value from a dataset, you can identify the center of the data distribution. Measures of central tendency do not provide information about individual data from the dataset; they provide a summary of the entire dataset. Generally, the central tendency of a dataset can be defined using some of the measures in statistics, including mean, median, mode, variance, and standard deviation.

Mean

The mean of a data set constitutes the average value of that dataset. It can be calculated as the sum of all the values in the dataset divided by the number of values found in the dataset. The mean is essentially a model of your dataset. It is the value that is most common. You will notice, however, that the mean is not often one of the actual values that you have observed in your dataset. Yet this is one of the most valuable aspects of the mean in that it can diminish error in the prediction of any one value in a dataset. That is, it is the value that produces the lowest amount of error from all other values in the dataset. An important property of the mean is that it includes all values from a specific dataset and is the only measure of central tendency where the sum of the deviations of each value from the mean is always zero.

Median

The median is the middle or center value from a dataset when the values are placed in order from smallest to largest or largest to smallest. Essentially, the median splits the distribution in half (there are 50% of observations on either side of the median value). In a distribution with an odd number of observations, the median value is the middle value. When there is an even number of values in a set of data, there is no single value representing the median. In this case, you take the two values in the center or the distribution, add them together, and divide the sum of those numbers by two. One of the most valuable aspects of the median is it is less affected by outliers and skewed data than the mean and is usually the preferred measure of central tendency used by statisticians when there is a data distribution that is not symmetrical.

Mode

The mode is the number (i.e., value) that is represented most frequently in a certain dataset. It is possible for a dataset to have one mode, more than one mode, or no mode at all. The mode is useful when a dataset has more than one segment, is badly skewed, or a statistician needs the impact of any outliers in a particular dataset.

Variance

Variance is the measurement of how far each number in a dataset is from the mean of that same dataset. Statisticians use variance to see how individual numbers relate to each other within a dataset rather than using broader mathematical techniques, such as arranging numbers into quartiles. The advantage of variance is that it treats all deviations from the mean as the same regardless of their direction.

Standard Deviation

Standard deviation is the measure of how spread out the data are. Its formula is simple: it is the square root of the variance for that dataset. A low standard deviation indicates that the values tend to be close to the mean (i.e., the expected value), while a high standard deviation indicates that the values are spread out over a wider range.

Chi Square

This statistic is a test that measures how a statistical model compares to observed data. When calculating a chi-square statistic test, the data must be random, raw (not cleaned), mutually exclusive (two or more events that cannot occur at the same time), and drawn from independent variables and a large enough sample. For example, the results of tossing a quarter meet these criteria. Chi-square tests are often used to test hypotheses and compare the size of any discrepancies between the expected results and the actual results given the size of the sample and the number of variables in the relationship.

t-Test

t-Tests are a type of statistic that is used to compare the mean of two separate groups. More specifically, it is used when a researcher wants to state with confidence that the obtained difference between the means of the sample groups is too great to have occurred by chance and that some difference also exists in the population from which the sample was drawn. For example, if we wanted to compare the mathematic achievement of boys and girls, we could use a *t*-test because we have one independent variable (i.e., sex of participants) with only two levels (i.e., male or female) and one dependent variable (mathematic achievement). For *t*-test calculations, the independent variable can have only two levels.

ANOVA

If the independent variable has more than two levels, a researcher would use a one-way analysis of variance (ANOVA). By using an ANOVA, researchers can test the differences between two or more groups. The independent variable has to have two or more categories, and it determines only that there is a difference between groups but does not indicate what is different. For example, if you wanted to figure out if test scores (i.e., mean test scores) differed based on what type of music students listen to while studying, you could do this using an ANOVA test where music types are the independent variable and test scores are the dependent variable.

ANCOVA

An ANCOVA is an extension of an ANOVA, which would be used if you wanted to determine if there is a difference between three or more independent groups after accounting for one or more covariates. If a teacher wants to know whether studying techniques have an effect on exam scores while accounting for the course grade the student currently has, they can use the student's current grade as a covariate and conduct an ANCOVA to determine if there is a difference between the mean exam scores of the three groups. By using an ANCOVA calculation, they can test whether studying technique has an effect on exam scores after the confound of the covariate has been accounted for. If that teacher finds that there is a difference in exam scores between the three studying techniques, they can be confident that the difference exists even after accounting for the student's current grade in the class.

MANOVA

Multivariate ANOVA (MANOVA) extends the usefulness of the ANOVA test by scrutinizing multiple dependent variables at the same time. As mentioned previously, the ANOVA test allows you to look at the differences between three or more group means. For example, if you have three different teaching techniques and you want to gauge the average scores for these groups, you could use an ANOVA, but you would be missing some potentially important information because when you use an ANOVA, you can look at only one dependent variable at a time. If you want to eliminate that problem, you can use a MANOVA to test multiple dependent variables at the same time.

MANCOVA

This statistical test is the same as a MANOVA except that with this test, you can control for one or more covariates that may influence the dependent variable. To clarify, let's look at another example. As a teacher, you could use a MANCOVA to explore whether exam outcomes differed due to the anxiety levels of students while controlling for revision time. You would set up your dependent variable as being social studies, science, and mathematics exam scores, all scored on a scale of 0 to 100. The independent variable would be anxiety level, which has been split into three groups: low-anxiety, moderate-anxiety, and high-anxiety students with the covariate being revision time. As the teacher, you may choose to control for revision time based on your belief that the effect of anxiety levels on overall exam performance will depend on the amount of time students spend revising.

Correlation

Correlation is a measure that expresses the magnitude and direction of a relation between two or more variables. It is important to note that just because a correlation exists between variables does not automatically mean that the change in one variable is the cause of the change in the values of the other variable. Simply stated, correlation does not equal causation. For example, there is a correlation between the per capita consumption of mozzarella cheese and civil engineering doctorates awarded (Vigen, n.d.). See Figure 4.1 for an example of this spurious correlation.

Figure 4.1 Correlation Does Not Equal Causation

Multiple Regression

Regression model statistical tests are deployed to describe relations between variables by fitting a line to the observed data. Regression allows you to estimate how a dependent variable changes as the independent variables change. Multiple regression is deployed to estimate the relations between two or more independent variables and one dependent variable. Multiple regression can also be used to assess how strong a relation is between two or more independent variables and one dependent variable (e.g., how hours of sleep, time of day, and amount of explicit instruction affect skill acquisition).

Path Analysis

This design is used to evaluate causal models by examining the relation between a dependent variable and two or more independent variables in the form of a path. Essentially, when deploying a path analysis, you are looking at the direct and indirect effects of the predictor variable. For example, a traumatic event may cause students to skip school, which may lead to dropping out of school and, in turn, lead to drug abuse.

Logistics Regression

The logistics regression model is a type of statistical model used for classification and predictive analysis. Simply stated, this model estimates the odds probability of the dependent variable occurring as the values of the independent variable change. For example, if we want to identify the odds of dropping out of college at different levels of alcohol consumption of students, we could use a logistics regression model to find those odds.

WHAT ARE THE CRITICAL COMPONENTS OF GROUP RESEARCH DESIGNS?

As we walk through the critical components of group designed research, we will lean on the *Publication Manual of the American Psychological Association, Seventh Edition*. We will focus on section three of the manual, titled Journal Article Reporting Standards, or JARS, which provides guidelines for authors of scholarly research on what information should be included in their journal articles (American Psychological Association [APA], 2020).

Title and Abstract

In group design articles, the title should explicitly state the design and the variables investigated. For example, "Reducing Child Problem Behaviors and Improving Teacher-Child Interactions and Relationships: A Randomized Controlled Trial of BEST in CLASS" by Sutherland and colleagues (2018) sought to test the BEST in CLASS intervention. This intervention assists teachers in systematically identifying students with chronic behavior problems and using targeted instructional practices. The study compared student outcomes of students who received the BEST in CLASS intervention to similar students who did not receive the intervention. When examining the title, we see that the authors explicitly stated that the study was conducted using a randomized controlled trial (the design) to test the BEST in CLASS intervention (variable of interest). So just by looking for keywords in the title, we can see this is a group design study.

The abstract should include accurate, nonevaluative, coherent, readable, and concise language. When reading the abstract of a group design study, you should be able to identify the problem being explored and with whom and where; research design; analytic strategy; data-gathering procedures; **sample size**; and basic findings, including effect sizes. When looking at the abstract from the Sutherland et al. (2018) study, we can see the criteria for an abstract, according to APA, was met.

> This study examined the effect of *BEST in CLASS*, a Tier-2 intervention delivered by teachers, on *child problem behavior, teacher-child interactions, and teacher-child relationships* using a *cluster randomized controlled trial design*. Participants were *465 children (3–5-year-olds)* identified *at risk for the development of EBDs* and their *185 teachers* from *early childhood programs* located in *two southeastern states*. Significant effects were found across both teacher-reported *(ES ranging from 0.23 to 0.42)* and observed child outcomes *(ES ranging from 0.44–0.46)*, as well as teacher-child relationships *(ES ranging from 0.26 to 0.29)* and observed teacher-children interactions *(ES ranging from 0.26 to 0.45)*, favoring the BEST in CLASS condition. *Results suggest* the promise of BEST in CLASS as a Tier-2 intervention for use in authentic early childhood classroom contexts and provide implications for future research on transactional models of teacher and child behavior.

Introduction

When you are reading the introduction to a group design study, think of it as an abbreviated literature review that includes many of the pieces discussed in Chapter 3, just shorter. The main purpose of the introduction here is to highlight the importance/rationale for the study, succinctly outline the historical factors surrounding the topic, and convey the study goals. When authors write high-quality introductions, you should be able to identify the primary and secondary hypotheses for the study and any exploratory hypotheses being explored as well as the **null hypothesis**. In statistics, a **hypothesis** is a statement of the relationship between variables of interest in terms of what is expected to happen. An example of a hypothesis statement to be tested might be students exposed to cooperative learning strategies will score higher on an achievement test than students who are exposed to a lecture-only format. On the other hand, a null hypothesis is a statement that no statistical significance exists between the independent variables and dependent variables. The null hypothesis in relation to the hypothesis above may look something like this: there will be no difference in achievement between students exposed to cooperative learning strategies and students exposed to a lecture-only format. This is the essential difference between introductions for literature reviews (Chapter 3) and single-case research (Chapter 5) in comparison to a group design study.

Method

The devil is in the details when it comes to the method section of scientific literature. When the author provides little or inaccurate information, it can lead to issues with **believability**, reproducibility, and replicability. Perceptions, whether true or not, serve as the foundation for people's beliefs and behaviors. Data believability relates to whether the data are regarded as being true, real, and credible (Wang & Strong, 1996) and is, therefore, based on an individual's perceptions of those outcomes. The term *reproducibility* refers to how much a tool can consistently yield the same outcome when used in the same way across multiple occasions. If that tool is used under similar circumstances and yields different results, those outcomes would not be considered reproducible. *Replicability* is the ability to accomplish consistent results through multiple research agendas, each involving a unique set of data, that try to tackle the same scientific topic. If the same results are not achieved through those research agendas, we would not consider the outcomes, data, or tools to be replicable. On the other hand, given the amount of uncertainty in the variables being studied, studies could be considered to have been replicated if they produced consistent results. So what does this mean for consumers of quantitative research? On its face, it means that if the information reported in a method section is poorly reported, it makes it extremely difficult for the consumer to take the authors at their word. Further, if there are multiple studies examining a variable under similar conditions and the results are not reproducible or replicable, the believability of those outcomes is much less than it would be if those results were reproduced and replicated. What this boils down to is author teams conducting their research with a high level of rigor.

One way to assess the rigor of a study is to use indicators of high-quality research, which we discuss later in this chapter. At a minimum, authors of this type of research need to report the inclusion and exclusion criteria, participant characteristics, setting descriptions, sampling procedures, sample size, data collection, measurement, materials, effect size and interpretation ranges, design, and their analytic strategy.

The essential characteristics of the target population that research teams employ to address their research question are known as inclusion criteria, which are the features that potential participants must possess to be included in a study. Geographic, setting, and demographic traits, such as age; gender; race; ethnicity; marital status; educational background; language; kind of work; physical activity; health conditions; and the existence of mental, emotional, or medical conditions, are typical inclusion criteria. If potential participants do not meet the inclusion criteria set forth by author teams, then they will be excluded from that study. Additionally, exclusion criteria are characteristics that match the inclusion criteria, but they might have variables that could thwart the study's progress. Inclusion criteria and exclusion criteria are needed because educational researchers rely on something called assumptions of normality.

Most special educators are familiar with or have heard of the bell curve. Relative to quantitative research, a bell curve is frequently referred to as a normal distribution. The bell curve represents data from a variable that are distributed in a bell shape among the population. Fundamentally, this means that a large number of people trend toward the center of the bell. Consequently, as the bell tails off in one direction or the other, the individuals included in those sections of the curve become fewer and fewer.

But why is this level of reporting important for special educators consuming research? A solid foundation of quality research is required in the field of special education to deliver effective instruction to students with disabilities. Studies conducted with high levels of rigor demonstrate the efficacy of the strategy that was investigated. Research of the highest caliber should assist educators, administrators, parents, legislators, and researchers in determining what is worth investing in and what is not. Extensive research on special education ought to offer insights into the aspects of classrooms, school systems, and society that affect the practical efficacy of evidence-based strategies. It should enable us to explain the environments in which learning and teaching take place as well as the circumstances in which people live, work, and put the knowledge they've gained to use. Put another way, research in special education ought to improve the lives of people with disabilities and their families (Odom et al., 2004).

Results

Like the method section, there are many pieces that authors *should* be reporting in the results section. The fact is many studies in the past did not have this guidance and, therefore, are missing some of the critical information current research is reporting. However, many studies are being published today that still omit pertinent information in the results section. At a minimum, authors need to report the number of participants throughout the various stages of the study, the statistical outcomes and analysis of those data, and any issues the author teams encountered with the data and statistical outcomes. But of most importance to us is asking, "Did it work?" We can determine the effect of an intervention by examining the effect sizes being reported by author teams.

Effect Sizes

Effect sizes are a measure of a study's effect. The greater the number is suggests the more impactful the intervention was when compared to the control/comparison group. According to Valentine and Cooper (2003), there are generally three different approaches to assessing the magnitude of an intervention's effect: (a) assessing the statistical significance of the effects, (b) assessing practical significance based on the raw mean differences of experimental groups, and (c) assessing the relative size of the effects based on standardized estimates of effect size.

Statistical Significance

Statistical significance refers to the assertion that a set of observed data did not happen by chance but can be attributed to a specific cause/variable. Statistical significance is important for academic disciplines or practitioners who rely heavily on analyzing data and are research informed. If the outcome of the statistical test suggests a high statistical significance, this indicates that any observed relation is unlikely to be due to chance.

Practical Significance

Perhaps the most important concept consumers of research need to be aware of is practical significance. Practical significance is the measure that tells us if the outcomes or effects are large enough to have some sort of meaningful change for our learners in the real world. To highlight practical significance, let's take a look at self-injurious behavior. Imagine you have a pool of students who engage in head-banging behaviors. You have a sample size large enough to use a quantitative analysis and a strategy you would like to test. Your mean data score from the dataset you have acquired is 15 instances of head-banging in 6 hours. The strategy you have is implemented, and you collect more data. After collecting the data, the mean score of head-banging behavior was reduced to 13 instances in 6 hours. Although statistics might not identify a mathematical significance between 13 and 15 instances of head-banging, the practical significance of reducing any number of instances is helpful to those children.

Discussion

The discussion section should place the current study within the literature base and consider any interesting findings discovered during the study. Many researchers argue that the discussion section of an article holds the most value in comparison to other parts of a research article. Whether there is a consensus or not, the discussion section shows you that the authors understand the results and how those are situated in the existing literature. Consumers of research should anticipate the following areas being addressed in a discussion section of a quantitative study: (a) an interpretation of the authors' findings within the context of the existing literature, (b) a description of the significance of the findings in relation to what is already known, and (c) an explanation of novel insights gleaned from the research. Along with situating their findings within the existing information on a particular topic, authors will also discuss any limitations they are aware of as they conduct their research.

WHAT ARE THE LIMITATIONS OF GROUP RESEARCH DESIGNS?

Like any research methodology, there are limitations consumers must be aware of. The most common weaknesses in a group design study include (a) poorly described participant populations, (b) too narrow a participant population, (c) failure to use appropriate controls or comparison groups, (d) failure to demonstrate the comparability of participants in treatment and control groups, (e) confounding variables, (f) systematic errors or differences in measurement, (g) attrition, (h) inappropriate statistical analysis and planning, and (i) poorly described methodology, all of which can lead to misrepresented results from a study (Joy et al., 2005). One way these limitations are being minimized in the world of education is to provide quality indicators for rigorous group designed research. The two main documents that guide rigorous research practices in special education come from the What Works Clearinghouse (WWC) and Council for Exceptional Children (CEC).

Mitigating Limitations

The purpose of the WWC is to review and summarize the quality of existing research in educational programs, products, practices, and policies. The WWC refines its procedures and standards based on improvements in education research and research synthesis methods. The *WWC Procedures and Standards Handbook, Version 5.0*, contains the most up-to-date procedures and standards at the time of this writing that are used to review studies and synthesize and characterize findings (WWC, 2020). A revised list of what special education teachers need to know about critically examining research using the WWC standards can be viewed in Table 4.2.

Table 4.2 *Essentials Checklist for Teachers Examining Research Using* WWC Standards

Question to Answer Did the article . . .	Description
Intervention and Comparison Conditions	
. . . describe what happened in the intervention condition?	• Goals of the intervention, including intended outcomes and populations. • The intervention's key components, such as curricula, instructional strategies, coaching, or other activities or strategies. • The resources needed to implement the intervention. • Delivery method—individual, small group, whole class, school. • The timing of the start and end of the intervention. • Intended and actual duration, frequency, and dosage.
. . . describe what happened in the comparison condition?	• What did the comparison group receive or do in lieu of the intervention?
Study Sample and Context	
. . . describe the population of interest?	• The population to which the study findings should apply in other contexts.
. . . describe participants?	• Student grades and ages for early childhood and adult learners and learners with disabilities. • Student race, ethnicity, sex, gender, gender identity, disability status, English learner status, socioeconomic status, and other characteristics (e.g., homeless, migrant, and foster). • Educator characteristics—years of experience and credentials.
. . . describe settings?	• Country or state if in the United States. • Urban, rural, suburban, or town setting. • Number of schools or sites, school type (e.g., public, charter, or private), and format (e.g., in person or online). • Classroom type, including general or inclusion, self-contained special education, and designated English language development.

Question to Answer Did the article . . .	Description
Study Design and Measures	
. . . report the study design? . . . report measures used?	• Was the study design a randomized controlled trial, quasi-experimental design, or regression discontinuity design? • What were the names and versions of the baseline—or pretest—and outcome measures used in the study, and what constructs did they measure? • When were the measures collected? • What were the data collection procedures, and did they differ for the intervention and comparison groups?
Specific Reporting Guidelines for Randomized Controlled Trials and Quasi-Experimental Studies	
. . . describe how intervention and comparison groups were formed? . . . describe which participants were included in the analysis?	• How were participants recruited and assigned to the intervention and comparison groups? • Were participants assigned as individuals—students or teachers—or in clusters—classes, schools, or districts? • What were the reasons participants or clusters were not included in the analysis, such as eligibility rules, missing data, or other decisions the researchers made?
Descriptive Statistics	
. . . report descriptive statistics?	• Descriptive statistics for the analytic sample—for each measure and all conditions reported.
Study Results for Each Outcome Measure	
. . . include impact estimate? . . . include test statistics? . . . include statistical significance? . . . include effect size?	• A measure of the impact of the intervention relative to the comparison group. • The test statistic associated with the impact estimate. • The p-value associated with the impact estimate test statistic. • The WWC reports effect sizes in terms of Hedges' g, which is based on the adjusted means and the unadjusted standard deviations and includes an adjustment for studies with small samples.

CEC is an international community of professionals who are the voice and vision of special education. CEC's mission is to improve, through excellence and advocacy, the education and quality of life for children and youth with exceptionalities and to enhance the engagement of their families. As such, CEC provides an approach for categorizing the evidence base of practices in special education. The quality indicators and the criteria for categorizing the evidence base of special education practices are intended for use by groups or individuals with advanced training and experience in educational research design and methods. A revised list of what special education teachers need to know about critically examining research using CEC's standards for evidence-based practices can be viewed in Table 4.3.

Table 4.3 *Essentials Checklist for Teachers Examining Research Using* CEC *Quality Indicators*

Quality Indicator	Standards for Evidence-Based Practices	Information Required to Meet Indicator
#1	Context and setting	The study provides sufficient information regarding the critical features of the context or setting.
#2	Participants	The study provides sufficient information to identify the population of participants to which results may be generalized and to determine or confirm whether the participants demonstrated a disability or difficulty of focus.
#3	Intervention agent	The study provides sufficient information regarding the critical features of the intervention agent.
#4	Description of practice	The study provides sufficient information regarding the critical features of the practice (intervention) such that the practice is clearly understood and can be reasonably replicated.
#5	Implementation fidelity	The practice is implemented with fidelity.
#6	Internal validity	The independent variable is under the control of the experimenter. The study describes the services provided in control and comparison conditions and phases. The research design provides sufficient evidence that the independent variable causes a change in the dependent variable or variables. Participants stayed with the study, so attrition is not a significant threat to internal validity.
#7	Outcome measures/ dependent variables	Outcome measures are applied appropriately to gauge the effect of the practice on study outcomes. Outcome measures demonstrate adequate psychometrics.
#8	Data analysis	Data analysis is conducted appropriately. The study reports information on effect size.

HOW DO I INTERPRET GROUP RESEARCH DESIGNS?

Interpreting group design studies takes professional judgment because no empirical study is going to exactly match your students' demographics, your training, and your experience. Furthermore, there are likely other environmental variables that are present in your classroom that are different from the study's setting. Nevertheless, one of the strengths of group designed research is that **confounding variables** are controlled. This means any effect on student outcomes by the intervention can be attributed to the intervention with high degrees of confidence.

What You Should Be Looking For

If you have found yourself searching through the existing literature base to find a possible solution for a situation in your classroom, you may find that the number of search results is daunting. One way to reduce the number of returns is to set a date limiter for what is returned based on the terms used in the search. Generally, you will want to set a date limiter of 5 to 10 years of the current year. This is not to say that research before the limiter is worthless, but it is important to access the most current research around your topics because it will have the most up-to-date information available. Once you restrict the number of results you receive, you can start to look for studies that may be of help to you. Thinking back to earlier in this chapter, you should peruse the titles and abstracts of the results looking for keywords that align with your reason for the exploration of the literature.

Now that you have identified a study or two that appears, from the title and abstract, to align with your needs, you can start reading the articles. As you read through the group design articles, you will want to pay close attention to the hypothesis and null hypothesis to see if the authors' study purposes still align with your needs. If so, you will want to continue to the method section and identify a few major items: participants, settings, resources needed (e.g., materials and interventionist), independent variable, and dependent variable. Once you've identified these components of the study and you still feel as though the content in the article is a close match to your situation, it is time to dig into the results section with a particular eye on the effect sizes the authors report.

Interpreting Effect Sizes

As mentioned earlier in this chapter, effect sizes are a measure of a study's effect. They tell you how consequential the relations between variables or variances between groups are and indicate the practical significance of a research outcome. The larger the effect size, the larger the practical significance of the outcomes are, while a small effect size indicates insubstantial practical applications. Anyone consuming research can look to Cohen's suggestions for interpreting effect size: Large magnitudes of effect were $d = .80$ or $r = .50$. Medium-size effects were placed between these two extremes, that is $d = .50$ or $r = .30$, with anything falling below that being considered a small effect (Cohen, 2013).

WHERE CAN I FIND MORE INFORMATION ABOUT GROUP RESEARCH DESIGNS?

Council for Exceptional Children Standards for Evidence-Based Practices in Special Education: This statement presents an approach for categorizing the evidence base of practices in special education. The quality indicators and criteria for categorizing the evidence base of special education practices are intended for use by groups or individuals with advanced training and experience in educational research design and methods. CEC's standards for evidence-based practices can be found at https://exceptionalchildren.org/sites/default/files/2021-04/EBP_FINAL.pdf.

Institute of Education Sciences (IES): IES is the statistics, research, and evaluation arm of the U.S. Department of Education. It is independent and nonpartisan. Its mission is to provide scientific evidence on which to ground education practice and policy and to share this information in formats that are useful and accessible to educators, parents, policymakers, researchers, and the public. Its website can be accessed at https://ies.ed.gov/.

Publication Manual of the American Psychological Association, Seventh Edition: This manual (https://www.apa.org) is the official source for APA Style. With millions of copies sold worldwide in multiple languages, it is the style manual of choice for writers, researchers, editors, students, and educators in the social and behavioral sciences, natural sciences, nursing, communications, education, business, engineering, and other fields. It guides users through the scholarly writing process—from the ethics of authorship to reporting research through publication. The seventh edition is an indispensable resource for students and professionals to achieve excellence in writing and make an impact with their work.

What Works Clearinghouse (WWC): For more than a decade, WWC has been a central and trusted source of scientific evidence on education programs, products, practices, and policies. It reviews the research, determines which studies meet rigorous standards, and summarizes the findings. WWC focuses on high-quality research to answer the question "What works in education?" *WWC Procedures and Standards Handbook, Version 5.0* can be found at https://ies.ed.gov/ncee/WWC/Docs/referenceresources/Final_WWC-HandbookVer5_0-0-508.pdf.

DISCUSSION QUESTIONS

1. What are important considerations when interpreting group designed research?
2. Based on the information provided in this chapter, what are the three most critical components of a group design?
3. Search the literature and identify a group design study that might support you in providing high-quality effective special education instruction.
4. What was it about the article you identified in question 3 that lets you know that the independent variable was effective in increasing a student outcome?
5. What are the differences between ANOVA, ANCOVA, MANOVA, and MANCOVA?
6. How do you know if a study was conducted with high levels of scientific rigor? In other words, how do you know that the study and the information presented within are believable?

KEY TERMS

believability: The degree to which something is regarded as true, real, and credible.

between-group design: Has two or more groups of participants that are tested concurrently using different variables.

confounding variable: A factor that influences both the dependent variable and independent variable, causing a spurious association.

dependent variable: Represents a quantity whose value depends on how the independent variable is manipulated.

effect size: A quantitative measure of the magnitude of the experimental effect. The larger the effect size, the stronger the relationship between two variables.

hypothesis: A formal statement that gives an explanation of the relationship between two or more variables of a specified population.

independent variables: Variables that are manipulated or changed by researchers and whose effects are measured and compared.

null hypothesis: The hypothesis statement that there is no significant difference between specified populations, any observed difference being due to sampling or experimental error.
quantitative statistics: Using numerical data to describe objects, situations, or phenomena.
randomized controlled trial: A study design that randomly assigns participants to an experimental group or a control group.
sample size: Number of participants or observations used in a study.
***t*-test:** A test that is used to compare the means of two groups.
within-subject design: Researchers compare related measures from the same participants between different conditions.

REFERENCES

American Psychological Association (APA). (2020). *Publication manual of the American Psychological Association* (7th ed.). https://doi.org/10.1037/0000165-000

Bodmer, W., Bailey, R. A., Charlesworth, B., Eyre-Walker, A., Farewell, V., Mead, A., & Senn, S. (2021). The outstanding scientist, R.A. Fisher: His views on eugenics and race. *Heredity, 126*(4), 565–576. https://doi.org/10.1038/s41437-020-00394-6

Bothwell, L. E., Greene, J. A., Podolsky, S. H., & Jones, D. S. (2016). Assessing the gold standard—lessons from the history of RCTs. *New England Journal of Medicine, 374*(22), 2175–2181. doi:10.1056/NEJMms1604593

Cohen, J. (2013). *Statistical power analysis for the behavioral sciences*. Academic Press.

Cooper, J. O., Heron, T. E., & Heward, W. L. (2020). *Applied behavior analysis* (3rd ed.). Pearson/Merrill-Prentice Hall.

Hariton, E., & Locascio, J. J. (2018). Randomised controlled trials—the gold standard for effectiveness research. *BJOG: An International Journal of Obstetrics and Gynecology, 125*(13), 1716. https://doi.org/10.1111/1471-0528.15199

Joy, J. E., Penhoet, E. E., & Petitti, D. B. (Eds). (2005). *Saving women's lives: Strategies for improving breast cancer detection and diagnosis: Appendix D, common weaknesses in study designs*. National Academies Press. https://www.ncbi.nlm.nih.gov/books/NBK22323/

Odom, S. L. (2021). Education of students with disabilities, science, and randomized controlled trials. *Research and Practice for Persons with Severe Disabilities, 46*(3), 132–145. https://doi.org/10.1177/15407969211032341

Odom, S. L., Brantlinger, E., Gersten, R., Horner, R. D., Thompson, B., & Harris, K. (2004). *Quality indicators for research in special education and guidelines for evidence-based practices: Executive summary*. Arlington, VA: Council for Exceptional Children Division for Research.

Sutherland, K. S., Conroy, M. A., Algina, J., Ladwig, C., Jessee, G., & Gyure, M. (2018). Reducing child problem behaviors and improving teacher-child interactions and relationships: A randomized controlled trial of BEST in CLASS. *Early Childhood Research Quarterly, 42*, 31–43. https://doi.org/10.1016/j.ecresq.2017.08.001

Valentine, J. C., & Cooper, H. (2003). *Effect size substantive interpretation guidelines: Issues in the interpretation of effect sizes.* Washington, DC: What Works Clearinghouse.

Vigen, T. (n.d.). Per capita consumption of mozzarella cheese correlates to civil engineering doctorate degrees awarded. TylerVigen.com. https://tylervigen.com/spurious-correlations

Wang, R. Y., & Strong, D. M. (1996). Beyond accuracy: What data quality means to data consumers. *Journal of Management Information Systems, 12*(4), 5–33. https://doi.org/10.1080/07421222.1996.11518099

What Works Clearinghouse. (2022). *What Works Clearinghouse procedures and standards handbook, version 5.0.* https://ies.ed.gov/ncee/WWC/Docs/referenceresources/Final_WWC-HandbookVer5_0-0-508.pdf

Chapter 5

Single-Case Research Designs

One of the main characteristics of group design research is testing hypotheses on large groups to find treatments that are likely to be effective and to generalize to a larger population. However, there will always be participants for whom treatment does not work, and oftentimes, statistical tests used in quantitative research do not account for participants whose data are considered outliers. Furthermore, it may be difficult to gather a large number of participants with similar characteristics to examine control and experimental group effects. This is where many social scientists apply single-case research design (SCRD) to see what treatments may support smaller populations of participants or participants who need more individualized interventions.

Single-case, or single-subject, research is as old as psychology itself, and in the late 19th century, Wilhelm Wundt, one of the founders of psychology, developed the idea of focusing intensively on each of a small number of research participants as he studied sensation and consciousness. Early examples include Herman Ebbinghaus's work on memory and Ivan Pavlov's work on classical conditioning, both of which are still included in almost every introductory psychology textbook (Jhangiani et al., 2015). In the mid-20th century, B. F. Skinner clarified many of the assumptions underlying single-subject research and refined many of its methods (Skinner, 1938). He and other researchers used it to explain how rewards, punishments, and other external factors influence behavior over time. While much of this early research was conducted on nonhuman subjects (e.g., rats and pigeons), the science is now widely applied to human participants.

In this chapter, we will discuss SCRD and its application in special education as we answer the following essential questions:

1. What are single-case research designs?
2. What are the critical components of single-case research designs?
3. What are the limitations of single-case research designs?

4. How do I interpret single-case research designs?
5. Where can I find more information about single-case research designs?

WHAT ARE SINGLE-CASE RESEARCH DESIGNS?

The experimental approach we focus on in this chapter is called the **single-case research design** (SCRD), also known as single-subject research. Single-case studies are often used in special education and behavior analytic research. SCRD is an evaluation method that can be used to rigorously test the success of an intervention or treatment for a particular case with a rather small sample size. Although SCRD is often conducted with a small number of participants (one to four), researchers using this design can also test independent variables (IVs) with groups of people participating in one experiment. For example, if a researcher wanted to investigate the effect of a group contingency on the active participation of students in a resource classroom, they could employ an SCRD where the whole class is considered the "case." It is important to note that SCRD studies are *not* case studies. This is a common misunderstanding of SCRD. According to Backman and Harris (1999), a case study is a form of descriptive research that seeks to identify explanatory patterns for phenomena and generates hypotheses for future research, while SCRD is an experimental approach to investigating causal relations between IVs and dependent variables (DVs). An SCRD is characterized by repeated measures of an observable and clinically relevant target behavior throughout at least one pretreatment (baseline) and intervention phase.

Although SCRD goes by many names (e.g., n of 1, $n = 1$, single subject, or single case), the foundational principles of this family of design remains the same. SCRDs allow for the evaluation of treatments as they are used in the applied settings (e.g., schools and clinics). Inferences are drawn by using a participant as the source of **control** or comparison. The fact that the participant acts as their own control is significantly different than quantitative group design because that approach involves a separate control group to compare the treatment group against. A participant as their own control means that the effect of treatment is evaluated throughout time and in connection to the participants' behavior or other DV. Like group designs, there are quality indicators surrounding the rigor of the SCRD that must be adhered to for a valid evaluation to take place. Given these quality indicators, SCRD can be designed and conducted in a plethora of ways to satisfy the practical needs within the setting and with the participant of interest. The treatment focus, the means of monitoring progress, the specific intervention techniques, and how and when treatment is delivered can all be organized in such a way that service delivery remains a priority (Kazdin, 2019).

WHAT ARE THE CRITICAL COMPONENTS OF SINGLE-CASE RESEARCH DESIGNS?

An essential feature of SCRD is the letter designation of sequence conditions. Although this phrase may seem sophisticated, the rule is rather straightforward. Each phase in temporal sequence (in order by time) is assigned sequential letters of the alphabet (e.g., A, B, and C). Stated another way, the initial phase, usually baseline, is designated with an A. Baseline refers to the level of responding before any intervention is introduced. The second phase in the sequence is labeled with a B. The third phase's label will be determined by whether it is a repeat of the first phase (A) or a new phase (C). Because a control or baseline condition is frequently the first phase of a study, baseline conditions are commonly called A.

The acceptability of SCRD as an experimental approach for examining the effects of an intervention hinges on something called **steady state responding** and **baseline logic**. Steady state responding is a purposeful procedure in which the DV is repeatedly exposed to the IV, with the goal of controlling for and/or eliminating any extraneous effects on the DV and establish a stable response pattern before going on to the next condition. According to Cooper et al. (2020), baseline logic comprises three separate but equally important elements: prediction, verification, and replication.

Prediction is the expected outcome of a currently unknown or future measurement. It is the most elegant application of quantification upon which all scientific and technical endeavor is based (Johnston & Pennypacker, 1980, p. 2). Logically, after prediction comes verification. **Verification** focuses on the demonstration that the DVs would not change in the absence of intervention (i.e., IVs). However, only one instance of verification is not enough to determine if the IV is what is responsible for affecting the DV. What researchers need is additional representations of verification, and this comes in the form of replication. **Replication** entails removing the intervention, reinstating it, and achieving similar results. Essentially, researchers are trying to turn behavior on and off using these essential features of SCRD to show that there is control within the study leading to the believability of the outcomes.

Single-Case Research Designs

SCRD is made up of a family of designs, the foundation of which is the AB design. While the AB design is the girder for other SCRD designs, it is also the weakest for making any conclusions about if there is a **functional relation** or not. The reason is that in an AB design, a change in the behavior can be identified only one time, meaning there is no replication of the effect. When researchers are not able to replicate a result within a single-case study, they cannot be sure the intervention was the thing responsible for the change in behavior, bringing into question the believability of the data. This all hinges on baseline logic, which was discussed earlier in this chapter. To increase the believability of a single-case study, researchers need to add a replication component/phase to their studies. Replication is accomplished in several ways within a variety of SCRD designs.

Reversal Design

Researchers might consider choosing the reversal (e.g., ABAB and withdrawal) design to examine if a functional relation exists between the IVs and DVs. The reversal design involves collecting a set of initial business as usual (i.e., baseline) data that will act as the control. Next, the researchers will implement their intervention and continue collecting data on the DV. After the data have reached stability or a particular decision-making rule, the researchers remove the intervention while continually monitoring the DV; this is known as the second baseline in a reversal design. Once stability has been reached in the second baseline, the researchers reinstall the intervention and continue to collect data on the DV. By adding the additional phases to the AB design, researchers can add a layer of replication, which can increase the believability of those data. See Figure 5.1 for examples of an AB and a reversal design.

Multiple Baseline Design

A multiple baseline design, which does not require condition reversal to create experimental control, is one of the most utilized single-case designs represented in journals that publish SCRD studies. One of the major reasons multiple baseline designs are so popular among special education researchers is the fact that many of the skills we work on with children are unable to be reversed once they are learned; this means that a reversal design would not show experimental control. Another reason one might choose to use this design is there are times when removing a treatment would be unethical (e.g., cause harm). For example, if a teacher installed an intervention to reduce aggressive behaviors of one student toward another and the intervention is working, it would not be appropriate to remove the intervention.

Multiple baseline designs are classified into three types: multiple baseline across persons, multiple baseline across behaviors, and multiple baseline across settings. The most common is the multiple baseline across people, in which baselines for three or more people are established before introducing the intervention. It is important to note that the intervention is introduced in a staggered manner. The staggered introduction of the intervention component

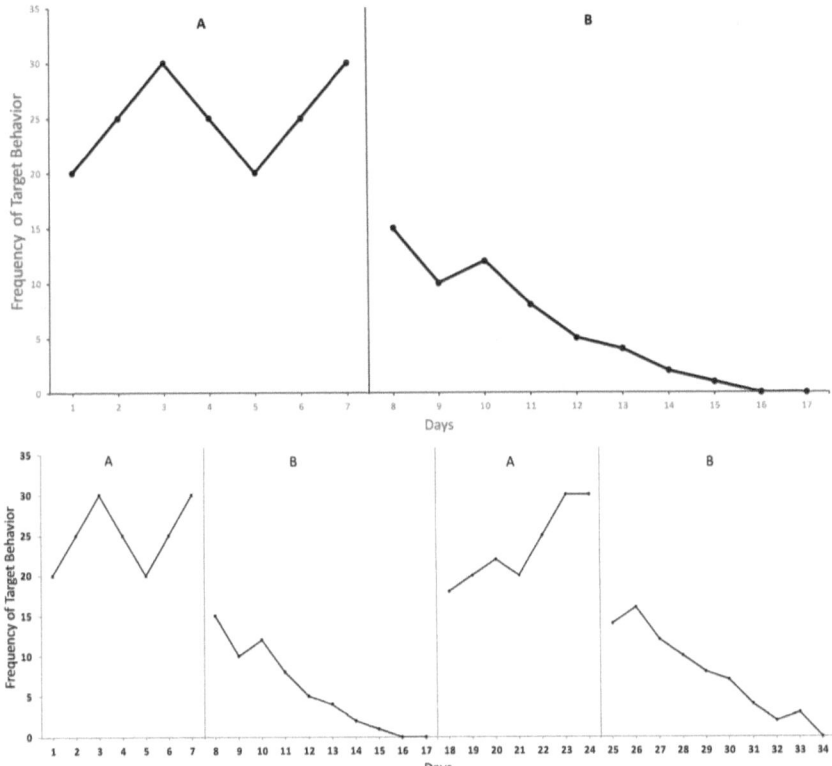

Figure 5.1 Example of AB and Reversal Designs

within a multiple baseline design is important because this is where single-case researchers assess the replication of results within their study. As with most of the SCRDs, there are variations to multiple baseline design.

One of those variations is the multiple probe design. This is where baseline data are periodically collected or probed. Not only is the burden of data collection reduced, but researchers may decide to take this approach if they believe repetitive measure of behavior or skills could cause frustration for the participant. The multiple probe design is an appealing choice when it is unethical or undesirable to collect many baseline data points, such as when the participant engages in self-injurious or aggressive behavior or when collecting baseline data would cause the participant to repeatedly fail or practice a skill incorrectly (Epstein & Dallery, 2022). If the outcomes do not change during baseline conditions and the changes occur across individuals only after the treatment is implemented, and this sequence is replicated across study participants, the single-case researcher has evidence to suggest that there is a functional relation between the IVs and DVs. See Figures 5.2 and 5.3 for examples of the multiple baseline and multiple probe design.

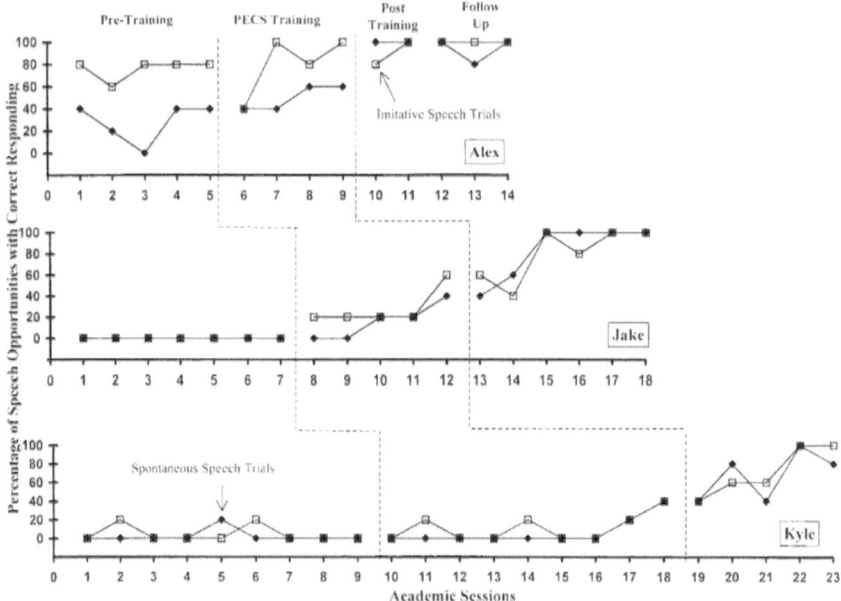

Figure 5.2 Example of a Multiple Baseline and Multiple Probe Design. Multiple baseline graph by Charlop-Christy et al. (2002).

Alternating Treatments Design

Sometimes single-case researchers are interested in examining which intervention is most effective for their learner. The alternating treatments, or multi-element, design is an approach used to assess the effect of various interventions on the frequency of problem behavior (Kodak & Halbur, 2021). For example, in an experiment conducted by Vollmer and colleagues in 1993, they wanted to compare the effect of one reinforcement schedule versus another reinforcement schedule and their effects on rates of problem behavior. In their study, they showed, via the data for all participants, that the same intervention was the catalyst for reducing the rate of problem behavior. However, this is not always the case because single-case researchers engage in work that involves humans and when we work with humans, there are several variables innate to the individual (e.g., setting, age, and disability) that can affect intervention research results. See Figure 5.4 for an example of the alternating treatments design.

Changing Criterion Design

Yet another design included in the family of single-case designs is a lesser-used design referred to as a changing criterion design (CCD; see Figure 5.5). The

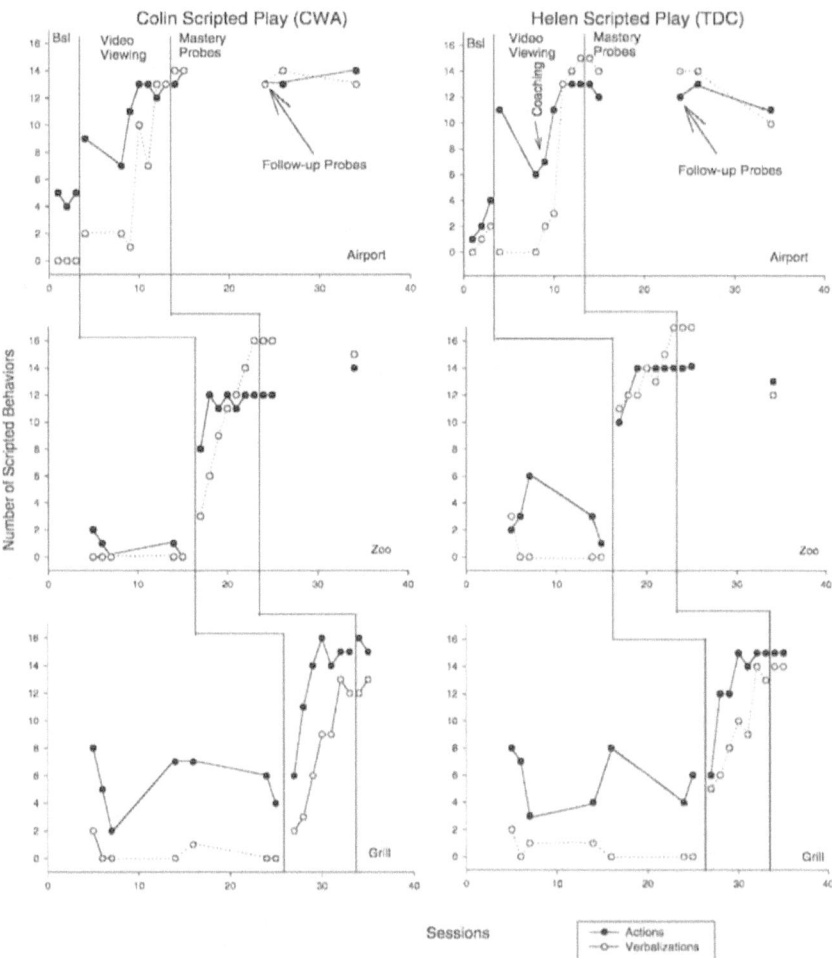

Figure 5.3 Example of a Multiple Probe Design. Multiple probe design by MacDonald et al. (2009).

CCD uses stepwise benchmarks for manipulating a dimension (i.e., accuracy, frequency, duration, latency, or magnitude) of a single behavior already present in an individual's repertoire (Cooper et al., 2020). The design has been used with behaviors where an immediate, considerable increase or decrease may be difficult to achieve or undesired; therefore, gradual shifts toward a desired goal are applied (Klein et al., 2017). The CCD requires initial baseline observations on a single target behavior, which is followed by the introduction of an intervention phase as well as subsequent intervention phases. Each phase is coupled with a change in criterion for the target behavior. Thus, each

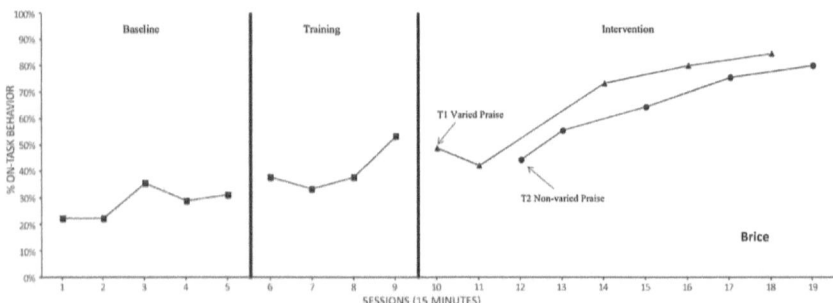

Figure 5.4 Example of an Alternating Treatment Design. Alternating treatment graph by Markelz et al. (2023), where treatment 1 was varied praise and treatment 2 was nonvaried praise.

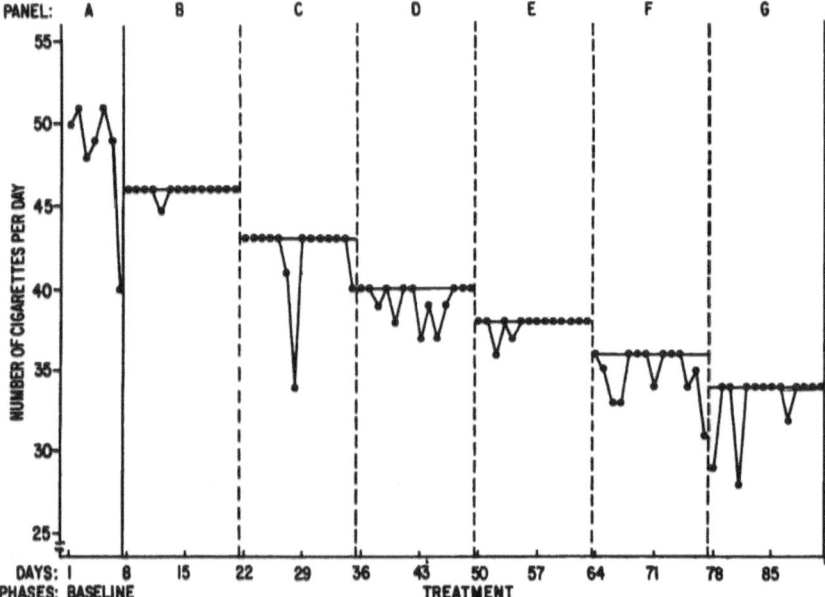

Figure 5.5 Example of a Changing Criterion Design. Changing criterion design example from Hartmann & Hall (1976).

phase of the CCD provides a baseline for the ensuing phase. When the rate of the target behavior changes in the direction anticipated in relation to the new criteria, experimental control has been demonstrated, and the researcher can safely suggest that the IVs and DVs have a functional relation.

Component Analysis

When undertaking intervention science, researchers and interventionists face a conundrum (Riden et al., 2022). Change must be realized swiftly for the benefit of the participants. Whether teaching self-regulation to a student with autism to improve social skills (Kornacki et al., 2013) or using behavior-specific praise to increase on-task behaviors in students with emotional and behavioral disorders (Markelz & Riden, 2019), researchers strive for interventions that effect positive change. Thus, interventions are developed on evidence-based methods, often in conjunction with other interventions (i.e., treatment packages), to achieve the most amount of change in the shortest amount of time. And while the development of treatment packages is appropriate, the shortcoming of some treatment packages is that the more components there are to implement, the less likely fidelity of implementation occurs as well as adoption by practitioners (Riley-Tillman & Chafouleas, 2003). Additionally, package interventions confound the ability of researchers to document which specific component (i.e., IV) contributed to the effect and in what variance. This is where the component analysis design comes in handy.

A component analysis is an SCRD that can be used to evaluate treatments made up of two or more IVs (components) that make up the package (see Figure 5.6). Component analyses are performed by researchers and clinicians to identify the active components of treatment packages that are responsible for behavior change. Component analyses may also improve the efficiency and social validity of behavioral treatments by eliminating ineffective and possibly time-consuming components and evaluating the necessity of more restrictive components (e.g., punishment procedures) or intervention

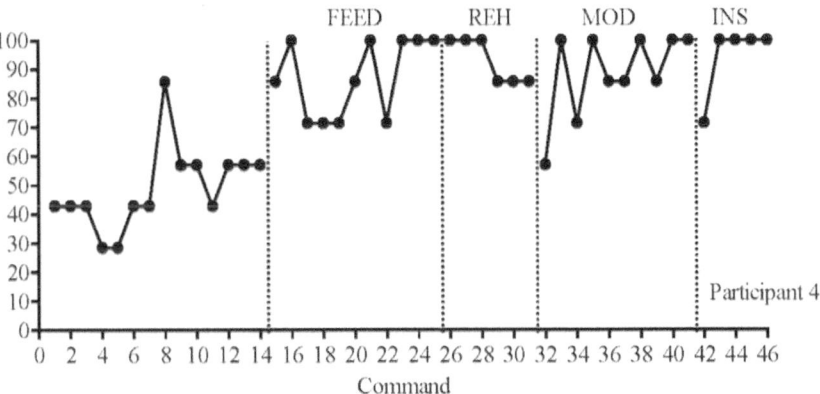

Figure 5.6   Example of a Component Analysis Design. From LaBrot et al. (2018).

components that are unnecessary (Ward-Horner & Sturmey, 2010). The design is accomplished through the systematic presentation or removal of individual components, which can provide an evaluation of the necessity and sufficiency of components and component combinations. When an element or a group of elements is determined to be adequate, it can also give researchers the chance to suggest interventions that are just as successful. Additionally, when all components of a treatment package are required, a component analysis can support the ongoing use of the full package. This is especially crucial when the treatment package contains a restrictive method (Riden et al., 2024).

Combination Designs

There are times when single-case researchers want to take advantage of the strengths of two different types of designs. This is possible by combining different types of designs to test the effect of the IVs on the DVs. One such example of combining designs can be found in an experiment by Markelz et al. (2021). In the study, they wanted to test a treatment package (i.e., training, goal setting, self-monitoring, and tactile prompting) intended to increase the use of teachers' using behavior-specific praise (BSP) in a day care setting. To analyze the effects between IVs and DVs, they combined a multiple probe design across teacher/child dyads with an add-in component analysis. The purpose of their study was to investigate the additive effects of training and goal setting, self-monitoring, and tactile prompting on early childhood educators' BSP toward children displaying off-task behavior, the relationship of components and use of BSP, and changes in child behavior as a result of the intervention (Markelz et al., 2021).

Variable behavior changes across the dyads reflect variable responses to intervention components by teacher participants and increases in BSP by target children. However, the results of their visual analysis revealed a functional relation between the intervention's first and second components as well as the frequency of BSP being delivered. The findings of this study imply that while gradual intensification of intervention components resulted in desirable behavior change, it may not be the most efficient approach for achieving that change. Ultimately, the researchers determined that although packaged treatments are sometimes required to quickly affect behavior change, each component must be evaluated for efficient and practical application because their findings showed that each component raised teachers' BSP rates; however, two out of three participants required the most intensive intervention (tactile prompting) to achieve mastery. What this means is that the author team may have been able to just implement the tactile prompting to increase all three teachers' rates of BSP and save valuable time in the process (see Figure 5.7).

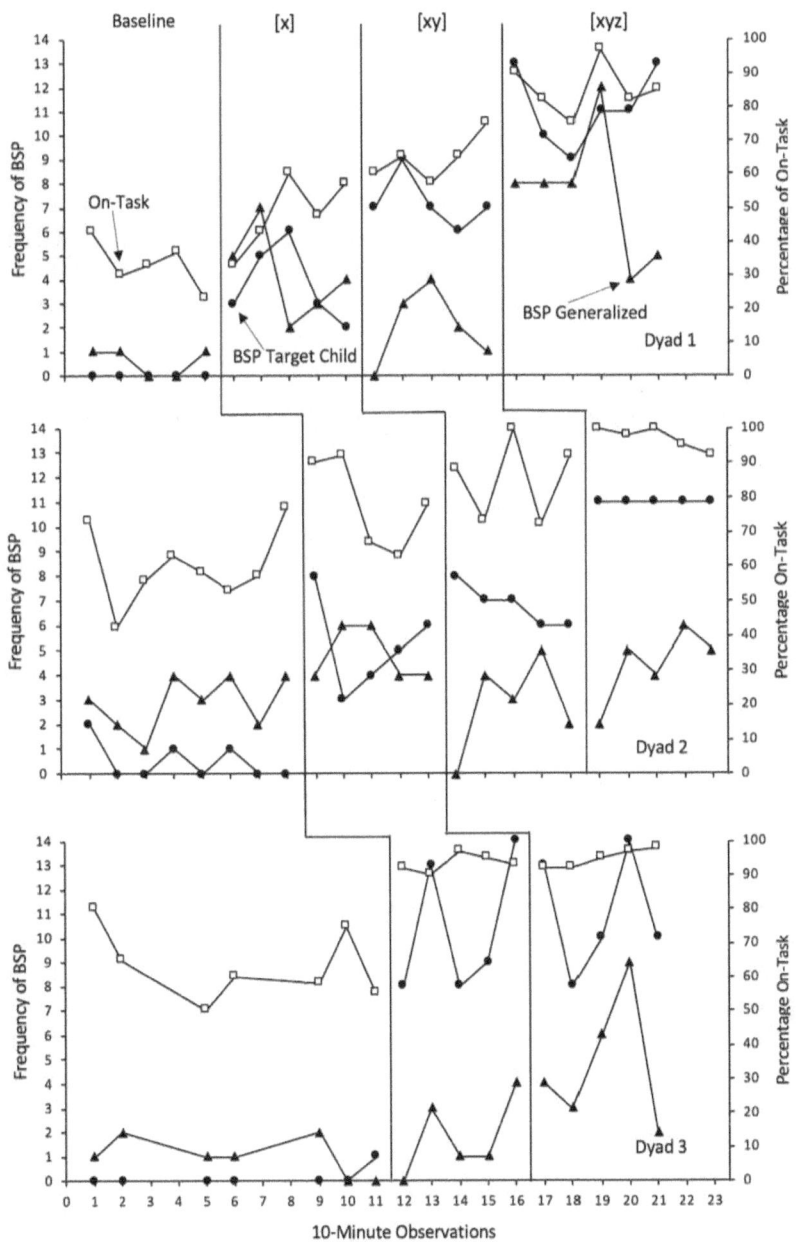

[x] = Training and goal setting; [y] = Self-monitoring; [z] = Tactile prompting

Figure 5.7 Example of a Combination Design. From Markelz et al. (2021).

WHAT ARE THE LIMITATIONS OF SINGLE-CASE RESEARCH DESIGNS?

The constraints of single-case research designs are many. The first of these concerns is the variable that surrounds someone each day that can either impede the effects of the intervention or cause change to the behavior, while the researcher might believe the intervention was the agent of change. Essentially, researchers must control for as many extraneous variables as they possibly can with the understanding that they cannot control for all of them. Given that the outcomes of interventions are examined over time, systemic environmental changes or **maturation** may influence the functional relation between the IVs and DVs, which can lead to error during the analysis and interpretation of the results. What is interesting and helpful for the SCRD researcher is the fact that replication and verification are inherent to many of the SCRDs (e.g., multiple baseline and reversal), which helps the researcher counteract any undue influence on the DVs by extraneous factors.

Another important limitation is the generalizability of the outcomes. The SCRD gives minimal evidence for conclusions about subject populations due to the small number of participants included in each study. Because of this, the field requires several replications surrounding interventions with a particular student population for it to be deemed evidence based and, therefore, providing credence to the generalization of intervention effects.

Mitigating Limitations

Much like the way limitations are mitigated with group design research, SCRDs must adhere to sets of standards to be considered quality research. This really began with an article written by Horner and colleagues in 2005, "The Use of Single-Subject Research to Identify Evidence-Based Practice in Special Education." The purpose of their article was to present the defining features of single-subject research methodology, clarify the relevance of single-subject research methods for special education, and offer objective criteria for determining when single-subject research results are sufficient for documenting evidence-based practices. Here, we will home in on the seven areas that researchers employing SCRDs must adhere to so the research results are sufficient when documenting evidence-based practices: (a) description of participants and settings, (b) DV, (c) IV, (d) baseline, (e) experimental control/internal validity, (f) external validity, and (g) social validity.

Under each category there are several criteria that must be met. When crafting the methodology section, the researchers must describe the participants with sufficient detail to allow other researchers to replicate their work by selecting individuals with similar characteristics. They must also describe in detail the process for choosing participants as well as critical features of the setting, which also supports replication. Next the SCRD researchers must turn their attention to the DVs by ensuring that they operationally define the target behaviors and describe the measurement system. The researchers must also ensure that the system is reliable and conducted repeatedly over time as well as conducting interobserver agreement (IOA) and ensuring that the result of that IOA is at the minimum standard of 80%. Next, the researchers must describe the IVs with such detail that they can also be replicated. They must also ensure that the IVs are systematically manipulated and under experimental control (think baseline logic) and that the treatment is being implemented as designed (i.e., fidelity). Horner and colleagues (2005) next discussed what the SCRD researchers must do during baseline and intervention phases. During baseline, they must ensure that repeated measurement of a DV occurs so that a pattern of responding can be established that can be used to predict the pattern of future responding before the IV is introduced as well as describe baseline conditions with replicable precision.

When implementing the IVs, researchers must keep a keen eye on experimental control and internal validity. Essentially, internal validity is looking to see if the treatment is the variable that is responsible for any behavior change or if there is some other unknown (confounding) variable that is responsible for that change. To do this, researchers must show at least three instances of behavior change. The final two areas that Horner and colleagues (2005) discussed are external and social validity. External validity is the extent to which you can generalize the findings of a study to other situations, people, settings, and measures. In other words, can you apply the findings of your study to a broader context? To establish external validity, researchers need to assess whether experimental effects can be replicated across participants, settings, or materials.

Finally, Horner and colleagues stated that the SCRD researchers must turn an eye to social validity. Social validity refers to the extent to which target behaviors are appropriate, intervention procedures are acceptable, and important and significant changes in target and collateral behaviors are produced. There are four areas that need to be assessed when examining social validity: (1) Is the DV socially important? (2) Is the amount of change meaningful to the participant and/or others around the individual? (3) Is the treatment practical and cost effective for the practitioner as an intervention? and (4) Can the social validity be enhanced by showing the IV implemented over time by different people in similar settings and with similar participants?

Since 2005, there have been several research groups and bodies that govern special education and special education research that have suggested areas of SCRD that must occur within a study to be considered high-quality and rigorous research. One such example comes from the Council for Exceptional Children (CEC). It also provides seven areas that SCRD researchers should abide by. Those categories are very similar to those suggested by Horner and colleagues in 2005 and include context and setting, participants, interventionist, description of the practice, internal validity, data analysis, and outcome. See Table 5.1 for a description of CEC's Quality Indicators.

Table 5.1 Checklist of CEC's Essential Quality Indicators for Single-Case Research Design Studies

Essential Quality Indicators for Single-Case Research	Yes/No
Context and Setting	
The authors provide information regarding the critical features of the setting/context. For example, the authors include type of classroom, geographic location, and socioeconomic status.	
Participants	
The authors provide and describe the demographics of the included participants, including, for example, age, grade level, gender, and race/ethnicity. The authors describe the disability or at-risk status of the included participants (e.g., specific learning disability and emotional or behavioral disorder).	
Interventionist	
The authors describe relevant information about the interventionist, such as teacher, researcher, peer tutor, as well as demographic information, such as age, gender, race/ethnicity, level of education, and years of experience. The authors describe any training or qualification the interventionist has or received to implement the intervention.	
Description of the Practice	
The authors provide details about the intervention. Those details may include the component making up the intervention or how often the intervention is received. This should be reported so a reader could implement the intervention as intended. When needed, the authors describe any required materials to implement the intervention.	
Internal Validity	
The authors describe in detail all conditions in the experiment, including baseline. The authors provide at least three demonstrations of experimental effect across three different points in time. Baseline phases include at least three data points.	
Essential Quality Indicators for Single-Case Research	Yes/No
Data Analysis	

The authors provide a single-subject graph clearly representing outcome data across all study phases for each unit of analysis (e.g., individual or classroom) to enable determination of the effects of the practice.
Outcome
The authors define and describe measurement of dependent variables. The authors report *all* the effects of the intervention.

HOW DO I INTERPRET SINGLE-CASE RESEARCH DESIGNS?

When it comes to interpreting the results of SCRDs, it is helpful to understand that there is a traditional approach and a more current approach. The traditional approach involves using systematic **visual analysis** to interpret the data collected during an SCRD study. A more current approach to interpreting the data obtained from SCRDs is applying statistics to the data so an effect size can be calculated. First, we will discuss visual analysis.

Visual Analysis

Researchers employing SCRD to examine the effect of an IV on a DV traditionally rely on visual analysis during data analysis. Visual analysis of graphic displays of data is a cornerstone of studies using an SCRD. Data are graphed for each participant during a study with level, trend, and stability of data assessed within and between conditions. Reliable interpretations of effects of an intervention depend on researchers' understanding and use of systematic procedures (Lane & Gast, 2014).

The first step SCRD researchers take when conducting their visual analysis is identifying the **level** of the data in each phase of the design. Researchers typically use the level in each condition to identify magnitude and direction of the change when comparing one condition to the level of the data in the next phase. Typically, level is calculated using the mean of the data within each phase. There are times when researchers may use the median, but typically, this is reserved for visual analysis when the datasets have outliers that will significantly skew a calculated mean. Whether researchers used the mean or median to calculate the level, typically, they will describe the level as either high, moderate, or low. See Figure 5.8 for a representation of level descriptions.

The next step in the visual analysis of SCRD is to use the split middle method for calculating trend lines. **Trend** refers to the overall direction taken by a data path. The trend within a dataset is represented with a straight line drawn through the data (i.e., trend line). When a change occurs surrounding

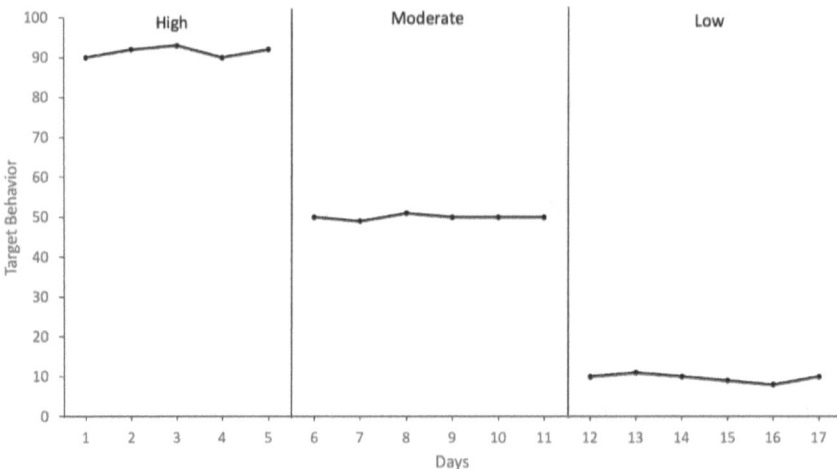

Figure 5.8 Descriptors for Level

the anticipated direction of the data from phase to phase, the power and believability are increased for that study. There are several terms used to describe the directionality of the data path. Some researchers use increasing and decreasing trends, others use accelerating and decelerating trends, and still others use therapeutic or contra-therapeutic trends. Regardless of the terms used when discussing trend, it is important for those consuming research to understand what the intended directionality of the data is and what the data are doing. See Figure 5.9 for a representation of trend labels.

Those engaging with the visual analysis process will now assess the data regarding **variability**. Essentially, variability is the "bounce" or the "peaks and valleys" of a given dataset. To examine variability systematically, researchers create a stability envelope for the data to determine if 80% of a phase's data points fall within plus or minus 25% of the level line that was calculated initially. If this is the case, the data are considered stable; if not and less than 80% of the data fall outside of the stability envelope, the data are considered variable. See Figure 5.10 for a representation of variability.

Immediacy of effect is another aspect of graphically depicted data that must be understood, even if less attention is paid to it than the previously mentioned level, trend, and variability. It is the difference in level between the final three data points of one phase and the initial three data points of the next. The faster (or more immediate) the effect, the more plausible the conclusion that the change in the outcome measure was caused by manipulating the IV (Cooper et al., 2020). Stated another way, immediacy is the magnitude to which data shifts concurrently with a condition change.

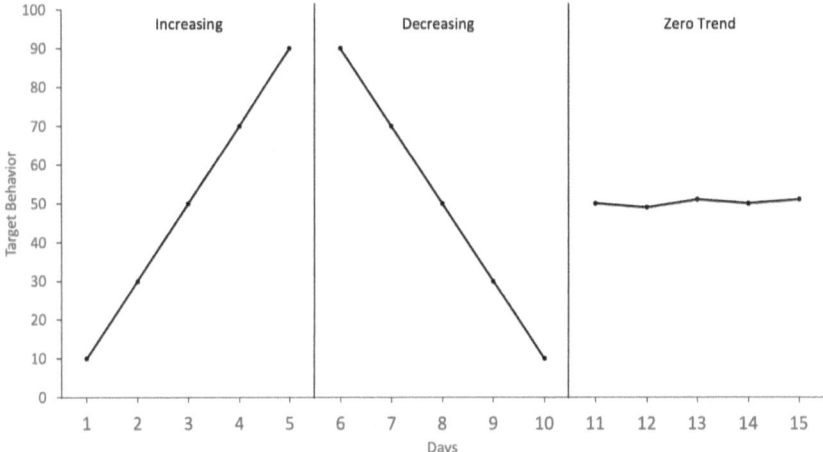

Figure 5.9 Descriptors for Trend

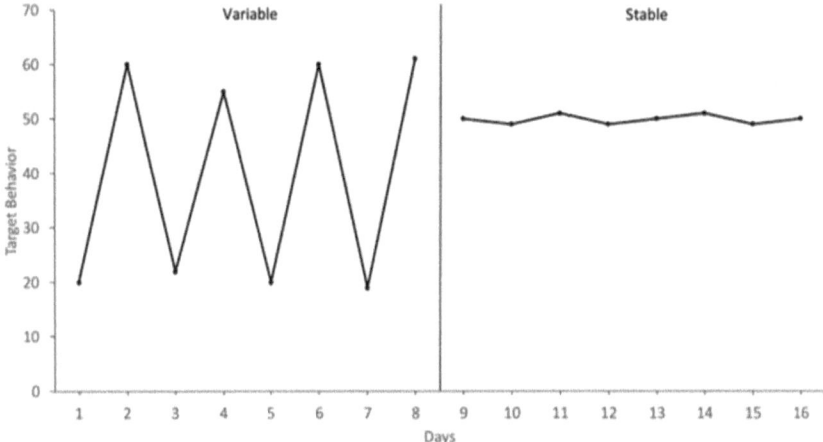

Figure 5.10 Descriptors for Variability

According to Ledford et al. (2018), when analyzing immediacy between conditions, the following questions should be considered: (a) Is there an immediate and abrupt change in the DV? (b) If not, is there a delayed increase in the DV (gradual therapeutic change in level and trend or a change that occurs several sessions after the condition change)? and (c) Is this pattern of responding replicated across similar conditions? For example, if a participant displays a delayed response to the intervention and all other participants display an immediate and abrupt change in the target behavior, first, researchers need to ensure procedures and data collection occurred as intended and then assess the idiosyncrasies of that condition compared to others (e.g., implementer and preintervention characteristics of participants).

The concept of **overlap** describes data as falling above or below an imagined line, separating a baseline range from an intervention range, and is fundamental in calculating the nonparametric indices. Nonparametric techniques are better matched to the type of data found in SCRD, easily calculated by hand, and more directly interpretable (Vannest & Ninci, 2015). In the following section, Statistics Applied to SCRD, we discuss the statistical indices used to determine the overlap of data points in the intervention condition that are not improved relative to baseline. Generally, the more overlap in the data, the less powerful is the effect of the intervention.

A functional relation exists in a study when the manipulations of the IV have an observable effect on the DV. Stated simply, the data show that the intervention we put in place after controlling for as many variables as possible has a clear effect on behavior of focus. As B. F. Skinner saw it, the term *functional relation*, which describes the relation between behavior and environment, essentially became synonymous with *cause-and-effect* relations (Dixon et al., 2012). In Skinner's words, "the external variables of which behavior is a function provide for what may be called a causal or functional analysis. We undertake to predict and control the behavior of the individual organism" (Skinner, 1953, p. 35).

Statistics Applied to SCRD

Recently, researchers have started to examine the application of statistical measures as a complement to the visual analysis of SCRD. In the early 2000s, the application of statistics being applied to SCRD research for calculating effect size started to show up in peer-reviewed journals. Due to the increased use of statistics in the world of SCRD, several experts in the field published articles that outlined a variety of statistical measures that can be applied to single-case research. One such article is from Parker and Brossart (2003), who examined and compared the performances of seven popular or promising techniques for analyzing between-phase differences in single-case research designs: (a) Owen White's binomial test on extended Phase A baseline, (b) Last Treatment Day technique, (c) Gorsuch's "trend analysis effect size," (d) Center's mean-only and mean-plus-trend models, and (e) Allison's mean-only and mean-plus-trend models. Since this publication, many other statistical tests have been suggested for SCRD, researched by prominent scholars in the field.

Parker and colleagues (2011) published a paper in *Behavior Modification*, "Effect Size in Single-Case Research: A Review of Nine Nonoverlap Techniques," that includes descriptions and formulas for calculating effect size, which can also be found in much of the recent published SCRD studies. Specifically, their work focused on nonoverlap indices, which are more robust than indices of mean- or median-level shifts across phases. The indices they described in their article are ECL, PND, PAND, Robust Pearson's phi, PEM, robust improvement rate difference (IRD), nonoverlap of all pairs (NAP), Kendall's tau for nonoverlap between groups, and tau for nonoverlap with baseline trend control (Tau-U). While all these terms may be confusing to those who are not statistically minded, the essential thing to remember is that these metrics are meant to be a companion to, not a substitute for, visual analysis. For those who want to run statistical measure to obtain an effect size on the effect of their intervention work in classrooms, there are a plethora of free online calculators that can be relied on. For example, Dr. James Pustejovsky, a statistician at the University of Wisconsin–Madison, has created software for just such occasions, which can be found on his website (see additional resources section below). See Table 5.2 for a snapshot of the most frequently used statistics in SCRD.

WHERE CAN I FIND MORE INFORMATION ABOUT SINGLE-CASE RESEARCH DESIGNS?

Council for Exceptional Children Standards for Evidence-Based Practices in Special Education: This report was commissioned by the Council for Exceptional Children Board of Directors. A work group, comprising seven special education researchers, developed, vetted, and piloted the new standards for determining evidence-based practices (EBPs) in special education. CEC's goal is that the standards will be applied to better understand the effectiveness of a range of practices for learners with disabilities. This report can be found at https://cecpioneers.exceptionalchildren.org/sites/default/files/2021-04/EBP_FINAL.pdf.

Single-Case Effect Size Calculator: This package provides R functions for calculating basic effect size indices for single-case designs, including several nonoverlap measures and parametric effect size measures, and for estimating the gradual effects model developed by Swan and Pustejovsky (2018). Standard errors and confidence intervals (based on the assumption that the outcome measurements are mutually independent) are provided for the subset of effect sizes indices with known sampling distributions. The calculator can be found at https://jepusto.shinyapps.io/SCD-effect-sizes/.

Table 5.2 Most Common Effect Sizes Found in SCRD Research

Effect Size Measure	Definition	Interpretation Scales
Percentage of nonoverlapping data (PND)	Represents the proportion of overlapping data between the phases compared based on the most extreme baseline value.	Ranges from 0% to 100%, with values greater than 70% considered large, between 50% and 70% considered moderate, and below 50% considered small.
Improvement rate difference (IRD)	Represents the ratio of improved to nonimproved data points in the phases compared.	Ranges from 0 to 1.0, with values greater than 0.70 considered large, between 0.50 and 0.70 considered moderate, and below 0.50 considered small.
Nonoverlap of all pairs (NAP)	Represents the ratio of improved to nonimproved data points, with all data points in each phase compared individually.	Ranges from 0 to 1.0, with values greater than 0.90 considered large, between 0.60 and 0.90 considered moderate, and below 0.60 considered small.
Percentage of all nonoverlapping data (PAND)	Represents the proportion of data points removed from the intervention phase to the total number of data points in the intervention and baseline phase.	Ranges from 0.50 to 1.0, with values greater than 0.90 considered large, between 0.60 and 0.90 considered moderate, and below 0.60 considered small.
Tau-U	Represents the proportion of data that improved between baseline and intervention phases after controlling for trends in the baseline data.	Ranges from 0 to 1.0 (though values can exceed 1.0), with values greater than 0.90 considered large, between 0.60 and 0.90 considered moderate, and below 0.60 considered small.

Spurious Correlations: Spurious Correlations is a project that is fun first and mildly educational second. It's great to occasionally break all the rules just to see what happens! The project can be found at https://tylervigen.com/spurious-correlations.

What Works Clearinghouse Single-Case Design Technical Documentation: In an effort to expand the pool of scientific evidence available for review, the What Works Clearinghouse (WWC) assembled a panel of national experts in single-case design (SCD) and analysis to draft SCD standards. In this paper, the panel provides an overview of SCDs, specifies the types of questions that SCDs are designed to answer, and discusses the internal validity of SCDs. This paper can be found at https://files.eric.ed.gov/fulltext/ED510743.pdf.

DISCUSSION QUESTIONS

1. What are the differences in case studies and single-case research designs?
2. Single-case research design hinges on three essential elements. What are they, and why are they essential in single-case research?
3. When conducting visual analysis of graphically depicted data, what are the patterns that researchers are looking at, and how are they calculated?
4. Recently, statistics have been applied to SCRD, particularly in the world of overlapping data. What are overlapping data, and why are they important?
5. In Chapter 4, we discussed quality indicators for group design research. In this chapter, we examined the quality indicators for single-case research. Looking back at Chapter 4, identify the similarities and differences in the quality indicators for group design studies with those for single-case design studies.

KEY TERMS

baseline logic: Refers to experimental reasoning inherent in single-subject experimental designs.

control: The impact of treatment is evaluated throughout time and in connection to the participants' behavior or other dependent variable.

external validity: The extent to which you can generalize the findings of a study to other situations, people, settings, and measures.

functional relation: When the manipulations of the independent variable have an observable effect on the dependent variable.

immediacy of effect: The difference in level between the final three data points of one phase and the initial three data points of the next. The faster (or more immediate) the effect, the more plausible the conclusion that the change in the outcome measure was caused by manipulating the independent variable.

internal validity: The extent to which you can be confident that the causal relation established in your experiment cannot be explained by other factors.

interobserver agreement: A measure of how closely two or more observers report the same values when observing and recording data on the same behaviors/events.

level: Relates to the dataset's "position" as measured along the y-axis.

maturation: Refers to the change in people over time from natural growth and development, such as physical growth and physiological changes.

overlap: The extent to which data from one condition are at the same level as data from an adjacent condition.

prediction: Prognosticating what you believe will happen in the future.

replication: Entails removing the intervention, reinstating it, and achieving similar results.

single-case research design: An evaluation method that can be used to rigorously test the success of an intervention or treatment on a particular case (i.e., a person, school, or community) and to provide evidence about the general effectiveness of an intervention using a relatively small sample size.

social validity: Refers to the extent to which target behaviors are appropriate, intervention procedures are acceptable, and important and significant changes in target and collateral behaviors are produced.

steady state responding: An intentional procedure in which the dependent variable is repeatedly exposed to the independent variable, with the goal of controlling for and/or eliminating any extraneous effects on the dependent variable and attaining a stable response pattern before going on to the next condition.

trend: The direction the data are moving. The data can be moving at an increasing, decreasing, on zero trend.

variability: Refers to the degree of difference among repeated measures of a particular behavior or response.

verification: Demonstrating that the dependent variables would not change in the absence of intervention (i.e., independent variables).

visual analysis: Method of evaluating graphical data by looking at them systematically.

REFERENCES

Backman, C. L., & Harris, S. R. (1999). Case studies, single subject research, and N of 1 randomized trials—comparisons and contrasts. *American Journal of Physical Medicine & Rehabilitation, 78*(2), 170–176. https://doi.org/10.1097/00002060-199903000-00022

Charlop-Christy, M. H., Carpenter, M., Le, L., LeBlanc, L. A., & Kellet, K. (2002). Using the picture exchange communication system (PECS) with children with autism: Assessment of PECS acquisition, speech, social-communicative behavior, and problem behavior. *Journal of Applied Behavior Analysis, 35*(3), 213–231.

Cooper, J. O., Heron, T. E., & Heward, W. L. (2020). *Applied behavior analysis.* Pearson UK.

Dixon, D. R., Vogel, T., & Tarbox, J. (2012). A brief history of functional analysis and applied behavior analysis. In J. L. Matson (Ed.), *Functional assessment for challenging behaviors* (pp. 3–24). Springer.

Epstein, L. H., & Dallery, J. (2022). The family of single-case experimental designs. *Harvard Data Science Review*, (Special Issue 3). https://doi.org/10.1162/99608f92.ff9300a8

Hartmann, D. P., & Hall, R. V. (1976). The changing criterion design. *Journal of Applied Behavior Analysis, 9*(4), 527–532.

Horner, R. H., Carr, E. G., Halle, J., McGee, G., Odom, S., & Wolery, M. (2005). The use of single-subject research to identify evidence-based practice in special education. *Exceptional Children, 71*(2), 165–179. https://doi.org/10.1177/001440290507100203

Jhangiani, R. S., Chiang, I. A., & Price, P. C. (2015). *Research methods in psychology* (2nd Canadian ed.) BCcampus. https://opentextbc.ca/researchmethods/

Johnston, J. M., & Pennypacker, H. S. (1980). *Strategies and tactics of human behavioral research.* Erlbaum.

Kazdin, A. E. (2019). Single-case experimental designs: Evaluating interventions in research and clinical practice. *Behavior Research and Therapy, 117*, 3–17.

Kodak, T., & Halbur, M. (2021). A tutorial for the design and use of assessment-based instruction in practice. *Behavior Analysis in Practice, 14*, 166–180.

Kornacki, L. T., Ringdahl, J. E., Sjostrom, A., & Nuernberger, J. E. (2013). A component analysis of a behavioral skills training package used to teach conversation skills to young adults with autism spectrum and other developmental disorders. *Research in Autism Spectrum Disorders, 7*(11), 1370–1376. https://doi.org/10.1016/j.rasd.2013.07.012

Klein, L. A., Houlihan, D., Vincent, J. L., & Panahon, C. J. (2017). Best practices in utilizing the changing criterion design. *Behavior Analysis in Practice, 10*, 52–61.

LaBrot, Z. C., Radley, K. C., Dart, E., Moore, J., & Cavell, H. J. (2018). A component analysis of behavioral skills training for effective instruction delivery. *Journal of Family Psychotherapy, 29*(2), 122–141. https://doi.org/10.1080/08975353.2017.1368813

Lane, J. D., & Gast, D. L. (2014). Visual analysis in single case experimental design studies: Brief review and guidelines. *Neuropsychological Rehabilitation, 24*(3–4), 445–463.

Ledford, J. R., Lane, J. D., & Severini, K. E. (2018). Systematic use of visual analysis for assessing outcomes in single case design studies. *Brain Impairment, 19*(1), 4–17.

MacDonald, R., Sacramone, S., Mansfield, R., Wiltz, K., & Ahearn, W. H. (2009). Using video modeling to teach reciprocal pretend play to children with autism. *Journal of Applied Behavior Analysis, 42*(1), 43–55.

Markelz, A. M., & Riden, B. S. (2019). Using apple watch to increase behavior specific praise and promote a positive learning environment. *Journal of Special Education Apprenticeship, 8*(2).

Markelz, A., Riden, B., & Hooks, S. D. (2021). Component analysis of training and goal setting, self-monitoring, and tactile prompting on early childhood educators' behavior-specific praise. *Journal of Early Intervention, 43*(2), 99–116. https://doi.org/10.1177/1053815120927091

Markelz, A. M., Riden, B. S., Morano, S., Hazelwood, A. L., & Taylor, A. M. (2023). The effects of varied and non-varied praise on student on-task behaviors. *Journal of Positive Behavior Interventions, 25*(4), 227–238. https://doi.org/10.1177/10983007221126568

Parker, R. I., & Brossart, D. F. (2003). Evaluating single-case research data: A comparison of seven statistical methods. *Behavior Therapy, 34*(2), 189–211. https://doi.org/10.1016/S0005-7894(03)80013-8

Parker, R. I., Vannest, K. J., & Davis, J. L. (2011). Effect size in single-case research: A review of nine nonoverlap techniques. *Behavior Modification, 35*(4), 303–322. https://doi.org/10.1177/0145445511399147

Riden, B. S., Markelz, A. M., Ruiz, S., Kent, S., Pavelka, S. K., & Chitiyo, A. (2022). The nature and extent of component analyses for improving or mitigating behavior: A systematic review. *Behavior Modification, 46*(1), 230–253. https://doi.org/10.1177/0145445520971256

Riden, B. S., Ruiz, S., Markelz, A. M., Sturmey, P., Ward-Horner, J., Fowkes, C. L., Wikel, K., Chitiyo, A., & Williams, M. (2024). The component analysis experimental method: A mapping of the literature base. *European Journal of Applied Behavior Analysis.* http://dx.doi.org/10.1080/15021149.2023.2297332

Riley-Tillman, T. C., & Chafouleas, S. M. (2003). Using interventions that exist in the natural environment to increase treatment integrity and social influence in consultation. *Journal of Educational and Psychological Consultation, 14*(2), 139–156. https://doi.org/10.1207/s1532768xjepc1402_3

Skinner, B. F. (1938). *The behavior of organisms: An experimental analysis.* Appleton-Century-Crofts.

Skinner, B. F. (1953). *Science and human behavior.* The Macmillan Company.

Swan, D. M., & Pustejovsky, J. E. (2018). A gradual effects model for single-case designs. *Multivariate Behavioral Research, 53*(4), 574–593. https://doi.org/10.1080/00273171.2018.1466681

Vannest, K. J., & Ninci, J. (2015). Evaluating intervention effects in single-case research designs. *Journal of Counseling & Development, 93*(4), 403–411. https://doi.org/10.1002/jcad.12038

Vollmer, T. R., Iwata, B. A., Zarcone, J. R., Smith, R. G., & Mazaleski, J. L. (1993). The role of attention in the treatment of attention-maintained self-injurious behavior: Noncontingent reinforcement and differential reinforcement of other behavior. *Journal of Applied Behavior Analysis, 26*(1), 9–21. https://doi.org/10.1901/jaba.1993.26-9

Ward-Horner, J., & Sturmey, P. (2010). Component analyses using single-subject experimental designs: A review. *Journal of Applied Behavior Analysis, 43*(4), 685–704. https://doi.org/10.1901/jaba.2010.43-685

Chapter 6

Qualitative Research Designs

Previously, we discussed quantitative research for investigating objective and measurable areas within special education. Quantitative research is associated with the scientific method of obtaining data in a systematic and predictable manner to generalize findings. Generally, this approach involves a large number of participants and is based on probabilities. Quantitative research uses p-values, power analysis, and other scientific methods to ensure the rigor and repeatability of the results.

In Chapter 5, we discussed single-case research designs (SCRDs). SCRDs are a family of research methodologies that are widely usedin behavioral experimentation, applied behavior analysis, and special education. This research methodology focuses on a small number of participants and monitors their behavior over time before and after an intervention is put in place.

There are times, however, when these research methods do not address nor allow for information to be collected that is pertinent to researchers in the field of special education. According to Miles and Huberman (2019), qualitative research provides well-grounded, rich descriptions and explanations of processes in identifiable local contexts. Qualitative research focuses on explaining human behaviors within the context of the social systems in which they occur. With qualitative data, researchers may maintain chronological flow, see which events cause which consequences, and derive fruitful interpretations. So in the context of special education, for example, researchers can investigate how students and teachers feel about their educational environment and their interactions with others. In this chapter, we will discuss qualitative research and its application in special education as we answer the following essential questions:

1. What are qualitative research designs?
2. What are the critical components ofqualitative research designs?
3. What are the limitations of qualitative research designs?

4. How do I interpret the results of qualitative research designs?
5. Where can I find more information about qualitative research designs?

WHAT ARE QUALITATIVE RESEARCH DESIGNS?

Qualitative research employs a systematic technique of gathering and interpreting data. When the topic in special education revolves around the life experiences or meaning of the individual or group of individuals, qualitative research is often preferred over quantitative methods. Qualitative research investigates the intricacies, depth, and richness of a specific situation through the perspective of the participant or others who may provide **germane** information. This could be the student, the student's caregivers or family members, or other relevant parties who have a role in the student's life. The knowledge may also come from the observations of the investigator or researcher. The foundational premise undergirding qualitative research is that reality is dependent on perceptions of humans and can change from person to person, often changing over time.

Qualitative research enables researchers to (a) characterize students' experiences and views, (b) investigate the meaning and processes underlying various occurrences, and (c) comprehend how and why **phenomena** occur in certain circumstances (Brantlinger et al., 2005). In the subject of special education, qualitative studies have been done to investigate a wide range of topics and concerns. Qualitative studies, for example, have explored the experiences of students with impairments and their families and the various stakeholders involved in their education (Ruppar et al., 2020). They have also investigated why long-standing educational disparities persist, especially for students of minority populations (Kozleski, 2017).

Furthermore, qualitative research has investigated the effects of teaching, learning, and curricular approaches on the results of students with disabilities and the quality of special education teachers (Scott et al., 2021). Qualitative methods have also been utilized to investigate social validity and intervention implementation (Leko et al., 2015). The goals of qualitative research are fundamentally distinct from those of quantitative research, in which data are quantified (i.e., as numbers) and statistically examined, as are the research methodologies and assumptions that guide the work (Leko et al., 2021). When conducting qualitative research, there are several methods from which special education researchers can choose, with the most common being interviews, case studies, ethnography, grounded theory, narrative inquiry, participatory research, and phenomenology (see Figure 6.1).

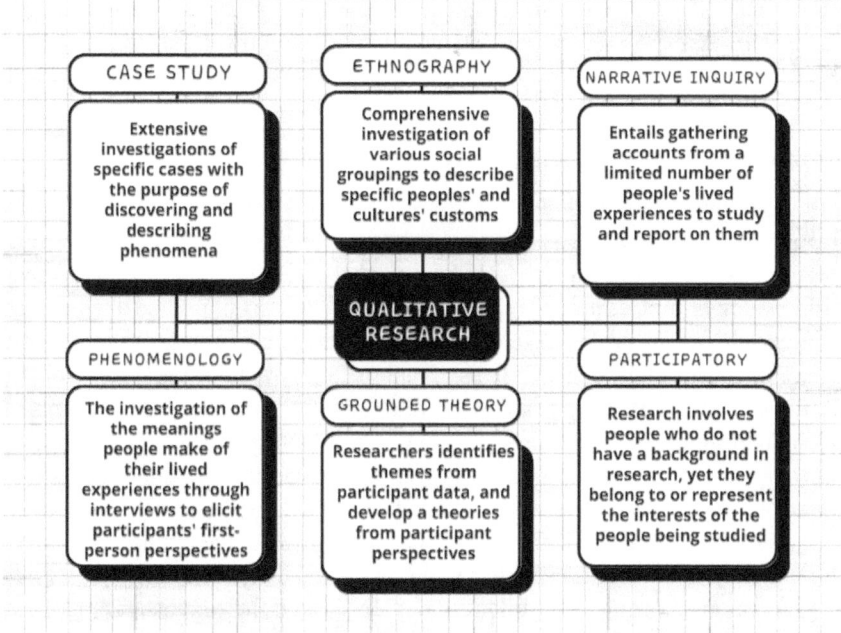

Figure 6.1 Types of Qualitative Research

Case Studies

Kenny and Grotelueschen (1984) define qualitative case studies as extensive investigations of specific cases to discover and describe phenomenon. Case studies entail the exploration of a case, which is described as an entity or object of study (Stake, 1995) that is bounded or separated for inquiry in terms of time, place, or physical boundaries (Creswell, 2008). Individuals, programs, events, schools, classes, and groups are all examples of instances. Once a case is determined, the researcher analyzes it methodically, often using a variety of data collection methods, such as interviews, field observations, and documentation.

For example, Scott et al. (2021) conducted a study using **focus groups** to address factors that might encourage the persistence of Black special education teachers (BSETs), who face numerous challenges that frequently lead to attrition. The research team conducted three focus groups with BSETs. The focus groups were conducted, and **grounded theory** analytic procedures were used to generate a preliminary grounded theory (discussed later in this chapter), Black special education teacher persistence in schools, to explain BSETs' persistence. Participants reported being motivated to change special education systems for students of color with disabilities. Participants described being motivated to change systems based on situational challenges (e.g., poor sense of belonging and bias toward qualifications) distinctively experienced by BSETs.

Ethnography

Ethnography research is a comprehensive investigation of various social groupings. Data is collected through observations, interviews, and existing documents. Ethnography is described as the scientific description of specific people's and cultures' customs. The researchers immerse themselves in a certain social group to understand its internal processes, structure, and functioning (McDuffie & Scruggs, 2008). Ethnography entails developing a framework of a group's behavior and beliefs over time. Ethnographies necessitate the researcher's engagement, either as a spectator or as an active participant, with the group under study over a prolonged amount of time. The concepts ungirding ethnography research is that absorption in the culture of the group allows the researcher to see the world through the eyes of the group.

Riitaoja and colleagues (2019) conducted an ethnographic study surrounding inclusion in a school in Finland. They conducted their investigation about how inclusion policies are implemented in a school with distinct special education (SEN) and general education (GE) courses. They performed a two-year ethnographic study concentrating on exclusion and the sense of belonging in a lower secondary school in Finland's capital region. Several students in the SEN class expressed an interest in switching to a GE class or in breaking down the barriers between SEN and GE classes in different ways throughout the fieldwork. Students who criticized the GE and SEN class divisions were offered the opportunity to switch to GE classes as part of talks with the school, but in the end, all of them preferred to remain in the SEN class. Their investigation shined a light on eventual problems, namely, the establishment of a sociocultural distinction between SEN and GE classes. The distinctive practices resulted in differentiating time–space paths and exclusion of students attending the SEN class from the school community by most teachers or peers within GE classes. In turn, this led to othering and stigmatization of students attending the SEN class, which was belittled in importance or made invisible to school personnel.

Grounded Theory

Another approach to qualitative research is grounded theory. This form of research begins with a broad research interest, and the researcher then identifies individuals who are most likely to clarify the original understanding of the research interest. Next, the researchers uses several approaches (e.g., interviewing and observation) to identify and construct a theory. This conceptual framework allows the voices of participants to emerge, requires that the researcher identify major themes or concepts from participant data, and provides an avenue to develop a theory from participant perspectives. One approach to conducting a grounded theory study is continually returning to the data and comparing experiences of participants, investigating similarities and differences, and focusing on the interrelationships among emerging themes (Stoner, 2010).

In 2020, Ruppar and colleagues sought to examine the processes that underlie involvement and progress in the general curriculum for students with extensive support needs. Using grounded theory methodology, they collected and analyzed qualitative data across three research sites, which allowed them to conclude how and why the intervention might work in various classroom and school contexts. Furthermore, they identified procedures that promote access to general education content in general education settings. They revealed that general and special educators' self-efficacy increased students' involvement and development in the general curriculum, developing a preliminary theory that might influence future investigations. The self-efficacy of special educators was influenced by their teacher preparation, adaptability, and material knowledge as well as the district's history and political background. Feelings of autonomy and role clarity and understanding of inclusive education all increased general educators' self-efficacy. Their findings highlighted the significance of instructors' self-efficacy in helping students with significant support needs to be involved and to advance in the main curriculum (Ruppar et al., 2020).

Narrative Inquiry

Narrative inquiry entails gathering accounts from a limited number of people's lived experiences to study and report on them (Clandinin & Connelly, 2000). Although interviews are a common data source in narrative inquiry, researchers may also rely on observations, records, or photographs. Researchers might delve into themes such as the story's substance, how it was given, and to whom it was addressed (Riessman, 2008).

In 2008, DeMik sought to determine what issues affected the choice to remain a special education teacher. Through their work and the use of narrative inquiry, they reported that although all participants had a passion for special education, the various personalities of individual respondents shed light on how each of them responded to the pressures of being a special education teacher, which caused some to remain in the field and others to leave. Additional themes gleaned from their narrative inquiry was a need for stronger collaboration and cooperation between general and special education teachers.

Phenomenology

Phenomenology investigates the substance of people's encounters with a phenomenon (Grbich, 2007). In other words, it is the investigation of the meanings people make of their lived experiences (Brantlinger et al., 2005). Interviews, which elicit participants' first-person perspectives, are the primary data source in phenomenological research. The qualitative method of phenomenology provides a theoretical tool for educational research because it allows researchers to engage in flexible activities that can describe and help to understand complex phenomena, such as various aspects of human social experience (Alhazmi & Kaufmann, 2022).

In 2018, Bryant deployed a phenomenological design to explore the experiences and perspectives of general education preschool teachers with the inclusion of students with disabilities in the regular classroom. The participants included eight general education preschool teachers who were interviewed using an open-ended interview format. The insight gathered from their interviews allowed Bryant to provide recommendations for inclusion practices for preschool-age children.

Participatory Research

Participatory research refers to research strategies, methods, and frameworks that use systematic inquiry in direct collaboration with individuals affected by a problem being examined to take action or effect change. This type of research involves people who do not have a background in research, yet they belong to or represent the interests of the people being studied. Researchers who use this approach select research methods that can be carried out in a collaborative, democratic manner that emphasizes true and meaningful participation in the study process (Vaughn & Jacquez, 2020).

One such example involved a research team in Northern Ireland that actively involved 36 young children with and without a recognized disability in all parts of the study. Six matched dyads of children in Northern Ireland determined the research topic and the methodology, acquired the data, and communicated their findings. Within- and between-group interactions were observed throughout the process to determine the children's level of engagement and ownership of the process. The findings indicate that when young children are regarded as equals, they will take ownership and actively participate in all stages of the process. Dyads appeared to encourage inclusivity and learning, with some children preferring to model behavior and others preferring to advise their peers on numerous aspects of the research. These findings demonstrate that with adequate support, young children with and without disabilities can completely participate in the research process (Gray & Winter, 2011).

WHAT ARE THE CRITICAL COMPONENTS OF QUALITATIVE RESEARCH DESIGNS?

It is necessary to understand how data are examined by researchers using this methodology in order to interpret qualitative research (covered later in this chapter). One of the critical components of qualitative research is data **confirmability**. Confirmability denotes that the researcher used certain procedures to determine the accuracy or reliability of the findings. Much like researchers in the quantitative world, those who engage in qualitative research should also be concerned with testing and confirming their hypotheses. Common approaches to confirmability are triangulation, respondent validation, strong data collection methods, and member checking.

Triangulation is the process of authenticating evidence from multiple people, data sources, and data collection methods (Creswell, 2008). In qualitative analysis, researcher triangulation involves the employment of numerous approaches to collect and interpret data. Think of triangulation as a sort of data control in qualitative research. Triangulation is deployed by qualitative researchers because their work is essentially interpretative. As a result, verifying the dependability and validity of the data through a scientific, objective perspective might be challenging. The theory behind researcher triangulation is that if multiple researchers use the same research technique and produce the same results, the data become more reliable. In a nutshell, researcher triangulation helps to demystify the research process (see Figure 6.2). When compared to using a single researcher, it helps to reduce biases and restrictions while also increasing data reliability.

Respondent validation is a procedure in which the researcher asks participants to verify the accuracy of the study's descriptions, themes, and interpretations (Creswell, 2008). Once the data is fully examined and the study concluded, the researcher meets with all the people who participated and shares the study's conclusions, utilizing a concept map as a visual representation of the findings. Verification happens when all participants are allowed to submit any additional information and confirm the findings' accuracy.

Employing rigorous data collection methods can help to enhance the data and hence corroborate the conclusions (Miles & Huberman, 2019). These tactics include (a) data collection after repeated contact, (b) behavior observation, (c) data collection in informal situations, and (d) the responder is alone with the researcher.

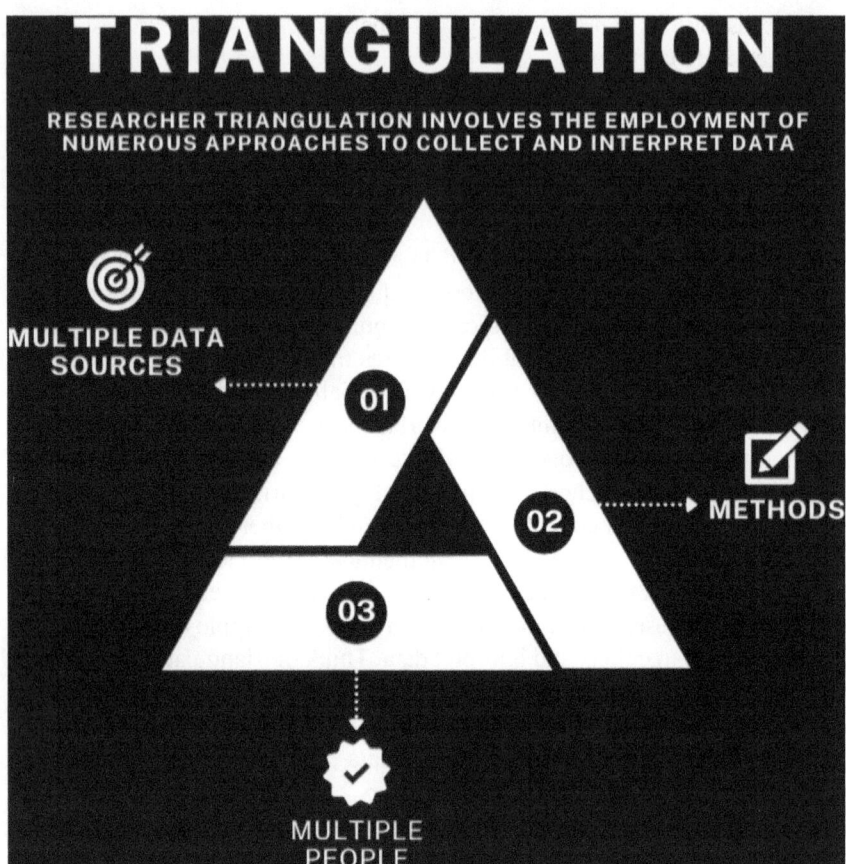

Figure 6.2　Data Triangulation

The trustworthiness of results is the bedrock of high-quality qualitative research. **Member checking**, also known as participant or respondent validation, is a technique for exploring the credibility of results. Data or results are returned to participants to check for accuracy and resonance with their experiences. Member checking is often mentioned in a list of validation techniques (Birt et al., 2016). Essentially, member checking is the process by which participants in qualitative research assess their data for accuracy and validity. Informally, member checking can occur during data collection when the researcher or evaluator summarizes and confirms their interpretation of what a participant said.

For example, Stoner et al. (2005) sought to examine the perspectives of parents of young children with autism spectrum disorder on their experiences, roles, and relationships with educators. Multiple interviews, observations, and documentation were used to obtain data. The data were analyzed using a cross-case analysis method. Triangulation, respondent validation, and member checking were used to confirm the findings. The findings revealed that the interaction between parents and educators is a dynamic and complex process. Three primary themes emerged: (a) the significant influences on parental perceptions, (b) frequent experiences that either decreased or increased parental trust, and (c) parental roles that were highlighted during parent engagement with education professionals.

Identifying the Quality of Qualitative Research

Quality indicators are the features of research that represent the rigorous application of methodology to questions of interest (Odom et al., 2005). They may serve as guidelines for (a) researchers who design and conduct research, (b) reviewers who evaluate the "believability" of research findings, and (c) consumers who need to determine the "usability" of research findings. In 2023, the Council for Exceptional Children (CEC) Division for Research published a special issue in the journal *Exceptional Children* introducing the next generation of quality indicators for research in special education (Lloyd & Therrien, 2023). The CEC is the largest international professional organization dedicated to improving the success of children and youth with disabilities and/or gifts and talents. In the introductory article to the special issue, Toste et al. (2023) stated that research methods in special education have advanced considerably since 2005. As such, there is a need to update the quality indicators for special education research and provide guidance for conducting research in the field.

Of particular interest to this chapter are the quality indicators introduced and described surrounding qualitative research by Joy Banks and colleagues (2023). Unlike quality indicators for conducting group design and single-case experimental research, there are different quality indicators for the various approaches to conducting qualitative research. Brantlinger et al. (2005) presented quality indicators for interview and observational studies as well as document and data analysis approaches. See Figure 6.3 for details of these quality indicators. In their article "Reflexive Quality Criteria: Questions and Indicators for Purpose-Driven Special Education Qualitative Research," Banks et al. (2023) discussed quality criteria focused on researcher reflexivity intended to complement and extend existing quality indicators (mentioned above) that have traditionally focused on credibility and trustworthiness of data to demonstrate the legitimacy of qualitative research. Olmos-Vega et al. (2022) defined **reflexivity** as a set of continuous, collaborative, and multifaceted practices through which researchers self-consciously critique, appraise, and evaluate how their subjectivity and context influence the research processes. According to Banks et al. (2023), there are three essential questions

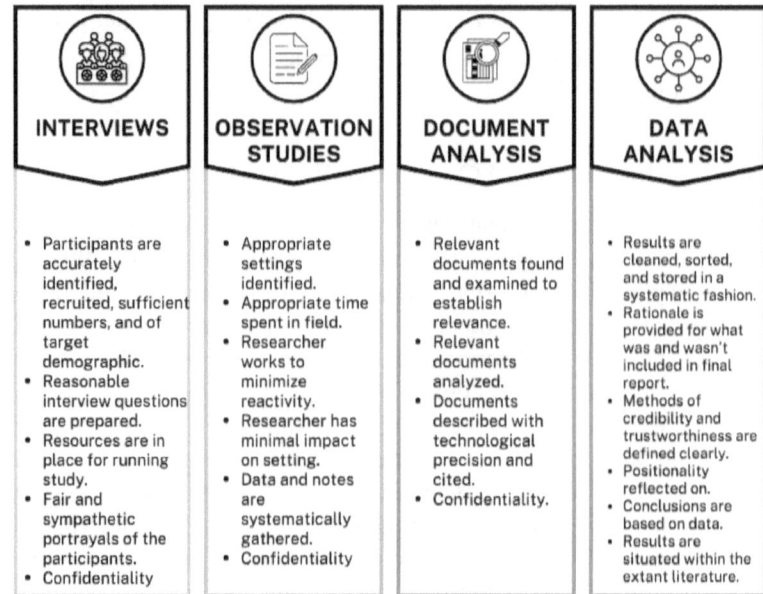

Figure 6.3 Quality Indicators within Qualitative Research

researchers must ask themselves when engaging in qualitative work: (a) Why do researchers conduct qualitative research? (b) By whom, with whom, and for whom is qualitative research conducted? and (c) Who is affected by the benefits and costs of research? See Figure 6.4 for a closer look at each of these essential questions and their associated quality indicators.

WHAT ARE THE LIMITATIONS OF QUALITATIVE RESEARCH DESIGNS?

When conducted properly, qualitative research is valid, dependable, believable, and rigorous. In qualitative research, there must be a method of determining the extent to which claims are supported by convincing evidence (Murphy et al., 1998). Although reliability and validity are generally related to quantitative research, they are increasingly being recognized as significant

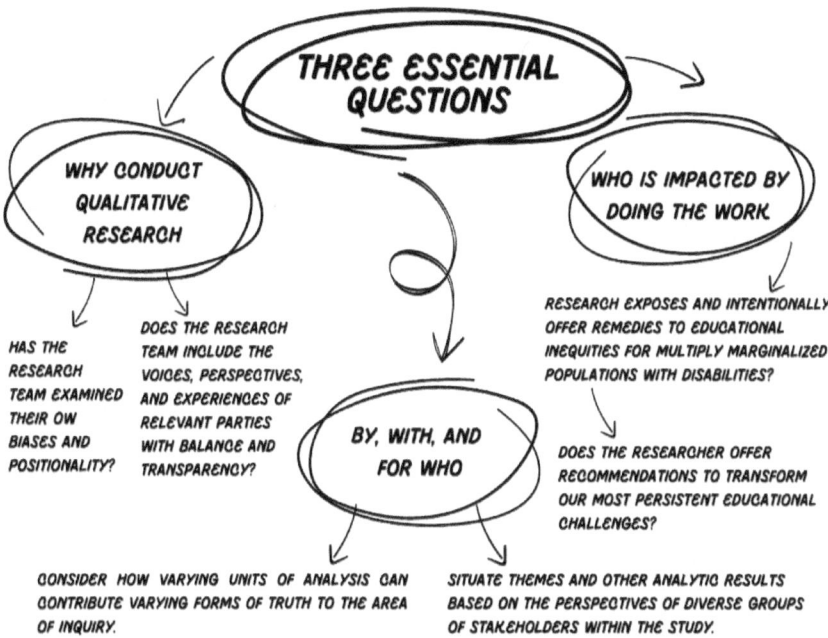

Figure 6.4 Essential Questions of Qualitative Research

ideas in qualitative research as well. Examining the data for reliability and validity evaluates the research's objectivity and credibility. Validity refers to the honesty and genuineness of the study data, whereas reliability refers to the data's reproducibility and stability (Anderson, 2010).

Like the quantitative approaches to research mentioned in previous chapters, qualitative research has its own set of limitations. Research quality is heavily dependent on the individual skills of the researcher and more easily influenced by the researcher's personal biases and idiosyncrasies. Rigor is more difficult to maintain, assess, and demonstrate, and the volume of data makes analysis and interpretation a time-consuming and laborious task. Sometimes it is not as well understood and accepted as quantitative research within the scientific community. The researcher's presence during data collection, which is often unavoidable in qualitative research, can affect the subjects' responses, but this is also true with particular types of quantitative research. As with other types of research, there can be issues of anonymity and confidentiality, which can result in problems when analyzing data. Further, findings can be more difficult and time consuming to characterize in a visual way.

Mitigating Limitations

One of the most important areas special education researchers face when conducting qualitative research is the **trustworthiness** and **credibility** of their research. Qualitative researchers are obligated to articulate evidence of four chief criteria to ensure the trustworthiness of the study's findings: credibility, transferability, dependability, and confirmability. Credibility is comparable to the concept of validity but is primarily concerned with internal validity. The credibility of qualitative data can be enhanced by using various viewpoints throughout the data collection process to guarantee that data are appropriate. This can be achieved through data, researcher, or theoretical triangulation; participant validation or member checking; or rigorous data collection approaches. Another area researchers can focus on to increase the rigor of their qualitative research is **transferability**.

Transferability is similar to but not the same as generalization in quantitative research. Transferability refers to the findings' application to similar circumstances or persons rather than broader ones. A robust description of the findings from several data collection methods that were used can help with transferability. In addition to the transferability of qualitative research results, there are two more areas the qualitative research can focus on that can increase the trustworthiness and credibility of this approach to research.

In quantitative studies, dependability is synonymous with reliability. **Dependability** can be ensured through rigorous data-gathering approaches as well as well-documented procedures and analysis. An inquiry audit conducted by an outside reviewer typically increases trustworthiness. Confirmability is like objectivity in quantitative studies; however, objectivity is not always required in qualitative investigations as long as personal biases are disclosed in the report. A bracketing interview or reflexivity can be used to unpack personal prejudice. Confirmability of qualitative data is ensured when data are reviewed and rechecked throughout the data-collecting and analysis process to guarantee that findings are likely to be repeated by others. A precise coding scheme that defines the codes and patterns observed in analysis can be used to document confirmability. This is referred to as an audit trail. It can also be secured by conducting a bracketing interview or exercising reflexivity to tackle potential personal prejudice.

The process of demonstrating the credibility of research is rooted in honest and transparent reporting of how biases and other possible confounders were identified and addressed throughout study processes. Such reporting, first described within the study's conceptual framework, should be revisited in reporting the work. Confounds may include the researcher's training and previous experiences, personal connections to the background theory, access to the study population, and funding sources (Johnson et al., 2020).

Rigorous qualitative investigations should contain a statement on reflexivity and **positionality**, in which researchers delineate their identities that may have an effect on the study and its conclusions (Trainor & Graue, 2014). This is sometimes referred to as a reflexivity statement. Researchers could share if they knew the participants before the study or if they had prior encounters with the topic under study. For example, researchers examining how kids with learning disabilities and their teachers view a new mathematics intervention may reveal whether they had ever worked as instructors, implemented the intervention themselves, or had prior ties with the students or teachers (Leko et al., 2021).

HOW DO I INTERPRET QUALITATIVE RESEARCH DESIGNS?

Practitioners often report enjoying reading qualitative more than quantitative research given qualitative research's narrative style of reporting. Both the quantitative and qualitative paradigmsproduce necessary and useful information, yet there are different criteria used to judge the "goodness" or "usefulness" of research using qualitative methods than those used for quantitative methods (Cruz & Tantia, 2017).

When consuming qualitative research there are several essential characteristics of the research that the reader must be able to identify. Those sections of a research article are the introduction, purpose statement, method, and results. The introduction of most any research article provides the reader with a brief literature review on the topic the authors are investigating. The purpose statement is typically where you would find the research questions the authors are attempting to address. The method section of a research article reports, in replicable detail, how a study was conducted, which includes a description of setting, participants, method of data collection, and data analysis. The next section of a research article is the results section. The results portion of the article is where the authors report the findings of their study. They are not necessarily interpreting them or positioning them in the extant literature though. For the practitioner or student looking to learn about the implication and/or application, the most essential sections of the article are the discussion and conclusion.

The discussion and conclusion sections should include an interpretation of the results as well as practical recommendations. The interpretation of first-level data or a literal description of observable behaviors, patterns, and themes from analysis should go beyond the literal description. The author's challenge is to provide a comprehensive examination and explanation of how distinct outcomes relate to one another, contribute to answering the research question, and accomplish the primary goal of the research endeavor. The discussion should position the study findings and analysis with the original conceptual framework (Johnson et al., 2020). The discussion sectionshould also include a concise narrative or graphical description and interpretation of study findings that improve understanding of the targeted phenomenonEssentially, those using quality indicators should be able to answer the following questions when reading qualitative research (see Figure 6.5).

Questions to Ask Yourself When Interpreting Qualitative Research

1. What was the guiding question?

2. What qualitative method was used and was it appropriate for the question asked?

3. How were the data generated? Did the researcher gather sufficient data to provide a holistic perspective of the phenomenon? How do you know?

4. How were the data analyzed? Has an understanding of the phenomenon been expanded?

5. Did the researcher evaluate his or her impact on the study? Was transparency adequately addressed?

6. Were mechanisms of credibility such as prolonged engagement, persistent observation, triangulation, peer debriefing and/or member checking used?

7. Is there a "thick description" of the phenomenon being studied which allows the reader to transfer applicability to his or her own work?

8. What is the relevance of the findings for those involved in the study as well as for those reading the study?

Figure 6.5   Questions to Ask When Interpreting Qualitative Research

1. What was the guiding question?
2. What method was used, and was it an appropriate fit?
3. How were the data gathered and generated?
4. How were the data analyzed?
5. How was the researcher's effect minimized?
6. Were methods to increase credibility used?
7. Was there a thorough description of the phenomenon of interest?
8. What is the relevance of study outcomes?

WHERE CAN I FIND MORE INFORMATION ABOUT QUALITATIVE RESEARCH DESIGNS?

Cochrane Qualitative and Implementation Methods Group: The focus of this resource is on the methods and processes involved in the synthesis of qualitative evidence and the integration of qualitative evidence with Cochrane intervention reviews of effects. The website can be found at https://methods.cochrane.org/qi/.

Council for Exceptional Children: In this article, the authors present an overview of mixed-methods research in special education and quality indicators for conducting and reporting such studies. The article can be found at https://journals.sagepub.com/doi/full/10.1177/00144029221141031.

QualPage: This resource provides links to free resources on qualitative and mixed-methods research. It can be found at https://qualpage.com/2020/11/05/free-resources-on-qualitative-research-and-mixed-methods/.

QuestionPro: QuestionPro is a survey software program that researchers can use to conduct their qualitative research. In this resource, what qualitative research looks like in comparison to quantitative research is discussed and examples of qualitative research are provided. The program can be found at https://www.questionpro.com/blog/qualitative-research-methods/.

University of North Carolina: Its website provides resources for qualitative training and support on how to search for and evaluate qualitative research, integrate qualitative research into systematic reviews, and report/publish qualitative research. The information includes some mixed-methods resources. The website is at https://guides.lib.unc.edu/qual.

DISCUSSION QUESTIONS

1. Identify what positionality is and state why is it important for authors to present their positionality within their research report.
2. In comparison to group design research and single-case research designs, how does qualitative research differ?
3. If someone stated that qualitative research is not real research, how would you respond to them to convince them that it is a valuable approach to conducting special education research?
4. Describe triangulation and why it is such an important factor in qualitative research.
5. Can the results of a qualitative research project be generalized?

KEY TERMS

confirmability: The steps to ensure that the data and findings are not due to participant or researcher bias.

credibility: A measure of how well a researcher can establish the accuracy and reliability of their findings.

dependability: In-depth description of the study procedures and analysis to allow the study to be replicated.

focus group: Interviews conducted by the researcher with a group of individuals at the same time.

germane: Relevant to a subject under consideration.

grounded theory: Research using an iterative design to produce a theory about aphenomenon.

member checking: A technique for exploring the credibility of results (also known as participant or respondent validation).

phenomena: A fact or situation that is observed to exist or happen, especially one whose cause or explanation is in question.

positionality: The social and political context that creates your identity in terms of race, class, gender, sexuality, and ability status.

reflexivity: The process of consciously examining your own subjective point of view as a qualitative researcher and identifying how your subjectivity could affect the outcomes of your research.

respondent validation: A procedure in which the researcher asks participants to verify the accuracy of the study's descriptions, themes, and interpretations.

transferability: The degree to which the results of qualitative research can be generalized or transferred to other contexts or settings.

triangulation: The process of corroborating evidence from different individuals, different types of data, and different methods of data collection.

trustworthiness: The degree of confidence in data, interpretation, and methods used to ensure the quality of a study.

REFERENCES

Alhazmi, A. A., & Kaufmann, A. (2022). Phenomenological qualitative methods applied to the analysis of cross-cultural experience in novel educational social contexts. *Frontiers in Psychology, 13*. https://doi.org/10.3389/fpsyg.2022.785134

Anderson, C. (2010). Presenting and evaluating qualitative research. *American Journal of Pharmaceutical Education, 74*(8), 141. https://doi.org/10.5688/aj7408141

Banks, J., González, T., Mueller, C., Pacheco, M., Scott, L. A., & Trainor, A. A. (2023). Reflexive quality criteria: Questions and indicators for purpose-driven special education qualitative research. *Exceptional Children, 89*(4), 449–466. https://doi.org/10.1177/00144029231168106

Birt, L., Scott, S., Cavers, D., Campbell, C., & Walter, F. (2016). Member checking: A tool to enhance trustworthiness or merely a nod to validation? *Qualitative Health Research, 26*(13), 1802–1811. https://doi.org/10.1177/1049732316654870

Brantlinger, E., Jimenez, R., Klingner, J. K., Pugach, M., & Richardson, V. (2005). Qualitative studies in special education. *Exceptional Children, 71*(2), 195–207. https://doi.org/10.1177/001440290507100205

Bryant, J. P. (2018). A phenomenological study of preschool teachers' experiences and perspectives on inclusion practices. *Cogent Education, 5*(1), 1549005. https://doi.org/10.1080/2331186X.2018.1549005

Clandinin, D., & Connelly, F. (2000). *Narrative inquiry*. Jossey-Bass.

Creswell, J. W. (2008). *Educational research: Planning, conducting, and evaluating quantitative and qualitative research*. Edwards Brothers.

Cruz, R. F., & Tantia, J. F. (2017). Reading and understanding qualitative research. *American Journal of Dance Therapy, 39*, 79–92. https://doi.org/10.1007/s10465-016-9219-z

DeMik, S. A. (2008). Experiencing attrition of special education teachers through narrative inquiry. *The High School Journal, 92*(1), 22–32. http://www.jstor.org/stable/40660784

Gray, C., & Winter, E. (2011). Hearing voices: Participatory research with preschool children with and without disabilities. *European Early Childhood Education Research Journal, 19*(3), 309–320. https://doi.org/10.1080/1350293X.2011.597963

Grbich, C. (2007). *Qualitative data analysis*. Sage.

Johnson, J. L., Adkins, D., & Chauvin, S. (2020). A review of the quality indicators of rigor in qualitative research. *American Journal of Pharmaceutical Education, 84*(1), 7120. https://doi.org/10.5688/ajpe7120

Kenny, W. R., & Grotelueschen, A. D. (1984). Making the case for case study. *Journal of Curriculum Studies, 16*(1), 37–51.

Kozleski, E. B. (2017). The uses of qualitative research: Powerful methods to inform evidence-based practice in education. *Research and Practice for Persons with Severe Disabilities, 42*(1), 19–32. https://doi.org/10.1177/1540796916683710

Leko, M. M., Cook, B. G., & Cook, L. (2021). Qualitative methods in special education research. *Learning Disabilities Research & Practice, 36*(4), 278–286.

Leko, M. M., Roberts, C. A., & Pek, Y. (2015). A theory of secondary teachers' adaptations when implementing a reading intervention program. *The Journal of Special Education, 49*(3), 168–178. https://doi.org/10.1177/0022466914546751

Lloyd, J. W., & Therrien, W. (2023). Introducing the next generation of quality indicators for research in special education [Special issue]. *Exceptional Children, 89*(4). https://journals.sagepub.com/toc/ecxc/89/4

McDuffie, K. A., & Scruggs, T. E. (2008). The contributions of qualitative research to discussions of evidence-based practice in special education. *Intervention in School and Clinic, 44*(2), 91–97. https://doi.org/10.1177/1053451208321564

Miles, M. B., & Huberman, A. M. (2019). *Qualitative data analysis: An expanded sourcebook.* (4th ed.). Sage.

Murphy, E., Dingwall, R., Greatbatch, D., Parker, S., & Watson, P. (1998). Qualitative research methods in health technology assessment: A review of the literature. *Health Technology Assessment, 2*(16). https://doi.org/10.3310/hta2160

Odom, S. L., Brantlinger, E., Gersten, R., Horner, R. H., Thompson, B., & Harris, K. R. (2005). Research in special education: Scientific methods and evidence-based practices. *Exceptional Children, 71*(2), 137–148. https://doi.org/10.1177/001440290507100201

Olmos-Vega, F. M., Stalmeijer, R. E., Varpio, L., & Kahlke, R. (2023). A practical guide to reflexivity in qualitative research: AMEE Guide No. 149. *Medical Teacher, 45*(3), 241–251. https://doi.org/10.1080/0142159X.2022.2057287

Riessman, C. K. (2008). *Narrative methods for the human sciences.* Sage.

Riitaoja, A. L., Helakorpi, J., & Holm, G. (2019). Students negotiating the borders between general and special education classes: An ethnographic and participatory research study. *European Journal of Special Needs Education, 34*(5), 586–600. https://doi.org/10.1080/08856257.2019.1572093

Ruppar, A. L., Knight, V. F., McQueston, J. A., & Jeglum, S. R. (2020). Involvement and progress in the general curriculum: A grounded theory of the process. *Remedial and Special Education, 41*(3), 152–164. https://doi.org/10.1177/0741932518806045

Scott, L. A., Brown, A., Wallace, W., Cormier, C. J., & Powell, C. (2021). If we're not doing it, then who? A qualitative study of Black special educators' persistence. *Exceptionality, 29*(3), 182–196. https://doi.org/10.1080/09362835.2020.1850453

Stake, R. E. (1995). *The art of case study research.* Sage.

Stoner, J. B. (2010). Qualitative research in education: Other methods of seeking knowledge. In F. E. Obiakor, J. P. Bakken, & A. F. Rotatori (Eds.), *Current issues and trends in special education: Research, technology, and teacher preparation* (pp. 19–39). Emerald.

Stoner, J. B., Bock, S. J., Thompson, J. R., Angell, M. E., Heyl, B., & Crowley, E. P. (2005). Welcome to our world: Parent perspectives of interactions between parents of young children with ASD and education professionals. *Focus on Autism and Other Developmental Disabilities*, *20*(1), 39–51. https://doi.org/10.1177 /10883576050200010401

Toste, J. R., Talbott, E., & Cumming, M. M. (2023). Special issue preview: Introducing the next generation of quality indicators for research in special education. *Exceptional Children*, *89*(4), 357–358. https://doi.org/10.1177/00144029231174106

Trainor, A. A., & Graue, E. (2014). Evaluating rigor in qualitative methodology and research dissemination. *Remedial and Special Education*, *35*(5), 267–274. https://doi.org/10.1177/0741932514528100

Vaughn, L. M., & Jacquez, F. (2020). Participatory research methods: Choice points in the research process. *Journal of Participatory Research Methods*, *1*(1). https://doi.org/10.35844/001c.13244

Chapter 7

Additional Research Methods

The scientific method is systematic, specific, and rigorous when done well and is used to acquire knowledge regarding a phenomenon of interest. The scientific method involves asking a question, engaging in research to build background information, developing a hypothesis, manipulating variables through experimental procedures to test a hypothesis, analyzing data obtained via intentional observation to draw conclusions about your hypothesis, and disseminating your research findings. In the previous chapters of this text, we presented a variety of methodologies researchers employ when engaging with the scientific method, including systematic literature reviews, group design (quantitative), single-case design, and qualitative methodologies. Yet there are other methodological approaches that can be used to explore questions in the social sciences.

Before introducing additional research methods, it is important to understand that there are many factors that determine the appropriate methodology. So how can a research team navigate the many approaches available to them and make the correct decision? First, they need to examine their research questions and populations of interest and then turn to the existing literature to see what the norms in the field are surrounding the phenomenon of interest. By doing this, they can see how similar inquiries have been addressed in the field. Next, the team must examine the practicality of the method, meaning that all research teams face barriers (e.g., funding, time, and labor) when conducting research and they must determine practically which methodology is best suited within their context despite other more rigorous methods.

Additionally, research teams should develop the purpose of their research and their research questions, lean on previous research, use the research method as intended, develop a research plan and a list of needed resources, and write the research method with precision. After moving through this process, researchers can determine if one of the methods previously described in Chapters 3, 4, 5, and 6 is appropriate or if there is a better fit methodologically. In this chapter, we will provide a tour d'horizon of mixed methods, case studies, surveys, secondary data analysis, teacher action research, the Delphi technique, and program evaluation as forms of research methodologies (see Figure 7.1). By the end of the chapter, we will have answered these essential questions:

1. What, why, and how are some additional research methods used in special education research?
2. Where can I find more information about these research methods?

WHAT, WHY, AND HOW ARE SOME ADDITIONAL RESEARCH METHODS USED IN SPECIAL EDUCATION RESEARCH?

The research design selected is the plan of attack that will be deployed to address the central research questions. This decision provides the overall structure for the steps a researcher will need to follow, the data that will be collected, and how the data will be analyzed (Leedy & Ormrod, 2001). Suffice it to say that selecting the correct approach to conducting research is critical. As we previously mentioned, there are several other methodologies special education researchers may select from depending on the purpose of their inquiry.

Mixed-Methods Research: What, Why, and How?

The first approach we introduce is referred to as **mixed-methods research**. This tactic focuses on the meaningful integration of quantitative and qualitative data that can provide a depth and breadth of data that a single approach may lack by itself (Ivankova & Creswell, 2009). This approach is used for collecting, analyzing, and mixing quantitative and qualitative data within a single study to understand a phenomenon of interest (Creswell, 2009). Ivankova and Creswell (2009) stated that during mixed-methods research, an investigator collects both numeric information (e.g., through closed-response items on questionnaires) and text (e.g., from face-to-face interviews and picture descriptions) to better answer a study's research questions. The word *mixed* suggests that at one or more points of a study, data are combined and/or linked. Because this research approach has gained momentum in the field, a working group led by John W. Creswell was established by the National Institutes of Health (NIH) to create a resource that would serve as a guide on how to develop and conduct rigorous mixed-methods research. In this resource, Creswell et al. (2011) states that mixed-methods research is defined as a research methodology that does the following:

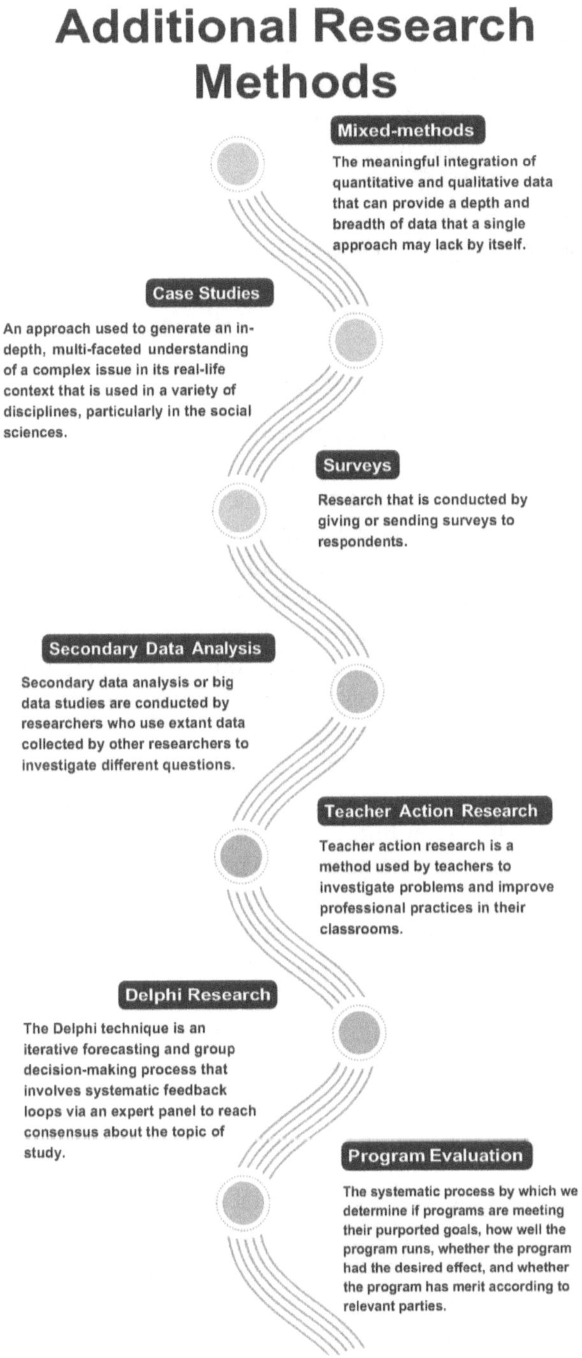

Additional Research Methods

Mixed-methods
The meaningful integration of quantitative and qualitative data that can provide a depth and breadth of data that a single approach may lack by itself.

Case Studies
An approach used to generate an in-depth, multi-faceted understanding of a complex issue in its real-life context that is used in a variety of disciplines, particularly in the social sciences.

Surveys
Research that is conducted by giving or sending surveys to respondents.

Secondary Data Analysis
Secondary data analysis or big data studies are conducted by researchers who use extant data collected by other researchers to investigate different questions.

Teacher Action Research
Teacher action research is a method used by teachers to investigate problems and improve professional practices in their classrooms.

Delphi Research
The Delphi technique is an iterative forecasting and group decision-making process that involves systematic feedback loops via an expert panel to reach consensus about the topic of study.

Program Evaluation
The systematic process by which we determine if programs are meeting their purported goals, how well the program runs, whether the program had the desired effect, and whether the program has merit according to relevant parties.

Figure 7.1 Additional Research Methods and Their Brief Descriptions

- Focuses on research questions that call for real-life contextual understandings, multilevel perspectives, and cultural influences
- Engages in rigorous quantitative research assessing the magnitude and frequency of constructs and rigorous qualitative research exploring the meaning and understanding of constructs
- Deploys multiple methods (e.g., intervention trials and in-depth interviews)
- Intentionally integrates or combines these methods to draw on the strengths of each
- Frames the investigation within philosophical and theoretical positions

Limitations of the Mixed-Methods Approach

Like all research methods, this approach is not without its limitations. The largest drawbacks to using a mixed-methods design is the amount of time, resources, and expertise it takes to conduct this type of research. Because of its complexity, time is not a friend to the mixed-methods researcher. If you think about this logically, it makes a lot of sense. Implementing a single research approach takes time, but when a research team uses more than one method, it is going to take double (or more) time to complete the research efforts. Regardless of the field of study, resources needed to conduct research can be hard to come by, and when combining research methods, one will need additional resources (e.g., people and funding). The needed resources for conducting mixed-methods research are a real consideration when tackling a question with this approach.

The last major limitation to mixed-methods research is researcher expertise. Many researchers have a depth of knowledge about a single research approach (e.g., single-case research and group design) but are only a mile wide and an inch deep with the other methods. This is a significant limitation when conducting rigorous research and increases the odds that a researcher will need to recruit experts in the methods they are mixing. Overall, a mixed-methods approach, while time consuming and resource heavy, can provide a rich investigation of a phenomenon of interest.

Case Studies: What, Why, and How?

Another research methodology that special education researchers deploy is **case study** research. A case study is a research approach that is used to generate an in-depth, multifaceted understanding of a complex issue in its real-life context and is used in a variety of disciplines, particularly in the social sciences (Crowe et al., 2011). This approach involves a detailed and intensive analysis of a particular event, situation, organization, or social unit. Typically, a case has a defined space and time frame: a phenomenon of some sort in a **bounded context** (Miles et al., 2014). When thinking about case studies, you might ask yourself, "What is considered a case to be studied?" The answer to that question is rather simple. For example, a case could be individuals, small groups, an organization, or a neighborhood. One might ask themselves, why or when would a research team consider using a case study approach? One of the main reasons is the benefits in terms of process and product. Case study research can support a team in focusing their research within a specific bounded context (e.g., space and time). A team may determine to use this approach because of the flexibility it provides in collecting a variety of data. The data can be collected through interviews, focus groups, records reviews, direct observations, and survey distribution. The variety of data obtained through case study research affords researchers an in-depth look at an organization or individual and the inner workings and interactions of that organization or individual (Schoch, 2020).

Concerning the products (i.e., outcomes), results from a case study provide an extensive comprehension of a bounded unit and aid the researcher in disseminating information in a consumer-friendly fashion. According to Schoch (2020), the results from case study research allow others to apply the principles and lessons learned in a case to other cases or situations and leads to transferability (i.e., the ability to apply the case to another situation), which is different from the generalization that occurs in quantitative studies. For example, if someone wanted to learn more about being a high school principal, a case study could help that person learn about that experience and apply it to another situation or help that person decide whether being a principal is their best career path.

Due to the range of application of the case study method, it is difficult to describe *how* this type of research is conducted. However, there is a consensus on key elements that must be included. The key elements of a case study design are (a) purpose of study; (b) type of research undertaken depending on the purpose (i.e., exploratory, explanatory, or descriptive); (c) research questions; (d) study of a single case or multiple cases depending on the purpose, research questions, and resource availability in terms of manpower, money, and time; (e) **epistemological** underpinnings determining the direction of the case study in the field; (f) literature review; (g) sampling; (h) methods of data collection adopted; (i) analysis of data; and (j) presentation of analyzed data in an effective and coherent way (Priya, 2021).

Limitations of Case Study Research

As mentioned earlier, all research approaches have their own set of limitations. This is nothing to be concerned with as long as the research teams are transparent about them. As we discussed earlier in this book, the discussion section of a paper is where the limitations of the study can be found. In this section, those engaging in case study research may consider including limitations such as responses from interviews are subjective in nature, subjects may tailor their responses to the researcher due to **reactivity**, replication of the method might be difficult based on boundaries put in place, data collection and analysis can take time, data collection and analysis can be resource intensive, and results may have limited transferability.

Survey Research: What, Why, and How?

Survey research is generally defined as the process of conducting research using surveys that researchers send to respondents. The data collected from surveys is then statistically analyzed to draw meaningful research conclusions (Bhaskaran, n.d.). Questionnaires are a useful survey tool that allow large populations to be assessed with relative ease. Despite a widespread perception that surveys are easy to conduct, to yield meaningful results, a survey needs extensive planning, time, and effort (Jones et al., 2013). Researchers use survey research to rapidly gather data that describes certain characteristics of a considerable sample of people who have insights surrounding the phenomenon of interest. To conduct this type of research in a rigorous fashion, there are several steps a researcher must take to determine if the results are valid. According to Yusoff et al. (2021), there are seven steps for conducting survey research (see Figure 7.2). The seven steps, presented in the order in which they are performed, are (1) set clear aims, (2) define attributes, (3) write a plan, (4) develop and write survey items, (5) assess and select the survey items, (6) standardize the scores, and (7) make the final preparations. By following these steps, research teams can systematically design a valid questionnaire for their research inquiry.

Limitations of Survey Research

Survey research can uncover a rich database regarding a phenomenon of interest. However, consumers of this approach to research must be aware of several limitations so they can interpret and situate the results of survey research with the correct degree of caution. The first limitation is that survey response rates are typically low. Low response rates can introduce bias when analyzing data because the responses on the survey pertain only to those who decided to complete the survey. This is also known as **nonresponse bias**. Another limitation of survey research is the speed in which respondents answer survey questions. Respondents typically answer a prompt with the first thought that comes to mind due to the objective nature of questions included in survey

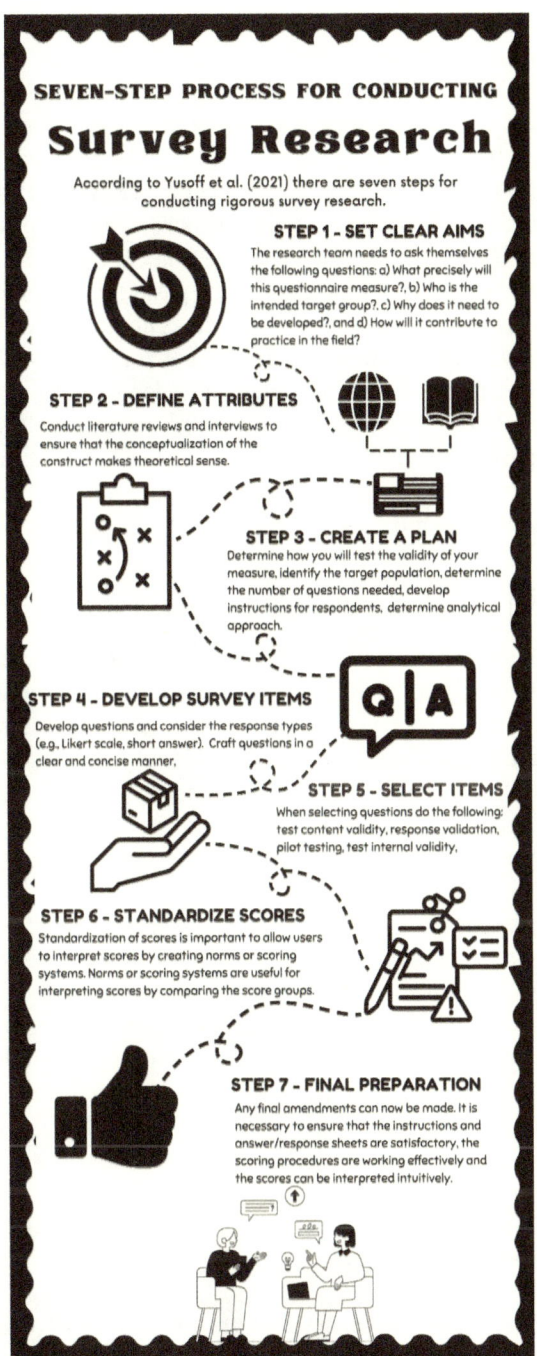

Figure 7.2   Seven-Step Process for Conducting Survey Research

research. This is inherently problematic for the researcher—and those reading about the research. Based on this information, it is safe to say that results of a survey provide only a snapshot of what is occurring rather than the rich, in-depth picture of the phenomenon researchers are intent on exploring. Another critical limitation of survey research is the potential for inaccurate responses to the survey questions. Many people are swayed by **social desirability**, meaning people tend to provide responses they believe are socially acceptable even if they are not fully accurate (Patten, 2021). A final limitation that has become more commonplace over the past few years is the infiltration of **bots** (Griffin et al., 2021). Bots are defined as computer software designed to perform automated tasks for users (Teitcher et al., 2015); such software can be created or downloaded within minutes and deployed to complete simple automated functions or find surveys offering incentives (Godinho et al. 2020). While survey research is intended to gather information from a large group of participants surrounding a particular idea, it is not the only research method that can be used to look at large amounts of data.

Secondary Data Analysis: What, Why, and How?

Secondary data analysis (SDA), or a big data study, is conducted by researchers who use **extant data** collected by other researchers to investigate different questions. Like **primary data** researchers, SDA investigators must be knowledgeable about their research area to identify datasets that are a good fit for an SDA. Researchers may opt for secondary data analyses for a variety of reasons, such as examining a different unit of analysis, posing different research questions that are more in-depth than in the original study, or combining multiple extant datasets (Lombardi et al., 2023).

An SDA researcher starts with a research question or hypothesis, then identifies an appropriate dataset or sets to address it. Alternatively, a researcher might already be familiar with a dataset and peruse it to identify other questions that might be answered (Cheng & Phillips, 2014). SDA researchers access primary data via formal (public or institutional archived primary research datasets) or informal data-sharing sources. There are numerous sources of datasets for secondary analysis. SDA may help a new investigator increase their clinical research expertise and avoid data collection challenges (Wickham, 2019). It may also allow for examining more variables than would be feasible in smaller studies, surveys of more diverse samples, and the ability to rethink data and use more advanced statistical techniques in analysis (Rew et al., 2000).

Yet until recently, there has been very little guidance on conducting this type of research rigorously in the field of special education. Thankfully, a group of authors published a special issue in the journal *Exceptional Children* that introduced the next generation of quality indicators in special education and features an article on secondary data analysis (Lombardi et al., 2023). In their article "Quality Indicators of Secondary Data Analyses in Special Education Research: A Preregistration Guide," the authors described the aspects of SDA that researchers should be engaging in when doing this type of research. The items on this list of quality indicators are intended to increase the believability of big data research and include how researchers should handle the following: (a) research questions and hypotheses, (b) variable reporting, (c) statistical power, (d) complex sampling designs, (e) analytical approach, (f) demographic variable, (g) missing data, and (h) software packages.

Limitations of Secondary Data Analysis

Despite the wealth of information that is available through secondary data analysis, there are several limitations we must recognize when reading and interpreting this type of research. One of the biggest limitations of SDA is that researchers have no control over database population, variables of interest, and study design because they likely did not have a role in collecting the primary data. This is concerning because researchers have different rationales for collecting data and they may not align with the phenomenon the secondary data analyst is exploring. Next, relevant demographic information (e.g., age, race, gender, and locale) may not be available, which can harm the **external validity** of the research findings. According to Wickham (2019), SDA research may be limited to descriptive, exploratory, and correlational designs and nonparametric statistical tests. Further, they state that SDA investigators are challenged to decide whether archival data can be shaped to match new research questions; this means the researcher must have an in-depth understanding of the dataset and know how to alter research questions to match available data and recoded variables.

Teacher Action Research: What, Why, and How?

The research approaches we have discussed in this chapter and throughout this book have been researcher driven. But research is not relegated to those who hold a PhD and work in academia. In fact, there is a research methodology dedicated to the boots on the ground (i.e., teachers in classrooms). This type of research is known as **teacher action research**. Teacher action research is a method teachers use to investigate problems and improve professional practices in their classrooms.

According to Johnson (2008), when engaging in action research, there are five essential steps that must be adhered to:

1. The first step, similar to all research methodologies, is for action researchers to identify a phenomenon of interest and develop research questions that will drive the investigation.
2. Next, action researchers need to determine how they intend to measure the phenomenon of interest. In other words, a plan (what, how, and when) must be developed regarding what data need to be collected to address the question formulated in step 1.
3. Step 3 is to move through the data collection process and analyze those data.
4. In step 4, action researchers should write up their findings regarding how those results can be used in classrooms and what resources are needed.
5. Step 5 involves disseminating findings from the action research to others and developing an action plan based on the results of the teacher action.

Engaging in this work is critical to implementing strategies and supports that are shown to be effective via other research methods but have for one reason or another failed to generalize to the natural setting (i.e., classroom).

The research-to-practice gap refers to the disparity between what research has shown to be effective and what practitioners actually do (Beahm & Cook, 2021). According to Greenwood and Abbot (2001), the research-to-practice gap is largely caused by the following:

1. The separateness of the research and practice communities (i.e., oftentimes, researchers fail to involve practitioners in the research process as meaningful and valued partners; hence, they miss the opportunity to discover exemplary classroom practices that have the potential for formal validation and widespread applicability)
2. The limited relevance of educational research as perceived by practitioners (i.e., research is often conceptualized and conducted in settings that are different from the realities of schooling)
3. The failure of researchers to produce usable interventions (i.e., with sufficient specificity and concreteness for use by practitioners)
4. The limited opportunities for meaningful professional development (i.e., there is often a heavy reliance on traditional models of professional development that call for a top-down transmission of information to teachers)

One of the major benefits that teacher action research provides is insights regarding the research-to-practice gap. Teacher action research can help address this gap through the examination and experimentation of identified best practices in relation to the activities in a real-life classroom setting. The information gleaned through this process can be used to help understand and inform the research conducted on best practices. Yet teacher action research is not without limitations.

Limitations of Teacher Action Research

When teachers are conducting research in their schools, they are doing so while continuing to engage in their daily duties as an educator. Because of this, the rigor of teacher action research can be minimized. Additionally, this type of work is typically conducted very quickly due to the limited time educators have with students in school, which can further reduce the rigor of this type of research. Further, preparing people to engage in research typically takes years of study and mentorship so research can be done at a high level of rigor and believability. This type of training is not afforded to teachers in their preparation programs, making the lack of training in research a limitation of teacher action research. Finally, the findings of teacher action research can have minimal generalizability due to the different contexts in which this type of research is conducted.

Delphi: What, Why, and How?

The Delphi technique was first developed in the 1950s by Norman Dalkey and Olaf Helmer to gain reliable expert consensus, which they named after the ancient Greek oracle of Delphi, who was known for predicting the future (Barrett & Heale, 2020). The Delphi technique is an iterative forecasting and group decision-making process that involves systematic feedback loops via an expert panel to reach consensus about the topic of study. The defining features of this approach include anonymity, iterative feedback, group responding, and consultation with experts of a particular area of inquiry. Much like other research methodology, there are essential steps that must be adhered to. Steps for conducting a Delphi study include (1) choosing a facilitator who has a dearth of knowledge around the phenomena of interest, (2) identifying experts in that field, (3) developing research questions that will drive the study, (4) conducting response and feedback rounds, and (5) analyzing and disseminating findings.

Limitations of Delphi Research

Like other research methodology, the Delphi approach is not impervious to limitations. One of the major limitations to this approach is the amount of time it takes to go through the iterative process. After each round of questioning and responding, the researchers need to meet with the expert panel and then go back to the respondents for another round of questioning. This is done a minimum of three times. One of the great things about Delphi studies is that they are flexible in nature. Flexibility is afforded through the allowance of respondents to alter their responses. But this is also problematic for research because bias can be introduced based on the social pressure to conform to the majority of respondents.

Program Evaluation: What, Why, and How?

Perhaps one of the lesser heralded types of research is known as program evaluation research, which is the systematic process by which we determine if programs are meeting their purported goals, how well the programs run, whether the programs had the desired effect, and whether the programs have merit according to relevant parties. Although held in less regard than other types of research, it is essential, particularly in fending off pseudoscientific approaches that have either a null or negative effect on student outcomes. Pseudoscience can be viewed as a system of theories and methods that have some resemblance to a genuine science but that cannot be considered as such. Examples include astrology, numerology, and esoteric magic (American Psychological Association, 2015). In education, strategies that claim to be effective but actually are not are pseudoscience; in fact, they can be harmful to those they claim to support and those around them.

In 2016, Lammert and colleagues developed a tool kit that can assist those who are engaging in the evaluation of special education programs. The authors state that a well-designed evaluation can have many benefits but to realize those benefits it is essential for those engaging in this work to create a purposeful plan. In their tool kit, the authors present a Gantt chart for purposefully planning an evaluation. Another group, Hanover Research, stated that conducting regular program evaluations is critical to ensuring consistent, successful outcomes yet it is a rigorous and demanding process. In 2023, Hanover Research provided a step-by-step planning tool to support program evaluation through a three-stage process. Stage 1 is the prioritization stage where the objectives for the evaluation process are identified and aligned with strategic goals and outcomes the team wants to progress monitor are identified. Stage 2 is the planning stage where the team answers these questions: (a) What are our goals for the evaluations? (b) How can we create buy-in from others relevant to the evaluation who may not be on the core team? and (c) When will the results be needed? The final stage is where the evaluation occurs. It is composed of the following main items: (a) identifying what can be learned from the data, (b) determining how to disseminate the results to those who need to see them, and (c) determining how to use this information to improve our programs.

Limitations of Program Evaluation Research

Much like all other research processes, there are limitations we must concern ourselves with as consumers of research. One of the major limitations of this or any other type of research is poor planning. Poor planning leads to poor measurement, which leads to inaccurate results. Another area of concern is the lack of readiness from the team and those outside the core team to conduct the evaluation. There are several other limitations one should be aware of when it comes to conducting program evaluations: deploying ineffective approaches, asking questions that are not aligned to the goals and objectives of the program evaluation, data that are not accurate, and overwhelming amounts of data that become too unwieldy to analyze.

WHERE CAN I FIND MORE INFORMATION ABOUT THESE RESEARCH METHODS?

Colorado State University: This guide examines case study research that is used to investigate phenomenon with individuals, small groups, or large groups. The guide can be found at https://writing.colostate.edu/guides/guide.cfm?guideid=60.

***Journal of Teacher Action Research*:** The *Journal of Teacher Action Research* is an international journal that publishes peer-reviewed articles written by teachers and researchers to inform classroom practice. The journal serves as a practical medium to read about and publish classroom-based research. The website for the journal is at http://www.practicalteacherresearch.com/.

National Institutes of Health (NIH): In November 2010, the Office of Behavioral and Social Sciences Research of the NIH commissioned a leadership team to develop a resource to provide guidance on how to rigorously develop and evaluate mixed-methods research applications. This resource can be found at https://obssr.od.nih.gov/research-resources/mixed-methods-research.

QuestionPro: This article outlines the things you need to know about survey research, such as types, methods, and examples, and is provide by QuestionPro, a survey software company. The article can be found at https://www.questionpro.com/blog/survey-research/

Westat: This tool kit was developed to support special education program evaluation as part of the Center to Improve Project Performance (CIPP) operated by Westat for the U.S. Department of Education, Office of Special Education Programs (OSEP). The tool kit can be found at https://osepideasthatwork.org/sites/default/files/Evaluating%20Special%20Education%20Programs%20Resource%20Toolkit_Section%20508_12.pdf.

DISCUSSION QUESTIONS

1. At your beginning of the year welcome meeting, your district's leadership states that they will be rolling out a new reading curriculum for students with disabilities. While many are excited about it, you as a scientific practitioner want to make sure that what you are being asked to do is effective. What research method discussed in this chapter would you select to do your own research regarding the effectiveness of this reading curriculum? Provide a rationale for your selection.
2. When discussing teacher action research, we mentioned several limitations to this approach. What might be some tactics to mitigate those limitations?
3. Identify a pseudoscientific practice, such as learning styles, and use the Westat tool kit to develop an evaluation process to examine the effectiveness of that approach.
4. At the beginning of this chapter, we introduced the mixed-methods design. Come up with three topics to investigate where this approach may be the best fit.
5. Many of the research approaches discussed in the chapter mention disseminating the results of your work. Come up with three very different audiences and venues for the meaningful dissemination of your work.

KEY TERMS

bots: Computer software designed to perform automated tasks for users.
bounded context: A conceptual boundary that defines a specific phenomenon.
case study: Research approach that is used to generate an in-depth, multifaceted understanding of a complex issue in its real-life context.
epistemological: The study of the nature, origin, and scope of knowledge.
extant data: Already collected and existing data.
external validity: Whether the findings of a study can be generalized to other contexts.
mixed-methods research: Combining quantitative and qualitative approaches to provide a depth and breadth of data around a phenomenon of interest.
nonresponse bias: When respondents who refuse to take part in a survey are systematically different from those who completed the survey.
primary data: Data that are collected by researchers directly from main sources through interviews, surveys, experiments.

reactivity: When participants in a study alter their behavior knowing that they are participants in a study.
social desirability: People tend to provide responses they believe are socially acceptable even if they are not fully accurate.
teacher action research: A research method teachers use to investigate problems and improve professional practices in their classrooms.

REFERENCES

American Psychological Association. (2015). *APA dictionary of psychology* (2nd ed.). APA.

Barrett, D., & Heale, R. (2020). What are Delphi studies? *Evidence-Based Nursing, 23*(3), 68–69. https://doi.org/10.1136/ebnurs-2020-103303

Beahm, L. A., & Cook, B. G. (2021). Merging practice-based evidence and evidence-based practices to close the research-to-practice gap. In B. G. Cook, M. Tankersley, & T. J. Landrum (Eds.), *The next big thing in learning and behavioral disabilities* (pp. 47–60). Emerald.

Bhaskaran, V. (n.d.). *Survey research: Definition, examples and methods.* QuestionPro. https://www.questionpro.com/blog/survey-research/

Cheng, H. G., & Phillips, M. R. (2014). Secondary analysis of existing data: Opportunities and implementation. *Shanghai Archives of Psychiatry, 26*(6), 371.

Creswell, J. W. (2009). *Research design: Qualitative, quantitative, and mixed-methods approaches* (3rd ed.). Sage.

Creswell, J. W., Klassen, A. C., Plano Clark, V. L., & Smith, K. C. (2011). Best practices for mixed methods research in the health sciences. *Bethesda (Maryland): National Institutes of Health, 2013,* 541–545.

Crowe, S., Cresswell, K., Robertson, A., Huby, G., Avery, A., & Sheikh, A. (2011). The case study approach. *BMC Medical Research Methodology, 11,* 100. https://doi.org/10.1186/1471-2288-11-100

Godinho, A., Schell, C., & Cunningham, J. A. (2020). Out damn bot, out: Recruiting real people into substance use studies on the internet. *Substance Use & Addiction Journal, 41*(1), 3–5. https://doi.org/10.1080/08897077.2019.1691131

Greenwood, C. R., & Abbott, M. (2001). The research to practice gap in special education. *Teacher Education and Special Education, 24*(4), 276–289. https://doi.org/10.1177/088840640102400403

Griffin, M., Martino, R. J., LoSchiavo, C., Comer-Carruthers, C., Krause, K. D., Stults, C. B., & Halkitis, P. N. (2021). Ensuring survey research data integrity in the era of internet bots. *Quality & Quantity, 56,* 2841–2852. https://doi.org/10.1007/s11135-021-01252-1

Hanover Research. (2023, March). *Step-by-step guide to K-12 program evaluation.* https://www.hanoverresearch.com/reports-and-briefs/k-12-program-evaluations-guide/?org=k-12-education

Ivankova, N. V., & Creswell, J. W. (2009). Mixed-methods. In J. Heigham & R. A. Croker (Eds.), *Qualitative research in applied linguistics: A practical introduction* (pp. 135–161). Palgrave Macmillan.

Johnson, A. P. (2008). *A short guide to action research*. Allyn & Bacon.

Jones, T. L., Baxter, M. A. J., & Khanduja, V. (2013). A quick guide to survey research. *The Annals of The Royal College of Surgeons of England, 95*(1), 5–7. https://doi.org/10.1308/003588413X13511609956372

Leedy, P. D., & Ormrod, J. E. (2001). *Practical research: Planning and design*. Merrill Prentice Hall.

Lombardi, A. R., Rifenbark, G. G., & Taconet, A. (2023). Quality indicators of secondary data analyses in special education research: A preregistration guide. *Exceptional Children, 89*(4), 397–411. https://doi.org/10.1177/00144029221141029

Miles, M. B., Huberman, A. M., & Saldaña, J. (2014). *Qualitative data analysis: A methods sourcebook* (3rd ed.). Sage.

Patten, M. L. (2021). *Questionnaire research*. Pyrczak.

Priya, A. (2021). Case study methodology of qualitative research: Key attributes and navigating the conundrums in its application. *Sociological Bulletin, 70*(1), 94–110. https://doi.org/10.1177/0038022920970318

Rew, L., Koniak-Griffin, D., Lewis, M. A., Miles, M., & O'Sullivan, A. (2000). Secondary data analysis: New perspective for adolescent research. *Nursing Outlook, 48*(5), 223–229. https://doi.org/10.1067/mno.2000.104901

Schoch, K. (2020). Case study research. In G. J. Burkholder, K. A. Cox, L. M. Crawford, & J. Hitchcook (Eds.), *Research design and methods: An applied guide for the scholar practitioner* (pp. 245–258). Sage.

Teitcher, J. E., Bockting, W. O., Bauermeister, J. A., Hoefer, C. J., Miner, M. H., & Klitzman, R. L. (2015). Detecting, preventing, and responding to "fraudsters" in internet research: Ethics and tradeoffs. *Journal of Law, Medicine & Ethics, 43*(1), 116–133. doi:10.1111/jlme.12200

Wickham, R. J. (2019). Secondary analysis research. *Journal of the Advanced Practitioner in Oncology, 10*(4), 395–400. https://doi.org/10.6004/jadpro.2019.10.4.7

Yusoff, M. S. B., Arifin, W. N., & Hadie, S. N. H. (2021). ABC of questionnaire development and validation for survey research. *Education in Medicine Journal, 13*(1). https://doi.org/10.21315/eimj2021.13.1.10

PART III

Reading and Implementing Research in Practice

Chapter 8

Classroom Management

Interest and investigation into why humans do what they do has a rich and tumultuous past. As far back as the late 1700s, social scientists turned their attention to the functions of the brain and how those processes determined the actions of individuals. These early scientists paved the way for the study of human behavior. Psychology as an experimental study originated in 1854 in Leipzig, Germany, when Gustav Fechner developed the first theory of how judgments about sensory experiences are made and how to experiment with them. The well-known idea of **classical conditioning** was initially investigated by Ivan Pavlov. His experiment in which dogs learned to drool at the sound of a tone is recognized as the pioneering work in this field. The genesis for Pavlov's classical conditioning began by gauging the amount of saliva generated for digestion in a variety of breeds. He soon discovered, though, that the dogs would begin drooling even prior to food delivery. He discovered later that the dogs connected the sound of his going down the stairs with the delivery of food. He then tested this notion by feeding the dogs while playing a tone at the same time (**stimulus** association). Eventually, he discovered that the dogs would salivate at the sound of a tone even in the absence of food. Through stimulus association, the dogs learned a novel reaction to a known stimulus. This taught reaction was dubbed a conditional reflex by Pavlov.

Following Pavlov, John B. Watson is recognized for having been the first to integrate behaviorism's diverse components. Watson's behaviorism is based on the tenet that consciousness, or introspective thoughts and feelings, should not be considered when analyzing behavior because it cannot be observed or controlled by science. According to him, psychology should be used to anticipate and manipulate only observable behavior; it should not interpret conscious experience in any way. Therefore, Watson characterizes learning as a change in discernible behavior. In his 1913 publication, "Psychology as the Behaviorist Views It," Watson characterizes behaviorism as "a purely objective experimental branch of natural science" that "recognizes no dividing line between man and brute." The defining feature of Watson's view on behaviorism relied on seeing and forecasting subjects' outward reactions to stimuli from external sources.

Based on Watson's behaviorism with some deviations, Burrhus Frederick (B. F.) Skinner became well known in the field for developing and using **operant conditioning**. According to Skinner's operant condition theory, an individual's conduct is influenced by their environment. The link between reinforcement and punishment, which is comparable to Thorndike's rule of effect, is the fundamental idea of operant conditioning. It is more likely for behaviors that are rewarded, rather than punished, to be repeated. Incorporating reinforcement into his behavior theory, Skinner noted that there was a high probability that a given behavior was the outcome of an environmental stimulus. In this sense, "rewards" that make a behavior repeat in the future are referred to as reinforcement. So what does any of this have to do with classroom and behavior management? More than you might think! Most of the intervention work implemented in schools to support classroom and behavior management adhere to the principles outlined by B. F. Skinner.

In this chapter, we will examine the issues concerning classroom management for students with disabilities and use a scenario to systematically examine how one can use research to address challenging student behaviors. By the end of the chapter, we will have answered these essential questions:

1. What are some of the issues concerning classroom management?
2. What are some of the best practices in classroom management?
3. How do I use research to address issues with classroom management?
4. Where can I find more information about classroom management?

WHAT ARE SOME OF THE ISSUES CONCERNING CLASSROOM MANAGEMENT?

If a student experiences trouble reading, we teach them to read. If a student is a poor speller, we teach them to spell. If a student struggles with double-digit addition, we teach them how to calculate double-digit addition problems. Yet when a student "misbehaves" in class, we punish them and hope they have "learned their lesson." But in actuality, we have taught them nothing. Instead, we should take a positive and proactive approach and teach students how to engage with the world in and outside of the classroom. After all, when you are teaching a little child to swim, you don't just toss them in the deep end of a pool and yell "Why are you drowning?" Instead, you should systematically teach them how to swim. The same concept should be applied to classroom behaviors.

Interfering behaviors in the classroom can affect the academic, behavioral, and social skills acquisition for all students in a classroom and lead to negative educational outcomes for students with disabilities (e.g., dropping out and change of placement). Students who display chronic interfering behaviors may face unfavorable consequences, such as suspensions, antisocial behavior, and involvement with the criminal justice system (Butler & Monda-Amaya, 2016). Interfering behaviors frequently jeopardize students' continued placement in general education settings, impede academic and social skill acquisition, spread to other classrooms or settings, and foster toxic teacher–student relationships and may persist into adulthood.

Improving outcomes for students who exhibit problem behaviors is critical. Traditional approaches to behavior management include student-centered approaches (e.g., differential reinforcement and time-out), classroom and teacher-centered tactics (e.g., **rules** and **routines** and clear expectations), teacher–student relationship focused (e.g., developing positive discourse with students), and school-wide initiatives (e.g., school-wide positive behavior interventions and supports). Interfering behaviors negatively affect teachers as well.

Behaviors that interfere with learning and instruction can have negative effects on teachers, particularly novice teachers (Gunter et al., 1994), and play a significant role regarding the ongoing teacher shortage issue in the United States. Interfering behavioral patterns among students can lead to teacher stress, burnout, and attrition (Bettini et al., 2020). Teachers identify student disruption, noncompliance, and disengagement as the most frequent challenging behaviors they need to manage daily (Gage et al., 2018), resulting in feelings of being underprepared to implement more targeted behavioral interventions to reduce interfering classroom behaviors (Riden, Taylor, Scheeler, et al., 2021). Education experts have developed, adopted, and examined practices that help support students in the classroom, many being classified as evidence-based practices (EBPs).

WHAT ARE SOME OF THE BEST PRACTICES IN CLASSROOM MANAGEMENT?

To increase the efficacy of the supports we implement, it is essential to think about why students do what they do. Equally important is understanding why we as teachers do what we do. In this section, we will highlight **functions** of behavior and the importance of rules and routines, antecedent-based strategies, consequence-based strategies, group contingencies, token economies, and tiered system of behavior supports.

Functions of Behavior

The human species engages in behavior for two reasons: to get something or to get away from something. We call these functions of behavior. If we can understand that students engage in behaviors to communicate something, we are halfway to understanding functions of behavior.

When working with students who exhibit interfering behaviors, we can classify them under one of two categories: social function and nonsocial function. Both functions are mediated by setting events. There are three subcategories under social function: (a) attention, (b) escape/avoidance, and (c) tangible. As a maintaining function, attention is when students engage in behavior that gains them attention. Students engage in attention-maintained behaviors for a variety of reasons, such as accessing interaction with others, expressing affection, and receiving or giving information and help. The next social function is escape/avoidance. Behaviors that are maintained by this function are motivated by escaping or avoiding an aversive (unpleasant) stimulus. Lastly, student behavior maintained by the tangible function results in the student's obtaining a "thing," such as a tablet to play games, food, clothing, or money.

As mentioned previously, there is a nonsocial function to behaviors. Automatically maintained behaviors are also known as *sensory behaviors*. Behaviors that fall under this category occur regardless of social interactions, meaning the individual is in control of the reinforcer that maintains the behavior. Automatically maintained behaviors may be engaged in to release tension, relax, end unpleasant thoughts, cope with stress, or to provide stimulation when bored. To increase the effectiveness of the support you choose, the function of the behavior is an essential consideration for educators. See Table 8.1 for additional examples pertaining to functions of behavior.

Importance of Rules and Routines

A classroom management plan creates a safe, positive, and consistent environment where teaching and learning can take place, guides student (and teacher) behavior, and communicates expectations. High-quality classroom management starts with establishing the rules and routines in your classroom. Rules are specific behaviors for which there are consequences (both positive and negative) and are applied across all classroom activities.

Routines create predictability, which lowers stress and anxiety and assists with regulating behavior in children (Wildenger et al., 2008). In addition to providing children with regularity, confidence, comfort, trust, and a sense of safety, routines enable teachers and students to predict what will happen next by helping them recognize patterns in the environment (Salmon, 2010).

Table 8.1 Four Functions of Behavior With Examples

Function	Definition	Student Example	Teacher Example
Attention	The behavior provides the individual with attention from others in the environment.	A student uses curse words to get their classmates to laugh at them.	The lead presenter at a professional development seminar stands in front of the audience and raises their hand in the air silently until everyone is paying attention.
Escape/avoidance	The behavior results in the removal of undesired activities, interactions, people, and/or situations.	A child leaves the class when a math curriculum-based measurement is presented to them.	The special education teacher knows that at 3:30 on Mondays the football coach seeks volunteers to help with home games on Friday nights. So each Monday, the teacher heads to their car as soon as students are dismissed so they can avoid the football coach's asking for help.
Tangible	The behavior results in the attainment of a preferred activity or item.	A student completes their assignment to access computer time.	A teacher is trying to gain access to a student file but needs the key. They walk to the office and ask the staff for the key to the file room.
Automatic (sensory)	A student engages in behavior because it physically feels good or relieves something that feels bad (e.g., provides relief or pleasure).	A student is completing a task at their desk and is repeatedly tapping their pencil on the desk. The teacher asks the student, "Why are you doing that?" The student states, "I like the sound the eraser makes on the desk."	A teacher is bouncing their knee as they wait to have their quarterly review with their principal. An office staff member asks the teacher if everything is OK. The teacher responds, "Oh yeah, everything is fine. I just bounce my legs when I am nervous. For some reason it helps calm me down."

Routines allow students to feel safe and predict interactions when they are explicitly introduced, modeled, and practiced (Leinhardt et al., 1987). Moreover, routines increase valuable instructional time for teachers and are important for students in adjusting to various school-related activities. For example, within the early childhood environment, there are routines that help students transition to different activities within the school day, such as the transition upon arrival (morning routine), transition to lunch (lunchtime routine), and transition at departure (afternoon routine).

Antecedent-Based Strategies

Antecedent interventions can be classified as a positive and proactive approach for addressing student behavior. They typically involve some type of environmental rearrangement; in other words, circumstances or factors are changed in some way so that they are no longer likely to cause or create the conditions that set the stage for problem behaviors to arise (Kern et al., 2002). As mentioned previously in the section on function of behavior, the success of behavior support strategies intently hinges on hypothesizing the functions of the behavior. Two examples of this are prompting and visual schedules. Prompting is a strategy that is used to support students as they learn new skills. The prompts are arranged in a hierarchy from least to most intrusive and are meant to be faded. The reason prompting is an effective antecedent strategy is that the student consistently contacts reinforcement during the skill acquisition process. Moving from least to most intrusive, the prompts are visual, verbal, gestural, modeling, partially physical, and fully physical (see Figure 8.1).

Another antecedent strategy that is low effort but effective is visual schedules. They are an intervention that can help students follow a routine, transition between activities, develop new skills, and reduce dependence on teachers when completing daily activities (Havlik, n.d.). To implement a visual schedule, a teacher can use a series of pictures, drawings, photos, symbols, or written directions to communicate the order in which a skill or activity needs to be performed. This type of antecedent intervention is typically leveraged to support students' understanding and managing the many things they must do during a particular activity or throughout a school day. There are simpler visual activity schedules that consist of just two images with the labels "first" and "then" to indicate a transition from one activity to another or involving multistep tasks with associated visuals (Fowkes, 2022). The essentials for creating a visual schedule are presented in Figure 8.2. The key to antecedent interventions is that they be put in place *before* the behavior occurs and that they be faded until the student can do the task independently.

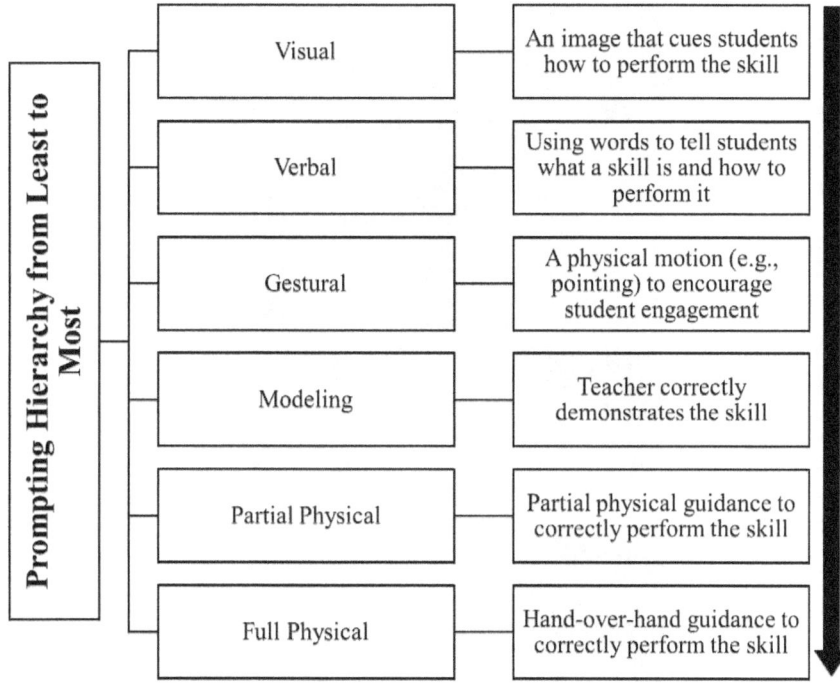

Figure 8.1 Prompting Hierarchy with Example

Consequence-Based Strategies

In contrast to antecedent interventions, consequence-based strategies are implemented after a behavior has been emitted by a student to reduce reinforcement for problematic behavior and boost reinforcement for desired ones. The purpose of consequence-based strategies is to react to student conduct properly, which necessitates reacting to the desired behaviors to increase them and appropriately reacting to behaviors of concern when they arise. To protect the safety of the learner and others, they also entail redirecting the student toward other behaviors of action and offering crisis prevention techniques. By comprehending the mechanism sustaining a problematic behavior (i.e., the function of behavior), teachers (along with their team) can build functional assessment-based interventions to minimize undesired behavior, improve quality of life, and foster positive relationships. An example of this would be extinction. Despite what some might think, extinction *is not* ignoring the student. When we ignore the whole child, we miss out on opportunities to provide reinforcement for the desired behaviors we seek. If we look at

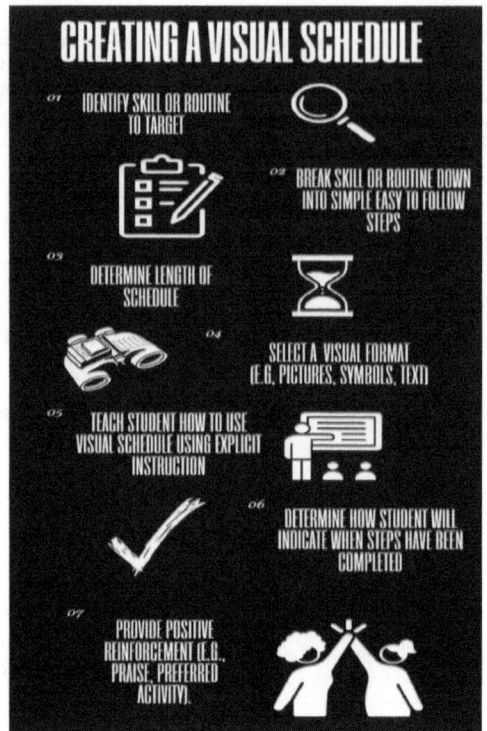

Figure 8.2 Essentials of Creating an Activity Schedule

the definition of extinction regarding student behavior, we see that it means to withhold reinforcement. So by definition, if we are placing a behavior on extinction, we are not providing reinforcement for them. For example, if we are using an extinction procedure with a child to reduce the number of times they call out, we must withhold our attention (presuming that is the maintaining function) when they call out instead of telling them to not talk out of turn, to be quiet, or to wait their turn. Then, what we would do is provide some praise (initially) when they raise their hand or are waiting patiently to respond. By doing this, we are making the calling-out behavior ineffective when attempting to access attention and making the raising of hand behavior effective for obtaining praise.

Group Contingencies

A group contingency is when the reinforcer is contingent upon one member of a group, a segment of the group, or the whole group. There are three types of group-oriented contingencies: independent, dependent, interdependent. When implementing an independent group contingency, each student can earn their reinforcer regardless of the behavior of their peers. A dependent group contingency, also known as the hero contingency, is when the reinforcement of an entire group is contingent upon one student's (the hero's) behavior. Teachers should use this approach with caution because it can lead to unwanted stress and anxiety in students as well as opening the door for potential bullying. If a teacher is to choose this approach, we suggest using the mystery hero, meaning only the teacher knows who the target student is. The final group contingency is the interdependent group contingency, which means that reinforcement of the group is contingent on the behavior of the whole class.

Token Economies

According to Kazdin (1977), a token economy is a type of contingency management wherein students receive tokens for exhibiting desired behavior. These tokens can then be swapped for prearranged backup reinforcement. A menu of meaningful reinforcement possibilities must be systematically linked to the tokens. As a result, in traditional monetary systems, the tokens gain symbolic value like that of everyday currency (Wolery et al., 1988).

According to Wolery et al. (1988), five components are necessary when installing a token economy in your classroom: (a) identifying specific target behaviors, (b) identifying tokens for conditioned reinforcement, (c) developing a menu of backup reinforcement options to award appropriate behavior, (d) developing an explicit protocol for exchanging conditioned reinforcers for backup reinforcers, and (e) developing procedures for fading the use of the token economy system. Consequently, the token economy is merely an instance of an array of behavioral strategies that associate the distribution and procurement of tokens with behavioral expectations (Maggin et al., 2011).

Tiered System of Behavior Supports

A framework called the multitiered system of supports (MTSS) assists teachers in offering behavioral and academic strategies to students with a range of support needs. The merging of response to intervention (RtI) and positive behavior intervention support (PBIS), two further intervention-based frameworks, gave rise to MTSS. Providing a framework for an integrated support program that is responsive, flexible, and varies in intensity for every student is the aim of a tiered system of supports. This method is intended to mitigate obstacles to learning and development both within and outside of the classroom to fulfill a student's academic, physical, social, emotional, and identity needs.

Tier 1, which is the biggest tier, provides core instruction and fundamental interventions to the entire school. Staff and students can develop positive relationships with each other because of this arrangement. It contains proactive classroom management techniques meant to foster a positive learning environment. The strategies in tier 1 are effective for supporting 75% to 90% of students in the school. Yet some students need a little extra assistance in meeting academic and behavioral goals, which they will find in tier 2. Supports and interventions are frequently delivered in small-group settings in tier 2 and often include interventions such as check-in/check-out, **daily behavior report cards**, check and connect, behavior contracting, and peer tutoring. The strategies in tier 2 are effective for supporting the remaining 10% to 20% of students in the school.

Significant challenges regarding behavior are present in some students who do not respond to strategies put in place in either of the first two tiers. In most schools, there are 1% to 5% of students for whom tiers 1 and 2 supports are not effective. At tier 3, these students receive more intensive, individualized support to improve their behavioral and academic outcomes. A functional behavior assessment (FBA) needs to be in place for students entering tier 3, the reason being that any intensive, individualized intervention should be based on evidence for the function of behavior. Included in the FBA are interviews with relevant parties, records reviews, antecedent–behavior–consequence (ABC) data collection, behavior screening tools, operational definitions, and competing pathways. When creating a competing pathways model, educators can identify the contingency in place, the desired behavior, a replacement behavior, and maintaining consequences (see Figure 8.3).

HOW DO I USE RESEARCH TO ADDRESS CLASSROOM MANAGEMENT ISSUES?

As we elaborated on earlier in this chapter, there are several negative impacts associated with challenging classroom behaviors and the effect they can have on students and teachers. Although solutions to these challenging situations may seem daunting (and they can be), in the previous section, we called attention to some of those challenges. We identified a variety of EBPs that can be implemented to mitigate any impact that interfering behaviors may be having on a class. In the following section, we examine, through a fictitious vignette, how one can use research to address an issue with classroom and behavior management. We provide a scenario with context, which is critical in understanding for scientific practitioners. Then, we provide a full-text, single-case research article as practice for becoming a scientific practitioner, which follows these four essential steps:

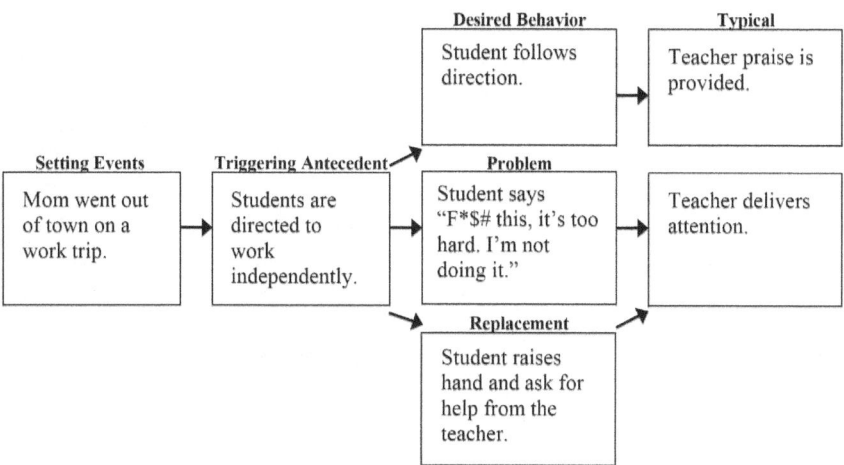

Figure 8.3 Example of a Competing Pathways Model

1. Identify and understand a problem in the classroom.
2. Know where to look for potential researched solutions.
3. Read and understand a variety of research articles to gather information.
4. Use professional judgment to implement researched strategies across individual contexts.

Identify and Understand a Problem in the Classroom

Mrs. Warren is a self-contained middle school teacher who works to include her students in inclusive settings to the greatest extent possible. Students on her caseload span several disability categories, including autism and emotional disturbance, and display several behaviors that can be described as interfering. All her students are provided services via their individualized education programs (IEPs) to foster their academic, emotional, and behavioral growth.

Mrs. Warren holds weekly meetings with the general education teacher (Mr. Rooney) about one student in particular, Hines. Hines engages in behaviors that distract his peers (i.e., crude language and inappropriate jokes), and he arrives late to class. Further, Hines has a difficult time attending to the tasks at hand, which has become a concerning barrier to knowledge acquisition. Mrs. Warren and Mr. Rooney have worked collaboratively for several years and have had great success with a variety of strategies to support their students regardless of their needs. In the past, they have found success using token economies, check-in/check-out, visual supports, behavior-specific praise, and noncontingent reinforcement, but when they tried them with Hines, none of them had any meaningful effect on his behavior.

While Mrs. Warren was eating her lunch in the teachers' lounge, she saw one of the district's behavior coaches (Mr. Cowher) making a cup of coffee, and she decided to approach him for some advice on how to best support Hines. Mr. Cowher mentioned that he had attended the Teacher Educators for Children with Behavioral Disorders conference and that while he was there, he had gone to a session on daily behavior report cards (DBRCs). Mr. Cowher described an example of a student the speaker gave whose behavior had many commonalities with Hines's and suggested that a DBRC might be the intervention she has been looking for. Being that Mrs. Warren had exhausted all the tools in her toolbox, she decides to investigate DBRCs as a possible intervention to promote Hines's positive classroom behaviors.

Know Where to Look for Potential Research Solutions

Like most individuals looking for answers to questions they have, Mrs. Warren turned to internet search engines. Upon entering the search term "daily behavior report cards" into the search engine, she is dismayed by the 97,300,000 results she received. Some relief is provided in the form of videos on creating a behavior tracker and images of DBRCs as well as links to what appear to be reputable websites. But Mrs. Warren remains skeptical because she is aware that much of the information found on websites dedicated to special education teachers has little if any empirical support via research. After combing through several videos, blogs, and websites, Mrs. Warren decides that she needs to be confident in the sources she chooses to use when trying to support her students.

She decides that the first course of action is to use a more academic search engine (e.g., Google Scholar). She types in her search term so that the results she receives are targeted toward DBRCs, and gets back only 821 hits. She did this by putting quotation marks at the beginning and end of her search term. Mrs. Warren feels a bit of relief because 821 articles to comb through seems much more doable than the millions she received using nonacademic search engines. As she scrolls through the returns of her search, she identifies several articles from what appear to be academic and peer-reviewed journals. She downloads a few of those and uses the information gleaned from the search results to navigate to several journals' home pages in search of just the right articles that she can use to craft her only DBRC. As she is sifting through the articles, she sees an article, "Using a Daily Report Card to Reduce Off-Task Behaviors for a Student With Autism Spectrum Disorder," by Riden, Taylor, Ruiz, et al. (2021), which was published in the *Journal of Behavioral Education* (*JOBE*).

She believes that this article is a reputable source because it was published in partnership with Springer, a leading global scientific publisher. Upon visiting *JOBE*'s website, she sees in their overview that they present empirical research investigating best practices and innovative methods that address the needs of diverse learners and implementation. The journal focuses on a core audience of educational researchers, practitioners, and school personnel and has an **impact factor** of 2.0, signifying that researchers in the field are reading this journal and citing the papers published in it. She determines that this article is the one she wants to use as a guide for setting up and implementing a DBRC with Hines.

Read and Understand a Variety of Research Articles to Gather Information

In the following section, the full article by Riden, Taylor, Ruiz, et al. (2021), "Using a Daily Report Card to Reduce Off-Task Behaviors for a Student With Autism Spectrum Disorder," is provided. Also included in this section are guiding questions that will support you as you read, glean, and interpret the content in a single-case research design article.

Using a Daily Report Card to Reduce Off-Task Behaviors for a Student with Autism Spectrum Disorder

Benjamin S. Riden[1] · Jontè C. Taylor[2] · Sal Ruiz[3] · David L. Lee[2] · Mary Catherine Scheeler[2]

Abstract

Daily behavior report cards (DBRCs) have shown promise in reducing problematic classroom behaviors. The effectiveness of DBRCs has been used widely examined with respect to students with attention deficit hyperactivity disorder, specific learning disabilities, and other high incidence disabilities. Past research has primarily focused on students in primary grades, with a limited number of studies examining students in secondary grades, in particular students in high school. Even fewer studies have examined the effectiveness of DBRCs implemented by novice special educators. The purpose of the current study was twofold: (1) to examine the effectiveness of a DBRC in reducing off-task classroom behavior for a high school student with autism spectrum disorder (ASD) and (2) to evaluate the delivery of an intensive intervention by a novice special education teacher. A preservice special education teacher implemented the intervention. A changing criterion design was used to examine the effectiveness of the intervention. We analyzed the data using visual analysis and calculated effect sizes using Tau-U. The results suggested that DBRCs are an acceptable and effective treatment for reducing off-task behavior with a student with ASD when implemented by a novice special education teacher. Data were collected to measure the novice teacher's implementation fidelity. Additionally, the results showed that a novice special education teacher can be trained to implement a behavior management program for a student presenting inappropriate classroom behaviors with high fidelity

Keywords Daily behavior reports cards · Preservice teacher · Autism Spectrum Disorder · Off-task · Behavior

---

Corresponding author:
Benjamin S. Riden
ridenbs@jmu.edu

1. Educational Foundation and Exceptionalities Department, James Madison University, Memorial Hall, 395 S. High, Harrisonburg, VA 22807, USA

2. Department of Educational Psychology, Counseling, and Special Education, Pennsylvania State University, University Park, PA, USA
3. College of Education, University of West Florida, Pensacola, FL, USA

Introduction

Problematic and disruptive academic and social classroom behaviors can have a dire impact on students with disabilities and their teachers, especially novice teachers (Gunter et al. 1994). These impacts can include removal from inclusive settings (Butler & Monda-Amaya 2016), interfering with the learning process (Sutherland et al. 2002, 2003) and loss of teaching efficacy (Klassen and Chiu 2010; Perrachione et al. 2008). Along with students with emotional behavioral disorders (EBD), learning disabilities (LD), and attention deficit hyperactivity disorder (ADHD), students with autism spectrum disorder (ASD) can present unique challenges in the classroom. Specifically, students with ASD can present problem behaviors (e.g., repetitive behaviors, intellectual disabilities, and symptoms of attention deficit hyperactivity disorder; Mayes et al. 2012; White et al. 2011). These behaviors can become barriers to effective educational and social development (Horner et al. 1992, 2002). For students who engage in chronic problem behaviors, the outcomes can be negative (Butler & Monda-Amaya 2016). Problem behaviors often threaten continued placement in general education settings, interfere with academic and social skill acquisition, generalize to other classrooms or settings, create toxic teacher–student relationships, and may follow students into adulthood (Butler & Monda-Amaya 2016; Neitzel 2010; Sutherland & Morgan 2003; Walker et al. 2004; Wehby et al. 1998).

Improving outcomes for students with problem behaviors is essential. Traditional approaches to behavior management include an assortment of approaches ranging from student-centered approaches (e.g., differential reinforcement, time-out), classroom and teacher-centered tactics (e.g., rules and routine, clear expectations), teacher-student relationship focused (e.g., developing positive discourse with students), and school-wide initiatives (e.g., school-wide positive behavior interventions and supports; Horner & Sugai 2000; Korpershoek et al. 2016; Sugai & Horner 2002). One intervention that has been shown to be particularly effective is the daily behavior report card (DBRCs; Lebel et al. 2013; Owens et al. 2012; Taylor & Hill 2017). DBRCs have been used to reduce problem behaviorin the classroom and are effective, efficient, and economical for special education teachers to implement.

Results of research on DBRCs suggest positive impacts on academic and social behaviors for students with disabilities (Atkeson & Forehand

1979; Barth 1979; Burke & Vannest 2008; Chafouleas et al. 2002; Riden et al. 2018; Smith et al. 1983; Vannest et al. 2010). Vannest et al. (2010) conducted a meta-analysis of single-case research analyzing 17 single-case research design studies, from 1970 to 2007, involving 107 participants. They reported a broad range in effect sizes for interventions (range = − 0.14 to 0.97) using improved rate difference (IRD) as the meta-analytic measure.

Updating the work of Vannest et al. (2010) and Riden et al. (2018) conducted an examination and analysis of single-case and group design DBRC research from 2007 to 2017. Their review included 390 participants identified as at-risk, eligible for 504 services, or as having a disability (e.g., ADHD, specific LD, EBD). Single-case DBRC research had an aggregated Tau-U effect size of 0.66 that canbe interpreted as a medium effect (range = 0.51–0.81). Further they reported a broad effect size range for group research designs (range = 0.03–0.72) which is interpreted as low to medium effect.

Ultimately, past research has suggested that DBRCs can be viable tools for teachers to use for classroom/behavior management. Yet, with the range of effects of this intervention in the past, additional research is needed to determine their effectiveness when working with students in academic settings. DBRCs have been consistently shown to have a low-to-high range of effectiveness for increasing desired academic and social behaviors of students considered to have disruptive behaviors including those with disabilities (Atkeson & Forehand 1979; Barth 1979; Burke & Vannest 2008; Chafouleas et al. 2002; Smith et al. 1983; Vannest et al. 2010). Further, the research base on using DBRCs in high school is minimal.

Daily behavior report cards are individualized rating forms used to appraise target behaviors of students on a daily basis, provide feedback to the students on hisor her performance, increase home-school communication, and deliver reinforcement contingent on student behavior (Atkenson & Forehand 1979; Barth 1979; Riden et al. 2018; Vannest et al. 2010). The flexibility, adaptability, and economical nature of DBRCs make them an efficient way to provide direct feedback about students' academic and social behaviors (Chafouleas et al. 2002). Throughout the research on DBRCs, five components have been shown to be necessary when creating the DBRC: (a) operationally defining the target behavior or constellation of behaviors; (b) rating of behaviors using simple numbers or symbols on a behavior scale; (c) daily monitoring of behaviors; (d) providing feedback to students on their behavior(s); and (e) communicating performance of DBRCs between the student's teacher and home (Chafouleas et al. 2002, 2007; Long & Edwards 1994; Riley-Tillman et al. 2007).

The inclusion of feedback and regular check-ins with the student about their behavior have the potential to create predictable schedules of reinforcement for some students. By utilizing instruments such as the function assessment screening tool (FAST), teachers are able to identify potential functions of target behavior that may be an effective means for deciding which students DBRCs are most likely to be effective. In our study, the results of the FAST suggest attention is maintaining the target behavior. In this instance using a DBRC was appropriate as the intervention is designed to provide students with attention via feedback on exhibited behaviors.

DBRCs are highly flexible in nature pertaining to settings and behaviors. We conducted our study in a high school setting where there is a need for highly flexible interventions that can travel from setting to setting with students. In comparison to elementary school where students receive the majority of their instruction in one setting, high school students receive instruction in various settings from several teachers throughout the day. A DBRC can be completed, and behaviors reinforced, by different teachers in different settings which can also promote the generalization of the target behavior. The factors mentioned above suggest DBRCs can be used efficiently by different teachers with multiple students in varying settings.

For example, Schumaker et al. (1977) implemented a daily report card system for use with problem behavior displayed by students in a secondary setting. In their study, the authors recruited three male students, each displaying disruptive behavior, truancy, tardiness, and limited completion of academic tasks, to participate in the DBRC intervention. The authors developed the DBRC which included sections for rules, classwork, grades, and teacher satisfaction with corresponding boxes the teacher could check to indicate whether the student had met a particular expectation. Reinforcement was provided to the participants at home by their parents/caregivers that included praise and additional privileges (e.g., snacks, TV time, bowling) contingent on their performance at school. Specifically, parents were taught about basic rules of exchange regarding points for privileges. If a student received all "yes" checks in a particular class for following classroom rules, the student earned two points. If the student broke only one rule in that class the student earned one point. Any more than that zero points were awarded.

A similar scale was used for classwork, grades, and teacher satisfaction. Parent-interventionist communication occurred via home visit once a week with the goal of collecting previous week's DBRC and troubleshooting any problems that may have occurred. Results suggest behavior trending in a therapeutic direction across all participants for all target behaviors.

The purpose of the current study was to extend the literature base and examine the effects of a DBRC treatment package on off-task classroom behavior exhibited by a high school student with ASD implemented by a preservice special education teacher. Previous reviews (i.e., Vannest et al. 2010; Riden et al. 2018) found that only five of 26 studies were conducted in secondary school settings leaving a gap in the literature. As such this study focuses on a student in high school implemented by a preservice special education teacher. Specifically, the purpose of the current study was to evaluate whether a DBRC would be a viable behavior management tool for a preservice special education teacher working with a student with ASD and a history of problem behavior. Additional purposes included the evaluation of (a) the effects of a DBRC on off-task behaviors of a student with ASD; (b) the extent to which a preservice teacher would implement a DBRC with fidelity in the classroom setting; and (c) the acceptability of the DBRC intervention by stakeholders.

METHODS

Participants and Setting

One female preservice special education teacher acted as the interventionist and one female high school student with ASD was the participant. Inclusion criteria for the interventionist consisted of (a) entering the culminating special education student teaching practicum, (a) working with students with disabilities, and (c) being placed in a K-12 academic setting. The interventionist was selected from a large public university in the northeast from an eligible pool of 15 that also met the inclusion criteria. The interventionist was a 21-year-old, white female entering her student teaching placement.

The inclusion criteria for the participant consisted of (a) attending a public K-12 school, (b) receiving services as an eligible student with a disability, and (c)engaging in high rates of behavior that result in being off-task during instructional classroom time. The participant was a 15-year-old white female in 9th grade diagnosed with ASD with a history of problem behavior and chronic absenteeism resulting in several ineffective interventions. The participant spent the majority of her time in special education settings throughout the day where she received services for mathematics, English language arts, and writing. She regularly attended history, science, and specials (e.g., physical education) in an inclusive setting always with the support of a paraprofessional. The participant had age appropriate expressive and receptive language skills.

The study was conducted in a public high school serving students in 8th–12th grade (total high school population = 2301) in the central Pennsylvania. Further, the intervention was implemented in both an autism support classroom during the System 44™ period (a reading and writing program) and an inclusive science classroom. During System 44™, the classroom consisted of 10 students including the participant. Instruction during this time was delivered with the student participant sitting at a table with three peers facing the teacher. During this time, the interventionist implemented the intervention as the classroom teacher led the class. The science class consisted of 12 students facing the science teacher. The participant sat at a table with her paraprofessional in the back of the classroom. The interventionist implemented the intervention as the science teacher instructed the class. The interventionist sat at a table behind the participant during instruction and approached her only after the 10-min interval expired to provide feedback and review goals in both settings.

Independent Variable

The DBRC form was adapted from Vannest et al. (2011). A DBRC package consisting of operational definitions of target behaviors, a simple number rating system, daily monitoring of behaviors, feedback provided to student on her behaviors, and communication of performance between the student's teacher and home was developed. The DBRC included the following: (a) a brief welcome note to the mother of the participant; (b) two questions in which the interventionist had to circle *yes* or *no* [i.e., (a) today we did a "check-in" with yesterday's card and (b) today we did a "check-out" with today's card]; (c) space for the participant's name, the date, and who the DBRC should be returned to (i.e., the interventionist); (d) the behavior rating scales, which described how many points could be earned contingent on student performance;

(e) a section for the target behavior to be reduced; (f) a section for the class period to be named and three subsequent boxes that labeled the target behaviors; (g) space for the interventionist to provide the rating for each behavior; (h) a space for the interventionist's signature and a space describing how many points were earned during that class; (i) a section for how many points had to have been earned to earn the reward (i.e., reinforcer); (j) two boxes at the bottom of the DBRC for teacher comments; the other for parent comments; (k) a space for the parent to sign the form prior to sending the DBRC back to school with the student the next day.

Dependent Variables

The first author and interventionist operationally defined each target behavior prior to data collection. Target behaviors included *talking out*, *looking at others*, and *picking fingers*. *Talking out* was defined as any instance the participant made an unauthorized or unsolicited verbal statement during whole group instruction, independent work, or silent reading. Verbal statements included academic or non-academic utterances (e.g., answering without raising hand) but did not include non-contextual vocalizations (i.e., stereotypy) or group work interactions. Verbal statements do not include talking to her paraprofessional (e.g., asking her paraprofessional a question, asking a paraprofessional for help). *Looking at others* was defined as any instance the participant looked at another student's work during independent work time, looking at others in the classroom during whole class instruction, or during silent reading. *Picking fingers* was defined as any instance in which the participant picked her fingernails with her hand or mouth during whole group instruction, independent work, or during silent reading which led to her being further off-task.

Experimental Design

The effects of the DBRC were evaluated using a changing criterion design (CCD) across three behaviors. Changing criterion designs require initial baseline data on a single target behavior followed by implementation of a treatment in a series of phases in a stepwise change in criterion rate for the target behavior each prior phase acting as baseline (Hartmann & Hall 1976).

Pre-experimental Procedures

Training

The author provided three 1-h trainings to the interventionist. After the training, the first author and interventionist met with the mother of the participant to define her responsibilities during intervention (e.g., daily review of the DBRC, contingent reinforcement, signing and returning DBRC). The final training was conducted by the interventionist and was delivered to the participant as the first author monitored the meeting. PowerPoint presentations were developed to aid the interventionist in training the parent and student so no pertinent information was left uncovered during the trainings.

Interventionist Training

Three days of training were provided prior to pre-baseline data collection. On the first day of training, the rationale for the DBRC intervention was presented along with the essential components of the intervention, implementation procedures, operational definitions, and a question-and-answer period. Day two consisted of a review of day one materials, instruction on conducting the functional assessment screening), the multiple stimulus without replacement preference assessment (Deleon & Iwata 1996), practice on data collection procedures, as well as baseline and intervention procedures. During training, the interventionist was required to meet a mastery criterion of 100% on data collection procedures. The interventionist recorded the first author engaging in *talking out, looking at others*, and *picking fingers* to gain reliability of behavior data collection procedures. A third day of training was conducted prior to intervention phase entailing a review of behavior definitions, intervention training, parent training materials introduced, and weekly intervention meetings scheduled.

Parent Training

The first author and interventionist met with the mother in the autism support classroom. A PowerPoint presentation was conducted to explain the benefits of DBRCs, a review of the target behaviors, introduction of the DBRC, and her role in the intervention. During the parent training reinforcers at home were discussed and extra phone time and watching a television show with the mother was agreed upon. Time was allotted at the end of the presentation to answer any questions the mother had about the intervention.

Student Training

Following the baseline phase, a participant training session was conducted. The interventionist delivered a PowerPoint presentation to the participant. The presentation included why we were providing this support, how the support would be delivered, what the DBRC would look like, and instruction on replacement behavior. Replacement behaviors included: (a) raising her hand to speak as opposed to talking out, (b) focusing on her own work and area rather than looking at others work or other distractions in the classroom, and (c) lacing her fingers and placing them on the desk or on her lap instead of picking at her cuticles. While replacement behaviors are not required for a DBRC intervention, best practice suggests identifying functionally equivalent replacement behaviors that achieve the same outcome as a less desirable problem behavior. When the replacement behaviors were introduced and modeled for the participant by the interventionist, the interventionist prompted the participant to practice the replacement behaviors until the behaviors were demonstrated correctly. During participant and parent training sessions positive language was emphasized at all times by the researcher and interventionist (e.g., "we are doing this to help you have better days at school," "we are not doing this because you are in trouble. We are doing this to help you become a successful young woman").

Pre-baseline Observation and Interviews

Two weeks prior to baseline, we determined the appropriateness of a behavior change program. Next, behavior pinpoints were defined according to Hawkins & Dobes (1977) that stated behavior definitions have to be objective, clear, and describe what the behavior is and what the behavior is not. Interviews were conducted with the interventionist, the full-time classroom special education teachers familiar with the participant, and the mother of the participant. Interview questions were adapted from the functional assessment interview (O'Neil et al. 1997). Three 1-h direct observation sessions were conducted on noncontiguous days based on answers to interview questions. Continuous measurement was used to collect antecedent-behavior-consequence data so all instances of the behaviors of interest were detected during the observation sessions (Johnston & Pennypacker 2009). The first author conducted the pinpointing and choosing of target behaviors.

Functional Assessment Screening Tool (FAST)

The FAST was designed to prompt informant verbal reports about conditions under which problem behavior might occur and to organize those reports according to common contingencies that maintain problem behavior: positive and negative reinforcement (Iwata et al. 2013). The interventionist facilitated the completion of a FAST with two classroom teachers familiar with the participant. A FAST was also provided to the mother but was never returned. The results suggested that the behaviors were maintained by attention.

Multiple Stimulus Without Replacement (MSWO)

The interventionist conducted three MSWO assessments across three days to identify possible reinforcers to be included in the evaluation. Three possible reinforcers were identified during the administration of the MSWO. During each session, the top three items selected out of five possible choices were snack, phone time, and nail time; but never with the same ranking. Thus, we allowed the participant to choose the reinforcer prior to the beginning of each intervention session (i.e., snack, phone time) with a secondary reinforcer (i.e., nail time) provided at the end of the week contingent on meeting the goal three out of five days.

Experimental Procedures

Data Collection

Data collection occurred during baseline and intervention phases. Baseline data collection occurred during one and a half hour classroom periods. The classroom periods were divided into six 10-min intervals for five days during baseline. A frequency count of target behaviors was collected during each of the six 10-min intervals. We decided to divide the period into intervals so we could check in with the student during intervention phases after each interval. The rationale for this is that reinforcement must be delivered as close to the behaviors as possible to maximize the effect on the target behaviors. We decided that waiting until the end of the class would be too long for the student to contact reinforcement. The reason for using one hour of the period opposed to the full one and a half hour class was to account for check-ins before instruction behavior, after each interval, at the end of all intervals, and time to deliver reinforcement at the end of the period contingent on the student's performance. During baseline, the interventionist and classroom teachers did not change the way they delivered instruction or managed their classroom.

Intervention data were collected in the same manner as baseline, every 10-min for 6 intervals during one class period. At the beginning of each observation the interventionist had data collection sheets and the DBRC ready, collected the previous day's DBRC (except on first day of implementation), reminded the participant to return the DBRC each day if the participant forgot to do so, reviewed behaviors necessary to earn points, reviewed behavior goals with the participant, remindedher about reinforcers that could be earned contingent on performance, and worded expectations positively. Throughout the DBRC period, the interventionist collected frequency during each interval, reviewed performance on targeted behaviors at the end of each interval with the participant, assigned point totals for behavior demonstrated, reviewed points not earned in a neutral tone and described how she could earn points during the next interval, and praised her for goals met during each interval. During end-of-interval-review sessions, the interventionist discussed how often the participant engaged in the target behaviors as well as praised the participant for engaging in the replacement behavior. Following this review the next 10 min interval began. During the observation intervals the interventionist did not address the participant's behaviors. The teachers were instructed to conduct their class as they always have. At the end of the observation the interventionist reviewed overall performance toward DBRC goals with the participant. Next, the participant was granted access to reinforcers contingent on her performance that day. The interventionist maintained neutral affect if goals were not met and reviewed behaviors that should be demonstrated next time to earn points and reminded the participant that tomorrow was a new day and the point sheet starts over. Last, the interventionist provided feedback for parents on the DBRC, signed the form, and sent it home with the participant for parent review and delivery of reinforcement contingent on her performance.

Intervention Phase Changes

Initial criterion for the first intervention phases across all three behaviors was set at 10% below the mean obtained during baseline. For *talking out* the initial criterion during intervention phase one was set at 64. For *looking at others* behavior,the initial criterion in intervention phase one was set at 40. The criterion for *picking fingers* was set at 10 during intervention phase one. Phase one continued until the participant met criterion three out of five days for each behavior. Criterion for *talking out* and *looking at others* during intervention phase two was set at 10% below the mean obtained during intervention phase one, 14 and 18, respectively. Due to the reduction in *finger picking* behavior during intervention phase one, the criterion during intervention phase two was set at six (i.e., one per interval). Phase 2 continued until the participant met criterion three out of five days for each behavior. Criterion for *talking out* and *looking at others* during intervention phase three was set at six during intervention phase three due to the significant drops in level. *Picking fingers* was moved to maintenance phase for the remainder of the study. Following intervention phase three *talking out* and *looking at others* behaviors were moved to maintenance. In total there were five phases including baseline and maintenance for the talk out and looks at others behavior and four phases including baseline and maintenance for the picking fingers behavior. Criterion selection was response guided. No procedural changes occurred during the course of the intervention after the start of the study.

Maintenance

Maintenance data were collected on all three behaviors. Data were collected on two behaviors (i.e., talking out, looking at others) for two days after intervention was removed. Data were collected for seven days for the picking finger behavior after intervention was withdrawn. These data were collected to see if the participant engaged in the desired behavior after intervention was removed.

Data Analyses

The current study used visual analysis as the primary method to determine experimental control (i.e., functional relations between the DBRC and positive changes in the dependent variables). Specifically, level, trend, and variability in the data were examined visually to evaluate experimental control (Cooper et al. 2020). Additionally, we calculated means for each condition for all three target behaviors to determined level changes, split middle to determine trend (Lane & Gast 2014). A positive trend equates to a decrease in target behaviors. A negative trend equates to an increase in target behaviors. We set a predetermined criteria of 75% of data must be within 25% of the mean to be considered stable.

A Tau-U statistical analysis was also used to examine the effectiveness of DBRCs on three target behaviors within phases and between phases. Tau-U combines nonoverlap between phases with trend from within the intervention phase and controls undesirable Phase A trends (Parker et al. 2011a, b). Tau-U was calculated for baseline data and phase one data (to detect immediate effect) and baseline data and total intervention (overall effectiveness) data for all target behavior separately using the Single-Case Research Tau-U Calculator. A strength of this web application is the ability to analyze data for several phase contrasts from a single design independently. The software then permits for the calculation of a properly averaged omnibus effect size (Vannest et al. 2016). Tau-U is calculated using the formula: Tau-U = S/number of pairs (Parker et al. 2011a, b) where S represents The Kendall Score (Brossart et al. 2018). Tau-U can be interpreted for significance as small effect (< 0.65), medium to high effect (0.66–0.92), or strong effect (0.93–1.0) (Parker & Vannest 2012).

Reliability, Fidelity, and Validity

Interobserver Agreement (IOA)

The first author conducted mean count per interval IOA during 40% of baseline phases. We followed the guidelines presented by Cooper et al. (2020) for calculating mean count per interval. We divided the entire observation period into six 10 min intervals. During each interval, two observers recorded the number of occurrences of the target behavior within each interval. We then calculated the agreement between each observers' counts within each interval. Next, we used the agreements per interval as out basis for calculating IOA. The formula for calculating mean count per interval is as follows:

$$\frac{\text{Int1IOA} + \text{Int2IOA} + \text{Int3IOA} + \text{Int4IOA} + \text{Int5IOA} + \text{Int6IOA}}{n \text{intervals}} = \text{mean count per interval IOA\%}$$

Mean count per interval IOA data for baseline was 90.8% across all behaviors (range = 83–96%). Mean count per interval IOA for intervention and maintenance across all three behaviors was 98.3% (range = 95–100%).

DBRC Implementation Fidelity

The first author conducted treatment integrity checks on 30% of intervention and maintenance phases. A 16-item integrity checklist was used to assess the extent to which the interventionist correctly implemented the DBRC. The checklist was separated into three sections: (1) upon arrival, (2) throughout the DBRC period, and (3) end of DBRC review period. Additionally, a second observer who was blind to the study used the DBRC treatment integrity checklist to calculate treatment integrity during 40% of the treatment integrity observations. IOA for implementation fidelity was 100%.

DBRC Social Validity

Adapted versions of The Usage Rating Profile-Intervention (Chafouleas et al. 2009; Schwartz & Baer 1991) were used to develop the social validity surveys. The interventionist, participant, and mother completed social validity surveys to assess the acceptability of the DBRC intervention. Each social validity survey used a Likert-type scale of one through six (i.e., 1 = strongly agree, 2 = agree, 3 = somewhat agree, 4 = somewhat disagree, 5 = disagree, and 6 = strongly disagree). The total possible score for the interventionist ranged from 10 (highest social validity) to 60 (lowest social validity). The total possible score for the participant ranged from seven (highest social validity) to 42 (lowest social validity). The total possible score for the parent ranged from eight (highest social validity) to 48 (lowest social validity).

RESULTS

Does a DBRC Reduce Off-Task Behaviors of a Student with ASD?

Visual Analysis

The results of the evaluation are depicted in Fig. 1. Visual analysis was used to evaluate the results. Specifically, trend, level, and variability in the data were examined to determine the effectiveness of DBRCs.

We conducted trend analysis by using the split-middle approach. The results pertaining to *talking out* showed a positive trend during baseline, zero trend during Phase 1, zero trend during Phase 2, zero during

Phase 3, and a zero-trend during maintenance. The results pertaining to *looking at others* showed a negative trend during baseline, a negative trend during Phase 1, a negative trend during Phase 2, a positive trend during Phase 3, and a positive trend during maintenance. Visual analysis of *picking fingers* data resulted in a zero trend during baseline, and a positive trend in Phase 1, a positive trend in Phase 2, and a zero trend in maintenance. Overall, we see a positive trend in the data across all conditions for all three target behaviors.

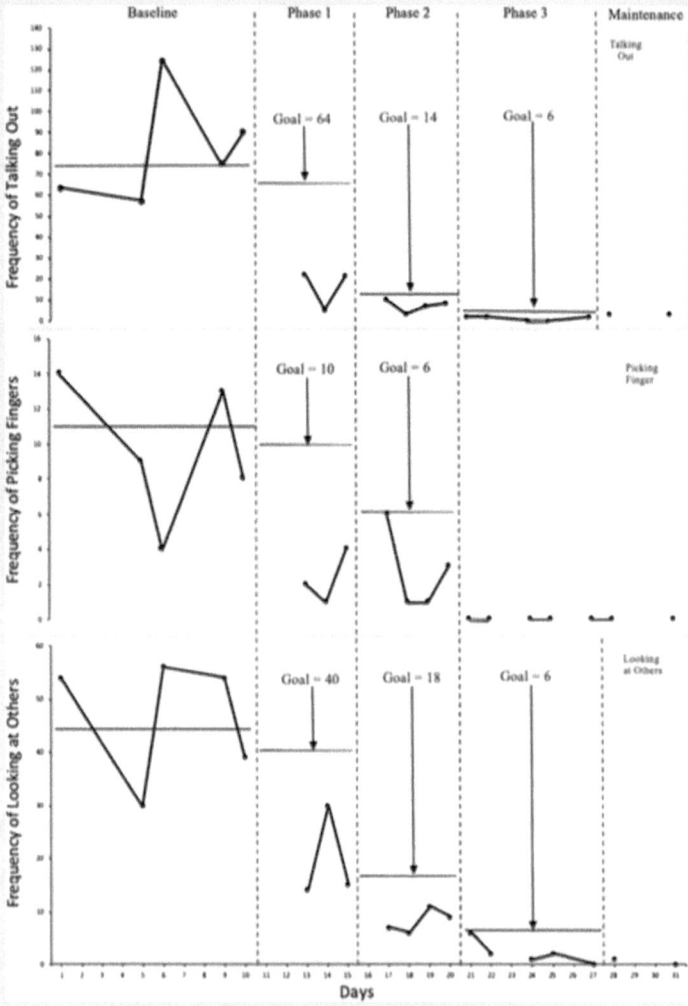

Figure 1. Frequency count of student's target behaviors

Frequency of *talking out* is depicted in the top panel of Fig. 1. During baseline, *talking out* occurred at a high level ($M = 71.25$). We observed an immediate drop in level of frequency of *talking out* during intervention Phase 1. We set a goal of 64 occurrences of *talking out* in Phase 1 and observed an immediate drop to low levels ($M = 16$). Subsequently, we set a goal of 14 occurrences of *talking out* in Phase 2 and continued to observe drops in level ($M = 7$). Next, we set a goal of six occurrences for Phase 3 and observed a continued drop in level ($M = 1.2$). During maintenance we observed a further drop in level ($M = 3$). Overall, with *talking out,* we observed a level change from baseline ($M = 71.25$) across all intervention conditions ($M = 6.83$). Frequency of *looking at others* is depicted on the middle panel of Fig. 1. During baseline, *looking at others* occurred at a high level ($M = 44.25$). We observed an immediate drop in level of *looking at others* during intervention Phase 1. We set a goal of 40 occurrences of *looking at others* in Phase 1 and observed an immediate drop to low levels ($M = 22$). We set a goal of 10 occurrences of *looking at others* in Phase 2 and continued to see drops in level ($M = 8.25$). Next, we set a goal of six occurrences for Phase 3 and saw a continued drop in level ($M = 2.25$). During maintenance, we observed a further drop in level ($M = 0.5$). Overall, with *looking at others* we observed a level change from baseline ($M = 44.25$) across all intervention conditions ($M = 8.6$).

Frequency of *picking fingers* is depicted on the bottom panel of Fig. 1. During baseline, *picking fingers* occurred at a high level ($M = 11$). We observed an immediate drop in level during intervention Phase 1 for *picking fingers*. We set a goal of 10 occurrences of *picking fingers* in Phase 1 and observed an immediate drop to low levels of behavior ($M = 2.23$). We set a goal of six occurrences of *picking fingers* in Phase 2 and observed no level change ($M = 2.75$). Next, we set a goal of six for Phase 3 and observed a continued drop in level ($M = 2.25$). During maintenance we observed zero occurrences of *picking fingers* during the duration of the maintenance phase (i.e., seven sessions). Overall, for *picking fingers*, a level change from baseline ($M = 11$) across all intervention conditions ($M = 2.6$) occurred.

We observed variability during baseline with *looking at others* and *picking fingers*. Across all intervention conditions for all three target behaviors, we observed minimal variability in the data. Stability was demonstrated across all target behaviors according to our criteria. Baseline *talking out* data resulted in 75% of the data points falling within the predetermined criterion for variability. Baseline *looking at others* data resulted in 75% of the data points falling within the stability envelope. Baseline *picking finger* behavior resulted in 75% of the data points falling within the stability envelope. We used the same criterion to determine stability for intervention conditions. Stability for *talking out* behavior data were not stable in phase one, two, or three. However, we observed stability in maintenance data. Frequency of *Looking at others* was not stable in phase one, had stability in Phase 2, and was not stable in Phase 3 or maintenance. Frequency of *picking fingers* was not stable in Phase 1 or Phase 2. We did observe stability in the data during maintenance.

Effect Size Analysis

Tau-U was calculated for all three target behaviors. Tau-U was calculated for baseline to intervention Phase 1 (immediacy of intervention effect). A large effect was demonstrated with *talking out* [ES = 1.00, $p < 0.001$, confidence interval (90%) = 0.26–1.00]. Tau-U analysis for baseline and across all intervention phases (total intervention effect) for *talking out* resulted in a large effect [ES = 1.00, $p < 0.001$, confidence interval (90%) = 0.49–1.00]. Tau-U for baseline to intervention Phase 1 for *looking at others* data demonstrated a large effect [ES = 0.93, $p < 0.001$, confidence interval (90%) = 0.20–1.00]. Tau-U for baseline and total intervention data for *looking at others* demonstrated a large effect [ES = 0.98, $p < 0.001$, confidence interval (90%) = 0.46–1.00]. Tau-U for baseline to intervention Phase 1 for *picking finger* behavior demonstrated a large effect [ES = 0.93, $p < 0.001$, confidence interval (90%) = 0.20–1.00]. Tau-U for baseline and total intervention data on *picking finger* demonstrated a large effect [ES = 0.91, $p < 0.001$, confidence interval (90%) = 0.34–1.00]. Overall, a strong effect size across all three target behavior was demonstrated [ES = 0.97, $p < 0.001$, confidence interval (90%) = 0.66–1.00].

With What Level of Fidelity Does a Preservice Teacher Implement a DBRC?

The interventionist implemented the intervention with 100% fidelity during each fidelity probe conducted by the first author. Additionally, she implemented intervention with 100% fidelity during each fidelity probe conducted by the doctoral candidate who was blind to the study. The interventionist implemented the treatment package for all sessions at 100% fidelity.

How Acceptable was the DBRC Intervention?

The interventionist, the mother of the participant, and the participant completed social validity surveys with a Likert scale rated 1 through 6 at the conclusion of the study to assess the usefulness of the DBRC intervention as well as their attitudes towards its effectiveness and ease of implementation. On the 10-question survey, the interventionist scored all of the questions as Strongly Agree or Agree ($M = 1.3$) providing evidence of the social validity of the intervention from an interventionist's perspective. The participant also completed a seven-question survey and responded with Agree (M = 2) for all questions indicating that the DBRC intervention was considered socially valid for her. Finally, the mother was given a social validity survey consisting of eight questions ($M = 1.75$). Her responses had more variability with ratings ranging from Strongly Agree (i.e., 1) to Somewhat Agree (i.e., 3). Anecdotal conversations with the mother during the post intervention meetings indicated that the participant had been doing much better at home and the family was experiencing a significant reduction in problem behaviors.

Overall, the results indicated improvement across all three behaviors. Visual analyses indicated a strong functional relation between intervention and dependent variables. Aggregated Tau-U results suggest a strong effect [ES = 0.97, $p < 0.001$, confidence interval (90%) = 0.66–1.00]. Data from the DBRC treatment integrity checklist suggested the interventionist implemented intervention with 100% fidelity. Results indicated that a preservice teacher can implement a DBRC intervention with 100% treatment integrity. Social validity data indicated that the DBRC intervention is acceptable to the interventionist, participant, and parent of the participant.

DISCUSSION

Findings suggest that a DBRC implemented by one novice interventionist can reduce problem behavior of one individual with ASD. Specifically, we observed a significant and immediate change in level across target behaviors. Additionally, the target behaviors became stable at low levels throughout the duration of intervention and remained at low levels through maintenance.

Daily behavior report cards have been investigated and deemed effective in numerous studies for students in primary grades. However, there is a lack of studies looking at DBRCs and students in secondary settings. Further, the extant literature focuses on researchers or teachers acting as the intervention agents. The results of this study begin to address gaps in behavior research, specifically DBRC research, in secondary settings that focus on affecting change in a student with ASD when implemented by a preservice special education teacher. Equally important to conducting behavior intervention experimental research in high school is working with preservice teachers to implement complex behavior interventions in the natural setting. As noted in the introduction, educators struggle managing problem behavior and implementing complex interventions. Certainly, we have not solved this problem, however, a gap in the literature exists pertaining to working with preservice special education teachers as intervention agents. This study attempts to move the needle in preservice special education preparation to a position that preservice special education teachers are capable of implementing intensive interventions with the hope that this generalize to the classroom when they enter the field.

The participant met the criterion for earning reinforcers each day for the primary reinforcers and met her weekly goal (i.e., meeting criterion 3 out of 5 days) to earn the secondary reinforcer (i.e., nail time with teacher). The reinforcers identified during the MSWO matched the function of the behavior identified by the FAST. Although the FAST is not considered a substitute for a functional analysis of problem behavior, its use provided valuable information prior to conducting direct observation of the participant's behavior in the classroom. Additionally, the current results are encouraging with regard to the ease of implementation of DBRCs constructed of research-based components (i.e., feedback, reinforcement contingencies, home–school communication) by a novice interventionist. The interventionist implemented the intervention with 100% fidelity. Additionally, all three individual stakeholders (i.e., interventionist, participant, parent) provided support for the social validity of DBRCs. The results of the social validity assessment are highly meaningful as using a DBRC should include the teacher/interventionist, participant, and the parents/guardians at home to maximize its effectiveness (Riden et al. 2018).

The current results should be considered in light of several limitations. First, the significant and immediate change in level of all three behaviors made seeing the stepwise change in behavior we expect to see in a changing criterion design less clear. It is important to note that between phases two and three there was some variability in the data that brings into the question the extent to which experimental control may have been established. Specifically, Between Phases 2 and 3, the data continued on a downward trend for *looking at others* and we observed a small change in level with some overlap between phases two and three for talking out. Issues surrounding experimental control for *looking at others* may have been due to the replacement behavior becoming learned as the intervention had been in place for some time. The small change in level with some overlap with *talking* out was likely due to the small window remaining for behavior change (i.e., the goal change was small). Next, during the intervention phases in using a CCD it is recommended that at least one change in criterion phase should revert to a previous goal level and/or baseline phase to further demonstrate a functional relationship between the intervention and the target behaviors (Cooper et al. 2020). Due to significant time restraints, the current study did not adhere to that recommendation. Ultimately, although variability in the data limits somewhat inferences regarding experimental control, the data strongly suggest the DBRC, implemented by a novice interventionist, was responsible for the dramatic reduction in off-task behaviors.

Third, a functional analysis of the problem behavior did not occur; instead the FAST was used which has been shown to have limited reliability and validity (Iwata et al. 2013). Fourth, due to variability in high school schedules (e.g., work release, transition services) we were only able to implement the DBRC during one period each day that occurred in two different settings; thus, generalization was not assessed. Fifth, the operational definition of the *looking at others* was not as clearly defined as we initially thought. During initial interviews, this behavior was brought to our attention as a form of bullying. The participant would look at what others were doing in the classroom or what others in the classroom were working on and would then begin to tell them how they were wrong and would tell them why the way she would do the task was correct, even if it was incorrect; and did so in a condescending tone. In our behavior definition and subsequent data collection we would count a *looking at others* occurrence even if she looked at someone entering the room, per our definition. A more appropriate operational definition would have included a clear explanation of what was occurring during the occurrences of *looking at others* rather than the act of looking. Lastly, we did not collect fidelity of parent provided reinforcement. Future research should examine fidelity of reinforcement delivery to determine its impact on student outcomes.

The current findings support previous research on the use of DBRCs to reduce problem behavior (e.g., Atkeson & Forehand 1979; Chafouleas et al. 2002; Smith et al. 1983; Vannest et al. 2010). The DBRC has been shown to be a viable behavior change agent that can be used by expert and novice teachers alike. However, the most current research has shown variability in effectiveness of the DBRC interventions (Riden et al. 2018; Vannest et al. 2010). This may be due to inconsistent implementation by teachers in the field as there is a lack of guidance pertaining to explicit steps that teachers need to perform. Future research should include focus on specific and immediate feedback, preferred items as reinforcers, clearly defined behavioral definitions, and treatment integrity.

The results of the current study and previous research suggest that in implementing DBRCs, practitioners should focus on seven elements. First, practitioners should conduct initial observation to determine if there is a problem and what those behaviors might be. Second, the function of the behavior should be identified prior to intervention. Third, a preference assessment should be conducted to identify preferred items that may be used as reinforcement. Fourth, behaviors used to create scales on a DBRC should be operationally defined. Fifth, home-school communication is a critical component of DBRC and must be included in the implementation if DBRC interventions. Sixth, immediate performance feedback should be provided to students on the progress towards behavior goals on a DBRC. Lastly, those wishing to use DBRCs as a behavior intervention should implement daily behavior reports cards with fidelity in order for the intervention to be successful. Failure to ensure treatments are implemented as planned poses threats to internal and external validity of the experiments (Moncher & Prinz 1991; Gresham et al. 1993).

The research literature is brimming with evaluations of interventions addressing individual educational domains (e.g., social interactions, reading, self-management) for elementary and preschool students with ASD (Carter et al. 2010; El Zein et al. 2014), far less attention has focused on adolescents (Kucharczyk et al. 2015). While early intervention is warranted and critical for the success of individuals with ASD, we must not forget about them as they approach adulthood. Perhaps most disconcerting about the lack of research in this area is the high school years may be the last touch point educators have to effect behavior change before students transition out of high school.

Acknowledgements The contents of this report were developed under a grant from the US Department of Education, # H325D130021. However, those contents do not necessarily represent the policy of the US Department of Education, and you should not assume endorsement by the Federal Government. Project Officer, Patricia Gonzalez.

Compliance and Ethical Standards

Conflict of interest The authors declare that they have no conflict of interest.

Ethical Standards All procedures performed in studies involving human participants were in accordance with the ethical standards of the institutional and/or national research committee and with the 1964 Helsinki declaration and its later amendments or comparable ethical standards.

Informed Consent Informed consent was obtained from all individual participants included in the study.

REFERENCES

Atkeson, B. M., & Forehand, R. (1979). Home-based reinforcement programs designed to modify classroom behavior: A review and methodological evaluation. *Psychological Bulletin, 86,* 1298–1308.

Barth, R. (1979). Home-based reinforcement of school behavior: A review and analysis. *Review of Educational Research, 49,* 436–458.

Briesch, A. M., & Chafouleas, S. M. (n.d.). The daily behavior report card (DBRC) as an evidence-based tool in intervention and assessment with at-risk students. Retrieved May 28, 2019, from https:// www.researchgate.net/ publication/237401499.

Brossart, D. F., Laird, V. C., & Armstrong, T. W. (2018). Interpreting Kendall's Tau and Tau-U for single-case experimental designs. *Cogent Psychology, 5*(1), 1518687.

Burke, M. D., & Vannest, K. J. (2008). Behavioral progress monitoring using the electronic daily behavioral report card (e-DBRC) system. *Preventing School Failure: Alternative Education for Children and Youth, 52,* 51–60.

Butler, A., & Monda-Amaya, L. (2016). Preservice teachers' perceptions of challenging behavior. *Teacher Education and Special Education, 39*, 276–292.

Carter, E. W., Sisco, L. G., Chung, Y. C., & Stanton-Chapman, T. L. (2010). Peer interactions of students with intellectual disabilities and/or autism: A map of the intervention literature. *Research and Practice for Persons with Severe Disabilities, 35*(3–4), 63–79.

Chafouleas, S. M., Briesch, A. M., Riley-Tillman, T. C., & McCoach, D. B. (2009). Moving beyond assessment of treatment acceptability: An examination of the factor structure of the Usage Rating Profile-Intervention (URP-I). *School Psychology Quarterly, 24*(1), 36.

Chafouleas, S. M., Riley-Tillman, T. C., & McDougal, J. L. (2002). Good, bad, or in between: How does the daily behavior report card rate? *Psychology in the Schools, 39*, 157–169.

Chafouleas, S. M., Riley-Tillman, T. C., Sassu, K. A., LaFrance, M. J., & Patwa, S. S. (2007). Daily behavior report cards: An investigation of the consistency of on-task data across raters and methods. *Journal of Positive Behavior Interventions, 9*, 30–37.

Cooper, J. O., Heron, T. E., & Heward, W. L. (2020). *Applied behavior analysis* (3rd ed.). Upper Saddle River: Pearson/Merrill-Prentice Hall.

DeLeon, I. G., & Iwata, B. A. (1996). Evaluation of a multiple-stimulus presentation format for assessing reinforcer preferences. *Journal of Applied Behavior Analysis, 29*, 519–533.

El Zein, F., Solis, M., Vaughn, S., & McCulley, L. (2014). Reading comprehension interventions for students with autism spectrum disorders: A synthesis of research. *Journal of Autism and Developmental Disorders, 44*(6), 1303–1322.

Gresham, F. M., Gansle, K. A., & Noell, G. H. (1993). Treatment integrity in applied behavior analysis with children. *Journal of Applied Behavior Analysis, 26*, 257–263.

Gunter, P. L., Jack, S. L., Depaepe, P., Reed, T. M., & Harrison, J. (1994). Effects of challenging behaviors of students with EBD on teacher instructional behavior. *Preventing School Failure: Alternative Education for Children and Youth, 38*, 35–39.

Hartmann, D. P., & Hall, R. V. (1976). The changing criterion design. *Journal of Applied Behavior Analysis, 9*, 527–532.

Hawkins, R. P., & Dobes, R. W. (1977). Behavioral definitions in applied behavior analysis: Explicit or implicit? In B. C. Etzel, J. M. LeBlanc, & D. M. Baer (Eds.), *New developments in behavioral research: Theory, methods, and application* (pp. 167–188). Hillsdale, NJ: Erlbaum.

Horner, R. H., Carr, E. G., Strain, P. S., Todd, A. W., & Reed, H. K. (2002). Problem behavior interventions for young children with autism: A research synthesis. *Journal of Autism and Developmental Disorders, 32*, 423–446.

Horner, R. H., Diemer, S. M., & Brazeau, K. C. (1992). Educational support for students with severe problem behaviors in Oregon: A descriptive analysis from the 1987–1988 school year. *Journal of the Association for Persons with Severe Handicaps, 17*, 154–169.

Horner, R. H., & Sugai, G. (2000). School-wide behavior support: An emerging initiative. *Journal of Positive Behavior Interventions, 2*, 231.

Iwata, B. A., Deleon, I. G., & Roscoe, E. M. (2013). Reliability and validity of the functional analysis screening tool. *Journal of Applied Behavior Analysis, 46*, 271–284.

Johnston, J. M., & Pennypacker, H. S. (2009). *Strategies and tactics of scientific research* (3rd ed.). New York, NY: Routledge/Taylor & Francis Group.

Klassen, R. M., & Chiu, M. (2010). Effects on teachers' self-efficacy and job satisfaction: Teacher gender, years of experience, and job stress. *Journal of Educational Psychology, 102*, 741–756.

Korpershoek, H., Harms, T., de Boer, H., van Kuijk, M., & Doolaard, S. (2016). A meta-analysis of the effects of classroom management strategies and classroom management programs on students' academic, behavioral, emotional, and motivational outcomes. *Review of Educational Research, 86*, 643–680.

Kucharczyk, S., Reutebuch, C. K., Carter, E. W., Hedges, S., El Zein, F., Fan, H., et al. (2015). Addressing the needs of adolescents with autism spectrum disorder: Considerations and complexities for high school interventions. *Exceptional Children, 81*(3), 329–349.

Lane, J. D., & Gast, D. L. (2014). Visual analysis in single case experimental design studies: Brief review and guidelines. *Neuropsychological Rehabilitation, 24*, 445–463.

LeBel, T. J., Chafouleas, S. M., Britner, P. A., & Simonsen, B. (2013). Use of a daily report card in an intervention package involving home-school communication to reduce disruptive behavior in preschoolers. *Journal of Positive Behavior Interventions, 15*, 103–112.

Long, N., & Edwards, M. (1994). The use of a daily report card to address children's school behavior problems. *Contemporary Education, 65*, 152.

Mayes, S. D., Calhoun, S. L., Mayes, R. D., & Molitoris, S. (2012). Autism and ADHD: Overlapping and discriminating symptoms. *Research in Autism Spectrum Disorders, 6*, 277–285.

Moncher, F. J., & Prinz, R. J. (1991). Treatment fidelity in outcome studies. *Clinical Psychology Review, 11*, 247–266.

Neitzel, J. (2010). Positive behavior supports for children and youth with autism spectrum disorders. *Preventing School Failure: Alternative Education for Children and Youth, 54*(4), 247–255.

O'Neill, R. E., Horner, R. H., Albin, R. W., Sprague, J. R., Storey, K., & Newton, J. S. (1997). *Functional assessment and program development for problem behavior: A practical handbook* (2nd ed.). Pacific Grove, CA: Brooks/Cole.

Owens, J. S., Holdaway, A. S., Zoromski, A. K., Evans, S. W., Himawan, L. K., Girio-Herrera, E., et al. (2012). Incremental benefits of a daily report card intervention over time for youth with disruptive behavior. *Behavior Therapy, 43*, 848–861.

Parker, R. I., & Vannest, K. J. (2012). Bottom-up analysis of single-case research designs. *Journal of Behavioral Education, 21*, 254–265.

Parker, R. I., Vannest, K. J., & Davis, J. L. (2011a). Effect size in single-case research: A review of nine nonoverlap techniques. *Behavior Modification, 35*, 303–322.

Parker, R. I., Vannest, K. J., Davis, J. L., & Sauber, S. B. (2011b). Combining nonoverlap and trend for single-case research: Tau-U. *Behavior Therapy, 42*, 284–299.

Perrachione, B. A., Rosser, V. J., & Petersen, G. J. (2008). Why do they stay? Elementary teachers' perceptions of job satisfaction and retention. *The Professional Educator, 32*, 25–41.

Riden, B. S., Taylor, J. C., Lee, D. L., & Scheeler, M. C. (2018). A synthesis of the daily behavior report card literature from 2007 to 2017. *The Journal of Special Education Apprenticeship, 7*, 3.

Riley-Tillman, T. C., Chafouleas, S. M., & Briesch, A. M. (2007). A school practitioner's guide to using daily behavior report cards to monitor student behavior. *Psychology in the Schools, 44*, 77–89.

Schumaker, J. B., Hovell, M. F., & Sherman, J. A. (1977). An Analysis of daily behavior report cards and parent-managed privileges in the improvement of adolescents' classroom performance. *Journal of Applied Behavior Analysis, 10*(3), 449–464.

Schwartz, I. S., & Baer, D. M. (1991). Social validity assessments: Is current practice state of the art? *Journal of Applied Behavior Analysis, 24*, 189–204.

Smith, M. A., Williams, R. L., & McLaughlin, T. F. (1983). The daily report card as an intervention technique for classroom academic and social behavior: A review. *BC Journal of Special Education, 7*, 369–380.

Sugai, G., & Horner, R. (2002). The evolution of discipline practices: School-wide positive behavior supports. *Child & Family Behavior Therapy, 24*, 23–50.

Sutherland, K. S., Alder, N., & Gunter, P. L. (2003). The effect of varying rates of opportunities to respond to academic requests on the classroom behavior of students with EBD. *Journal of Emotional and Behavioral Disorders, 11*, 239–248.

Sutherland, K. S., & Morgan, P. L. (2003). Implications of transactional processes in classrooms for students with emotional/behavioral disorders. *Preventing School Failure, 48*, 32–37.

Sutherland, K. S., Wehby, J. H., & Yoder, P. J. (2002). Examination of the relationship between teacher praise and opportunities for students with EBD to respond to academic requests. *Journal of Emotional and Behavioral Disorders, 12*, 5–13.

Taylor, J. C., & Hill, D. (2017). Using daily behavior report cards during extended school year services for young students with intellectual and developmental disabilities. *Education and Treatment of Children, 40*, 525–546.

Vannest, K. J., Burke, M. D., Sauber, S. B., Davis, J. L., & Davis, C. R. (2011). Daily behavior report cards as evidence-based practice for teachers. *Beyond Behavior, 20*, 13–21.

Vannest, K. J., Davis, J. L., Davis, C. R., Mason, B. A., & Burke, M. D. (2010). Effective intervention for behavior with a daily behavior report card: A meta-analysis. *School Psychology Review, 39*, 654.

Vannest, K. J., Parker, R. I., Gonen, O., & Adiguzel, T. (2016). Single Case Research: Web based calculators for SCR analysis (Version 2.0) [Web-based application]. College Station, TX: Texas A&M University. Retrieved from singlecaseresearch.org.

Walker, H. M., Ramsey, E., & Gresham, F. M. (2004). *Antisocial behavior in school: Evidence-base practices*. Belmont, CA: Thomson Wadsworth.

Wehby, J. H., Symons, F. J., Canale, J. A., & Go, F. J. (1998). Teaching practices in classrooms for students with emotional and behavioral disorders: Discrepancies between recommendations and observations. *Behavioral Disorders, 24*, 51–56.

White, P. J., O'Reilly, M., Streusand, W., Levine, A., Sigafoos, J., Lancioni, G., et al. (2011). Best practices for teaching joint attention: A systematic review of the intervention literature. *Research in Autism Spectrum Disorders, 5*, 1283–1295.

Guiding Questions

1. On a scale of 1 to 10, what is your confidence in the reliability of the journal Mrs. Warren's article is published in? Provide evidence for your rating.
2. Based on the article title and abstract, is this a useful article given Mrs. Warren and Mr. Rooney's struggles to support Hines in the classroom? Explain why.
3. Does the introduction provide a rationale for the purpose of the single-case study? What is that rationale? Provide a summary of the introduction to this single-case article in your own words.
4. Are research questions explicitly stated? If they are, what are they trying to answer? If not, should they be and why?

5. On a scale of 1 to 10, how rigorous would you rate the method section of the single-case article Mrs. Warren identified? Provide evidence for this rating.
6. Are the results of the article presented clearly and in an objective manner? Explain your answer. Summarize the results section in your own words, including data.
7. On a scale of 1 to 10, how well does the discussion section answer the "so what?" question? In other words, do the authors explain why the results matter? Provide evidence for your rating.
8. On a scale of 1 to 10, how confident are you in the overall believability, reliability, and validity of the Riden, Taylor, Ruiz, et al. (2021) article. Provide evidence for your rating.
9. What criticisms do you have of the article Mrs. Warren located? Are there any limitations the authors did not address in the limitations section?
10. Given your answers for the previous questions, what conclusions can Mrs. Warren draw about a DBRC to support students engaging in interfering behaviors?

Use Professional Judgment to Implement Researched Strategies Across Individual Contexts

After reading the single-case article on DBRCs, Mrs. Warren is confident the intervention is effective in supporting students who display interfering behavior and thinks that a DBRC might be the thing she and Mr. Rooney can collaborate on, in partnership with Hines, to ultimately help Hines be successful in the classroom, both academically and behaviorally. Now that Mrs. Warren has identified an intervention, she sets off to create and implement a DBRC system that can be used by her and Mr. Rooney as well as any other teachers who interact with Hines.

During her search for supports in creating a DBRC, she avoided websites such as Teachers Pay Teachers or Pinterest because she was unable to connect any of those materials to any research or experts in the field. As she continues her search, she stumbles upon a website called Intervention Central. She is pleased to see the website offers content and materials surrounding, for example, the response to intervention framework and curriculum-based measures along with materials for academic and behavior interventions. However, Mrs. Warren wants to be sure that the materials she might access from this website are based on research. She finds the contact section of Intervention Central, where she reads about the individual who created the website. As she reads about them, she finds that they provide national trainings for schools and organizations on a broad range of topics relating to school improvement and they are a certified school psychologist with over 17 years of experience in public education. Further, she sees that they have developed several scholarly products aimed at supporting school-wide and teachers' classroom management and supports.

Feeling confident in the resources provided at Intervention Central, she begins exploring the materials available for teachers. As she is looking over the website, she finds a behavior report card maker. The online application allows teachers to create a DBRC that can be individualized. Now that Mrs. Warren has a plan and a way to create the DBRC, in collaboration with Mr. Rooney, they develop the DBRC with relevant behavior goals and get to work.

WHERE CAN I FIND MORE INFORMATION ABOUT CLASSROOM MANAGEMENT?

Council for Exceptional Children (CEC): The CEC is the largest international professional organization dedicated to improving the success of children and youth with disabilities and/or gifts and talents. By following this link, you can access several resources on classroom and behavior management: https://exceptionalchildren.org/taxonomy/term/35.

Intervention Central: Intervention Central provides teachers, schools, and districts with free resources to help support students in classrooms. Among the many resources provided, you can find additional information on classroom management at https://www.interventioncentral.org/behavioral-intervention-modification.

IRIS Module: The IRIS Center provides a wide variety of resources and services to suit a diverse set of instructional needs and circumstances. This module provides insights into key concepts and foundational practices as they relate to classroom behavior management. Visit the module at https://iris.peabody.vanderbilt.edu/module/beh1/.

WestEd: WestEd, a nonpartisan research, development, and service agency, works with educational and other communities to promote excellence; achieve equity; and improve learning for children, youth, and adults. The following link will take you to a free archived webinar that highlights the free online professional development modules and resources on classroom and behavior management provided by the IRIS (IDEA '04 and Research for Inclusive Settings) Center for Training Enhancements: https://www.wested.org/resources/behavior-and-classroom-management-online-professional-development-modules-and-resources-for-implementation/.

DISCUSSION QUESTIONS

1. What are some negative outcomes associated with students who display interfering behaviors in school settings and the teachers working to support them?
2. At the beginning of this chapter, you read about classical and operant behavior. How do those principles relate to supporting students displaying challenging behaviors?
3. Explain your experience reading the single-case research article provided in this chapter on DBRCs. What did you learn from that exercise? What questions remain about implementing DBRCs?
4. If a colleague asked you what steps you took when identifying DRBCs as a potential intervention to implement with one of your students, how would you describe the process so they can successfully identify single-case research articles that may be helpful in their classroom?
5. When you are scanning the internet for academic or behavioral supports, name a couple of ways you can assess the reliability of the content.

KEY TERMS

classical conditioning: Conditioning in which the conditioned stimulus (such as the sound of a bell) is paired with and precedes the unconditioned stimulus (such as the sight of food) until the conditioned stimulus alone is sufficient to elicit the response (such as salivation in a dog).

daily behavior report card: A tool that teachers and parents use to track a student's behavior in the classroom. It helps everyone to understand the student's strengths and the areas that need improvement and to work together to encourage desired behavior.

function: Refers to the source of environmental reinforcement for a behavior. There are four main functions of behavior: attention, escape, tangible, and automatic (sensory).

impact factor: Commonly used to evaluate the relative importance of a journal within its field and to measure the frequency with which the "average article" in a journal has been cited in a particular time period.

interfering behaviors: Behaviors that are disruptive or repetitive and interfere with a student's day-to-day activities.

operant conditioning: The process in which behavioral change occurs as a function of the consequences of behavior.

routines: A set of procedures for handling both daily occurrences (e.g., taking attendance, starting a class period, or turning in assignments) and minor interruptions of instruction, such as a student's broken pencil or the arrival of a note from the main office.

rules: These are specific behaviors for which there are consequences.

stimulus: An object or event that follows a response that increases or decreases the likelihood that the same response happens again in the future.

REFERENCES

Bettini, E., Cumming, M. M., O'Brien, K. M., Brunsting, N. C., Ragunathan, M., Sutton, R., & Chopra, A. (2020). Predicting special educators' intent to continue teaching students with emotional or behavioral disorders in self-contained settings. *Exceptional Children, 86*(2), 209–228. https://doi.org/10.1177/0014402919873556

Butler, A., & Monda-Amaya, L. (2016). Preservice teachers' perceptions of challenging behavior. *Teacher Education and Special Education, 39*(4), 276–292. https://doi.org/10.1177/0888406416654212

Fowkes, C. (2022). *Representation in visual schedules for individuals with disabilities* [Master's thesis, James Madison University]. Scholarly Commons: A Repository for James Madison University. https://commons.lib.jmu.edu/masters202029/143

Gage, N. A., Scott, T., Hirn, R., & MacSuga-Gage, A. S. (2018). The relationship between teachers' implementation of classroom management practices and student behavior in elementary school. *Behavioral Disorders, 43*(2), 302–315. https://doi.org/10.1177/0198742917714809

Gunter, P. L., Shores, R. E., Jack, S. L., Denny, R. K., & DePaepe, P. A. (1994). A case study of the effects of altering instructional interactions on the disruptive behavior of a child identified with severe behavior disorders. *Education and Treatment of Children, 17*(3), 435–444. https://www.jstor.org/stable/42900480

Havlik, A. (n.d.). *Visual schedules: A practical guide for families.* https://ed-psych.utah.edu/school-psych/_resources/documents/grants/autism-training-grant/Visual-Schedules-Practical-Guide-for-Families.pdf

Kazdin, A. E. (1977). *The token economy: A review and evaluation.* Plenum Press.

Kern, L., Choutka, C. M., & Sokol, N. G. (2002). Assessment-based antecedent interventions used in natural settings to reduce challenging behavior: An analysis of the literature. *Education and Treatment of Children, 25*(1), 113–130. https://www.jstor.org/stable/42900519

Leinhardt, G., Weidman, C., & Hammond, K. M. (1987). Introduction and integration of classroom routines by expert teachers. *Curriculum Inquiry, 17*(2), 135–176. https://www.jstor.org/stable/1179422

Maggin, D. M., Chafouleas, S. M., Goddard, K. M., & Johnson, A. H. (2011). A systematic evaluation of token economies as a classroom management tool for students with challenging behavior. *Journal of School Psychology, 49*(5), 529–554. https://doi.org/10.1016/j.jsp.2011.05.001

Riden, B. S., Taylor, J. C., Ruiz, S., Lee, D. L., & Scheeler, M. C. (2021). Using a daily report card to reduce off-task behaviors for a student with autism spectrum disorder. *Journal of Behavioral Education, 30*(3), 397–416. https://doi.org/10.1007/s10864-020-09382-6

Riden, B. S., Taylor, J. C., Scheeler, M. C., Lee, D. L., & McCloskey, A. V. (2021). The effects of an electronic daily behavior report card on student's challenging behavior. *Journal of Special Education Technology, 36*(3), 127–140. https://doi.org/10.1177/01626434211033580

Salmon, A. K. (2010). Engaging young children in thinking routines. *Childhood Education, 86*(3), 132–137. https://doi.org/10.1080/00094056.2010.10523133

Watson, J. B. (1913). Psychology as the behaviorist sees it. *Psychological Review, 20*, 158–177.

Wildenger, L. K., McIntyre, L. L., Fiese, B. H., & Eckert, T. L. (2008). Children's daily routines during kindergarten transition. *Early Childhood Education Journal, 36*, 69–74. https://doi.org/10.1007/s10643-008-0255-2

Wolery, M., Bailey, D. B., & Sugai, G. (1988). *Effective teaching: Principles and procedures of applied behavior analysis with exceptional students*. Boston: Allyn Bacon.

Chapter 9

Math Instruction

Mathematics is a core instructional content area that is critical for student success. Although educational scholars and math teachers have long understood the benefits of math instruction, even the general public cannot deny the integration of mathematical concepts in a technologically advanced society. In the past, it may have been common for math teachers to hear, "When will I ever need to know this?" But today we know math helps children have better problem-solving skills and reasoning abilities. It is true that as an adult, solving a math problem with a train that leaves the station at 2 o'clock going 60 mph may seem far-fetched, but the skills learned in framing the problem, identifying the knowns and unknowns, and taking steps to solve the problem are very important life skills. On a neurological level, scientist have identified the importance of math reasoning in brain development because it creates new neural pathways and strengthens existing ones (Zacharopoulos et al., 2021). Like an athlete who goes to the gym to lift weights to perform faster and stronger during games, math practice strengthens brain development. Children with greater math abilities have better academic outcomes across a variety of disciplines.

If a student has a disability in math or a teacher's math instruction is lacking in best practice, many aspects of the child's development may be negatively affected. It is imperative, therefore, that special education teachers be scientific practitioners in the design and delivery of math instruction to benefit students with disabilities. In this chapter, we will examine the issues concerning math instruction for students with disabilities and use a scenario to systematically examine how teachers can use research to address math instruction issues. By the end of the chapter, we will have answered these essential questions:

1. What are some of the issues concerning math instruction?
2. What are some of the best practices in math instruction?
3. How do I use research to address math instruction issues?
4. Where can I find more information about math instruction?

WHAT ARE SOME OF THE ISSUES CONCERNING MATH INSTRUCTION?

It is estimated that 3% to 9% of school-age children in the United States have a mathematics disability (Swanson, 2012). Although this percentage may seem relatively small, there has been consistent underperformance in mathematics among all students for decades. The National Association for Educational Progress (NAEP; 2022) continually reports that students are performing below basic levels in standardized mathematics assessments. In 2022, the percentage of fourth graders below basic was 24% and for eighth graders, 38% (NAEP, 2022). In an effort to understand how disability and math instruction affect student progress, researchers have examined characteristics of students with math disabilities. Figure 9.1 is a list of common characteristics that affect mathematics performance.

Many of the characteristics listed can be attributed to **working memory** limitations, which have been identified as contributing factors to math disabilities (Fuchs et al., 2014). Working memory refers to the simultaneous storage and processing of information (Baddeley, 1992). Students who have deficits in working memory often have slower and inaccurate processing of classroom instruction, which results in more difficulty learning the content. In addition, students with working memory limitations struggle to plan and organize tasks, filter relevant from irrelevant information, and regulate their attention (Li & Geary, 2013; Swanson et al., 2014).

Mathematical problem-solving requires working memory skills as well as other critical reading skills, such as decoding and comprehension. Vukovic

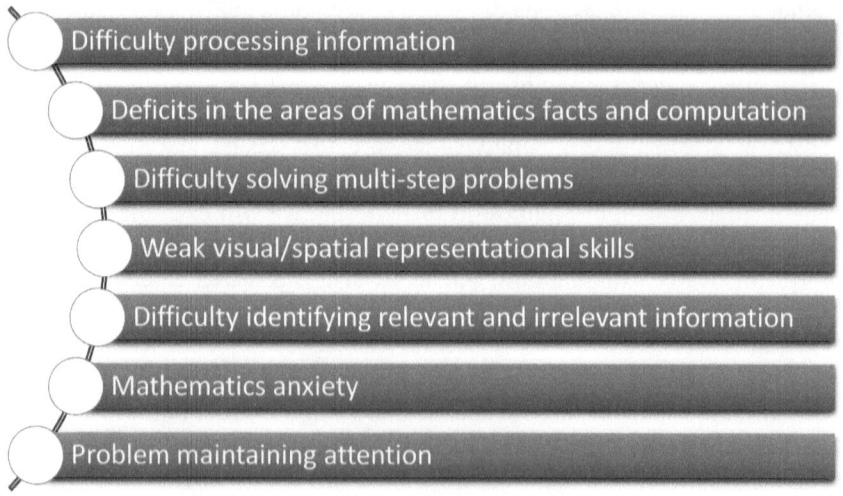

Figure 9.1 Common Characteristics That Affect Mathematics Performance

and Siegel (2010) pointed out that mathematical thinking requires both procedural and conceptual knowledge. **Procedural knowledge** refers to the step-by-step algorithms needed to solve math problems. Often taught through repetition and memorization, knowing which step to start with and how to continue the process until the problem is solved is vital for mathematics literacy. An example would be adding fractions with different denominators. Procedurally, one needs to (1) find the least common multiple of the denominators, (2) recalculate the nominators based on the multiple, (3) add across numerators, and (4) simplify. Procedural knowledge allows us to solve any fraction addition problem because the procedures are consistent across problems.

Conceptual knowledge is a more complex concept that includes knowledge of categories, relationships, principles, and representations. In other words, conceptual knowledge is an understanding of how and why the procedures of math work and in what context. Conceptual knowledge allows students to see relationships and patterns. It leads to the integration of new knowledge to solve unfamiliar problems. Take our fractions problem for example; solving the equation requires procedural knowledge, but understanding why those steps must be followed introduces conceptual knowledge. Understanding the concept of numerators and denominators is about knowing how many "pieces" are represented out of the "whole." When the whole is represented by different "sizes" (i.e., the denominator), comparing across entities (i.e., fractions) is challenging. Therefore, to make comparisons similar and assist in the analysis of two or more groups, modifying the groups to be similar in sizes allows for easier comparison of the pieces.

Instruction that exclusively focuses on procedural skills and fluency, without including conceptual understanding, does not facilitate **mathematics literacy**. Therefore, mathematics instruction for all students must include procedural and conceptual practice; however, students with mathematics disabilities likely need additional supports regarding their working memory issues.

WHAT ARE SOME OF THE BEST PRACTICES IN MATH INSTRUCTION?

Thankfully, educational researchers have examined mathematics instructional practices to support students with mathematics disabilities. In the next section of this chapter, we will introduce some best practices in mathematics instruction supported with empirical evidence.

Explicit Instruction

Explicit instruction is a systematic, direct, engaging, and success-oriented method of teaching (Archer & Hughes, 2010). The emphasis of instruction is on proceeding in small steps, checking for student understanding, and achieving active participation. Students are given opportunities for guided and independent practice, including practicing new skills and reviewing previously learned skills. Explicit instruction also utilizes immediate and frequent student feedback.

Research suggests that teaching mathematics with explicit instruction can significantly improve a student's ability to perform mathematics operations (e.g., adding and multiplying) as well as solve word problems (Gersten et al., 2009). The teaching method is effective across all grade levels and for diverse groups of students, including English language learners. Additional key components of explicit instruction include (a) clearly identifying skills of concepts to be learned, (b) connecting new content to previous content, (c) modeling concepts or procedures in a step-by-step manner, (d) verbalizing thought processes while demonstrating the concept or procedure, and (e) providing opportunities to practice using **scaffolded instruction**.

Self-Regulated Strategy Development

There is a collection of research-based strategies grounded in the **self-regulated strategy development** (SRSD) framework. SRSD math is designed to improve procedural and conceptual knowledge of mathematics while developing four basic self-regulation strategies: goal setting, self-monitoring, self-talk, and self-reinforcement (IRIS Center, n.d.).

With the use of explicit instruction, SRSD helps students regulate their own behaviors as they encounter academic challenges. First, students are taught goal-setting skills that include setting goals and breaking them into steps as needed, developing a plan for meeting those goals, implementing the plan, monitoring progress toward those goals, and revising the goals as needed. Second, students must be able to self-monitor their behaviors to ensure they are engaging in productive behaviors as opposed to unproductive behaviors that may not lead toward their goals. Self-monitoring consists of two parts, self-assessment and self-recording. Self-monitoring can assist a student to increase or decrease the frequency, intensity, or duration of a behavior. Third, SRSD supports self-talk. Self-talk is a strategy for students to talk themselves through a task or activity. It promotes the conscious understanding of the task at hand and supports positive thinking. Finally, self-reinforcement is a method through which students reward themselves for obtaining their goal. Often as simple as a positive self-statement (e.g., "I've finished 15 out of

20 problems, only five more to go. I'm proud of myself for staying focused and on task"), reinforcement encourages the student to continue the SRSD next time.

Schema-Based Instruction

Most students with mathematics difficulties, including those with disabilities, have trouble solving word problems. **Schema-based instruction** (SBI) is a word problem–solving strategy that teaches students to identify problem types by focusing on the underlying structure of the mathematical situation (Hott et al., 2021). There are two main types of **schemas**: additive and multiplicative. Additive schema includes addition and subtraction problems. Multiplicative schema includes multiplication and division problems. The core feature of SBI involves teaching students to build a rich schema for different word problem structures and to identify how surface-level information may vary but does not change the problem schema. Combined with explicit instruction, SBI helps students identify word problem types, represent them correctly, and use effective methods for solving them (Jitendra et al., 2016).

Concrete–Representation–Abstract

Concrete–representation–abstract, or CRA, is grounded in the early work of Bruner and Kenney (1965), who defined learning through "stages of representation." The three stages are (1) enactive—learning through movement and action, (2) iconic—learning through pictures, and (3) symbolic—learning through abstract symbols. CRA instruction creates meaningful mathematics connections among concrete, representational, and abstract levels of understanding. It is a three-stage learning process where students learn through physical manipulation of concrete objects, followed by learning through pictorial representations of the concrete manipulations, and ending with solving problems using abstract notation (Miller et al., 2011).

The concrete stage of instruction uses physical objects to model mathematical problems, such as cubes, colored chips, or fraction bars. The representational stage uses representations of the physical objects to model problems, such as circles, dots, tallies, other types of semi-concrete representations. Finally, the abstract level uses symbols to model problems, such as numbers and operational symbols (e.g., $+$, $\div$, $-$, and $=$). Research has shown that the CRA method can bridge the gap between procedural and conceptual understanding for students with disabilities (Bouck et al., 2018).

HOW DO I USE RESEARCH TO ADDRESS MATH INSTRUCTION ISSUES?

There are many issues concerning mathematics instruction. The previous section highlighted a few of those issues and presented a couple of evidence-based practices. In this next section, we examine, with a fictional vignette, how teachers can use research to address a common math instruction issue. We provide a scenario with context, which is critical in understanding for scientific practitioners. Then, we provide a full-text research article that follows these steps for, practicing to become a scientific practitioner:

1. Identify and understand a problem in the classroom.
2. Know where to look for potential researched solutions.
3. Read and understand a variety of research articles to gather information.
4. Use professional judgment to implement researched strategies across individual contexts.

Identify and Understand a Problem in the Classroom

Ms. Jackson is a fifth-grade special education teacher at Willow Creek Elementary School. She provides special education services to students with learning disabilities. Depending on her students' individual needs and their least restrictive environment placements, she sometimes co-teaches instruction and sometimes teaches small-group instruction in a resource room setting. Most of her students have individualized education program (IEP) goals to accelerate reading fluency and comprehension, but a few of her students have additional challenges in math and are a couple of grade levels behind their peers. Ms. Jackson has noticed that word problems are particularly problematic for these students because the reading component is one challenge and the mathematics component is another. Her students express frustration, often shut down, become defiant, and demonstrate other avoidance behaviors during math instruction.

After school one day, Ms. Jackson is chatting with a special education teacher colleague about her observations and challenges with a couple of her students. Coincidentally, her colleague recently returned from the annual Council for Exceptional Children conference, where they sat in on a session that discussed evidence-based practices for math instruction. Her colleague asks if she has tried SBI to teach word problems. Ms. Jackson is familiar with the term but is not really sure what it entails. She was taught that keyword identification was the best method for instructing word problems. For example, if the problem contains the word "altogether," the problem likely requires addition, or if the problem contains the word "fewer," it likely requires subtraction. Her colleague suggests that SBI could be a new strategy that she could implement with her students who are struggling in math. Ms. Jackson is grateful that her colleague mentioned SBI and says she will look into the practice further.

Know Where to Look for Potential Researched Solutions

Ms. Jackson sits down at her desk and searches online with the phase "SBI for math." After poking around the internet for a bit, she learns that SBI is a way to teach problem-solving skills by having students categorize math word problems based on the structure of the problem. Then, students use visual representations or number sentences to represent the schema and solve. She learns that the keyword approach that she has been using often leads to systematic errors. For example, here's a word problem: "Juan took the 14 baseball cards he no longer wanted and gave them to Kai. Now, Juan has 62 baseball cards left. How many baseball cards did Juan have to begin with?" The keyword approach may lead students to focus on the word "left" as well as the two numbers in the problem and decide to subtract. However, the operation required is addition because the structure of the problem is $x-16=62$. So to solve for x, the students need to add $62+16$, which equals 78.

SBI makes sense to Ms. Jackson, and she thinks it might help her students. But is this an evidence-based practice or just the new "strategy of the day" without any empirical support? Before she spends more time learning the strategy and implementing it with her students, she turns to the literature to see whether SBI is a valid practice.

Ms. Jackson opens Google Scholar on her computer. She enters "schema-based instruction" and "math" and "literature review" in the search bar. She sets the search year range from 2017 to the present. Ms. Jackson decides to include the search term "literature review" because she wants to see if there is a larger body of evidence on SBI. Rather than examine one study on SBI, she wants to see if multiple studies have been conducted and what the cumulative body of evidence suggests. Ms. Jackson scrolls the search results and sees the title "Schema-Based Instruction for Mathematical Word Problem Solving: An Evidence-Based Review for Students With Learning Disabilities," which is an article by Cook et al. (2020) published in the journal *Learning Disability Quarterly*. She is drawn to this article because the title contains the phrase "students with learning disabilities," which matches who her students are. The peer-reviewed journal is published by Sage, which is a reputable publishing company, and a quick search online shows that the journal has an impact factor of 1.8. There is also a PDF link available, so she knows she has free access to the full text of the article. Ms. Jackson clicks the link and downloads the article to read.

Read and Understand a Variety of Research Articles to Gather Information

In the following section, we provide the full article by Cook and colleagues (2020), "Schema-Based Instruction for Mathematical Word Problem Solving: An Evidence-Based Review for Students With Learning Disabilities." We also provide guiding questions to practice reading, gleaning, and interpreting research article content.

Schema-Based Instruction for Mathematical Word Problem Solving: An Evidence-Based Review for Students with Learning Disabilities

Sara Cothren Cook, PhD[1], Lauren W. Collins, PhD[2], Lisa L. Morin, PhD[3], and Paul J. Riccomini, PhD[4]

Abstract

The purpose of this review is to determine the evidence base classification of schema-based instruction (SBI) as an intervention to improve word problem-solving outcomes in mathematics for students with learning or mathematics disabilities in Grades K–12. Using the Council for Exceptional Children's quality indicators (QIs) and standards, we reviewed both single-case and group design studies to classify the evidence of SBI. Results of this review indicate that SBI is a potentially evidence-based practice (EBP) for students with learning disabilities. Implications and directions for research and practice are presented.

Keywords Learning disabilities, Mathematics, Mathematics difficulties, Schema-based instruction, Word problems

---

Corresponding Author:
Sara Cothren Cook
Email: cothren@hawaii.edu

1. University of Hawai'i at Mānoa, Honolulu, USA
2. San Diego State University, CA, USA

3. Old Dominion University, Norfolk, VA, USA
4. The Pennsylvania State University, University Park, USA

Introduction

It is estimated that 3%–9% of the entire school-age population in the United States has a mathematics disability (MD; Fuchs et al., 2010; Swanson, 2012). Despite the large population of students affected by MD (i.e., a learning disability [LD] in mathematics), this area is not as well researched or understood as the area of reading disabilities (Garrett, Mazzocco, & Baker, 2006; Watson & Gable, 2013). However, recent data indicate the percentage of students with disabilities who are proficient in mathematics is as low as 9% and only as high as 16 % in eighth and fourth grades, respectively (U.S. Department of Education, Institute of Education Sciences, National Center for Education Statistics, 2018). It is clear that despite a dearth of research in mathematics, students with MD are in dire need of more effective interventions.

In an effort to better understand how to effectively address the deficit characteristics of students with MD (see Powell, Fuchs, Fuchs, Cirino, & Fletcher, 2009; Vukovic & Siegel, 2010), researchers have identified cognitive characteristics of students with MD that negatively impact their ability to solve problems. Specifically, working memory (WM) deficits are directly linked to MD (Fuchs et al., 2014; Geary, Hoard, Byrd-Craven, Nugent, & Numtee, 2007; Swanson, 2012; Swanson, Jerman, & Zheng, 2009). WM refers to the concurrent storage and processing of information (Baddeley, 1992; Watson & Gable, 2010), and deficits in WM are evidenced by slow and often inaccurate processing of classroom instruction resulting in students struggling to learn. In addition, students with WM deficits often have difficulty planning and organizing tasks, filtering relevant from irrelevant information, and regulating their attention (Li & Geary, 2013; Swanson, Orosco, & Lussier, 2014; Watson & Gable, 2010). Mathematical problem solving requires the seamless blend of these skills in addition to a host of other critical skills, such as reading ability, including decoding and comprehension, and procedural and conceptual knowledge of mathematics. Demonstration of these skills can tax WM, further exacerbating the challenges students with MD experience in developing a thorough understanding of mathematics at both the conceptual and procedural level—both of which are essential for improving overall performance.

Vukovic and Siegel (2010) highlighted the importance of teaching mathematic concepts and skills in a manner that fosters deeper mathematical thinking. They pointed out that mathematics instruction that focuses exclusively on procedural skills and fluency, instead of including conceptual understanding, does not facilitate mathematics literacy (i.e., an integrated understanding of both conceptual and procedural knowledge that allows for the application of mathematics to solve real-world problems; National Council of Teachers of Mathematics, 2014; National Mathematics Advisory Panel [NMAP], 2008). Clearly, it is not an either/ or situation, but rather making use of instructional techniques to foster and support conceptual and procedural learning (e.g., problem solving) simultaneously as well as accounting for the WM issues that are often characteristic of students with MD.

One particularly important skill practitioners can emphasize to help students better develop their ability to solve problems is the application of schemas. Generally, schemas refer to knowledge that is organized and stored in long-term memory and can be applied to newly received information or experiences to make and strengthen connections that form new understanding (Kalyuga, 2006). Schemas are assembled by continuously adding new layers of knowledge to form deeper and broader understanding of concepts (Steele & Johanning, 2004). Consequently, several small units of content are organized into larger units, eventually freeing up WM (Kalyuga, 2006). Schemas are triggered when a student attempts to comprehend and organize new information, such as a mathematical problem. As students learn more mathematical concepts, connections are continuously made within and across these different ideas, thus, building deeper mathematical understanding that leads to more sophisticated problem-solving skills. Schema is an essential element in helping students develop mathematical problem-solving skills; however, students with MD require additional instructional scaffolding to facilitate the development of schema (Hwang & Riccomini, 2016; Jitendra, DiPipi, & Perron-Jones, 2002).

Schemas based on visual representations are especially important for students with LD during problem-solving instruction and can take many different forms including schema diagrams, bar models, generic diagrams, graphic organizers, tables, and charts (Hwang & Riccomini, 2016). Whereas an addition word problem involving picking apples and cherries could be very simply represented by a pictorial illustration of apple and cherry trees (i.e., a drawing of a tree with apples on it), the same problem could be represented with schema diagram (e.g., bar model, graphic organizer illustrating essential problem features). The variety of visual representations has encouraged researchers to determine what type of visual representations best support the understanding and mastery of mathematical concepts for students with LD (Edens & Potter, 2008; Hegarty & Kozhevnikov, 1999; van Garderen, 2007).

Hegarty and Kozhevnikov (1999) explained the differences between pictorial and schema representations; a pictorial representation is defined as a "vivid and detailed visual image" (p. 685), whereas schematic representations more explicitly illustrate "the spatial relationships between objects and imagining spatial transformations" (p. 685). In other words, schema representations illustrate the essential mathematical features. It is important to note that although a schematic representation *can be* pictorial, a pictorial representation is not necessarily schematic (e.g., pictures of apple trees do not illustrate mathematical features). That is, schematic representations require students to move beyond simply drawing the items represented in a word problem (e.g., cherry and apple trees) and instead use conceptual knowledge to visually represent a specific problem type (i.e., schema) and apply it to a novel situation. Hua, Woods-Groves, Kaldenberg, Lucas, and Therrien (2015) explained that schematic representations facilitate the generalization of conceptual knowledge across word problems that are similar in concept (e.g., adding) but different in content (e.g., word problems that require adding money as opposed to those adding other objects).

van Garderen and Montague (2003) investigated the extent and efficacy of students' use of pictorial and schematic diagrams during problem solving. Results indicated that students who used pictorial representations incorrectly solved word problems about 70% of the time. To the contrary, students who employed schematic representations solved the same word problems correctly about 70% of the time. Clearly, schema and visual representations focused on the schema features (i.e., pictorial vs. schema diagram) play an important role in learning mathematical problem solving, but the instruction accompanying the schema representation is also an important consideration.

NMAP (2008) advised using explicit systematic instruction along with the use of visual representations to teach word problem solving to students exhibiting low achievement in mathematics, including students with LD. To improve word problem solving for students with MD, researchers have investigated the effectiveness of the semantic approach for students with difficulties in mathematics (Jitendra,

Dupuis, Star, & Rodriguez, 2016; Morin, Watson, Hester, & Raver, 2017). As opposed to typical word problem instruction that teaches students to identify key words or use a checklist of steps, the semantic approach focuses on teaching conceptual ideas while also providing information about the structure of problems (Powell, 2011; Riccomini, Hwang, & Morano, 2016). The semantic approach allows students to generalize knowledge of problem structure to solve new, similarly structured problems. One example of the semantic approach is schema-based instruction (SBI).

SBI integrates the use of explicit instruction found effective in mathematics instruction (Montague, 2008) with the use of visual representations and incorporates other strategies such as paraphrasing, visualizing, hypothesizing about problem solutions, and checking work (NMAP, 2008; Palincsar & Brown, 1987; Rosenzweig, Krawec, & Montague, 2011). Swanson, Lussier, and Orosco (2013) asserted that visual-schematic strategies which form the basis of SBI support the visual-spatial WM of students with MD. SBI has produced favorable results for increasing outcomes for students with MD in word problem solving across a variety of grade levels and problem types (Hwang & Riccomini, 2016; Jitendra et al., 1998; Xin, 2008; Xin, Jitendra, & Deatline-Buchman, 2005).

Exploring the Evidence Base of SBI

Recently, Jitendra, Nelson, Pulles, Kiss, and Houseworth (2016) conducted an evidence-based review on the effects of using mathematical representations on mathematics achievement. As part of the inclusion criteria, Jitendra and colleagues only included experimental or quasi-experimental studies that focused on representation interventions (i.e., the authors made an a priori decision to exclude single-case studies from this evidence-based review). To classify the evidence of this research, Jitendra, Nelson, et al. (2016) applied the standards for group design studies proposed by Gersten et al. (2005). For the purpose of their review, mathematical representations were defined as "materials, visual sketches, diagrams or pictures that symbolized an abstract mathematical idea" (pp. 4–5). Although Jitendra, Nelson, et al. (2016) included SBI intervention studies, authors also included studies that incorporated concrete manipulatives as opposed to only schematic representations. It is critical to note that in addition to including students with LD, Jitendra, Nelson, et al. (2016) also included students who were not formally identified with LD but who were at risk, as evidenced by mathematics difficulties. Jitendra, Nelson, et al. (2016) noted that mathematical representations for students with LD or mathematics difficulties are considered an evidence-based practice (EBP) according to standards proposed by Gersten et al. (2005); however, the authors acknowledged that "fewer studies in this review would be considered methodologically sound on the basis of CEC's criteria for classifying the evidence base of practices" (p. 19).

Council for Exceptional Children (CEC) Quality Indicators (QIs) and Standards

In 2014, the Council for Exceptional Children published a set of standards for establishing EBPs for students with disabilities. When developing the CEC (2014) standards, the workgroup considered previous proposed standards (e.g., Gersten et al., 2005; Horner et al., 2005) and designed a set of standards that allows researchers to consider findings from both single-case and group design studies when classifying the evidence base of a practice. For a detailed explanation and comparison of the standards, see B. G. Cook et al. (2015).

There are three notable differences between the standards Jitendra, Nelson, et al. (2016) applied in their review (i.e., Gersten et al., 2005) and standards (i.e., CEC, 2014) we selected for our systematic review. First, unlike the Gersten et al. (2005) and Horner et al. (2005) standards that evaluate the quality of only one type of study (group experimental or group quasi-experimental design and single-case design, respectively), the CEC (2014) standards allow researchers to include both single-case and group design studies in their evaluation, making for a more comprehensive review of the extant literature. CEC provides measures of quality that are applicable to (a) both single-case and group design studies, (b) only single-case studies, or (c) only group design studies. Second, CEC (2014) standards require that 100% of applicable QIs be met for a study to be considered methodologically sound. In contrast, for a study to be considered "high quality" (p. 162) based on Gersten et al. (2005) standards, only 90% of essential QIs and 50% of desirable QIs need to be met. Finally, CEC (2014) proposed that reviews should "be specific to an outcome area and learner population" (p. 1). In other words, the target population included in evidence-based reviews that apply CEC (2014) standards should be narrow.

The Present Study

The purpose of this review is to expand on the work of Jitendra, Nelson, and colleagues (2016) by using the CEC (2014) QIs and standards to determine the evidence-based classification of SBI to improve word problem solving outcomes for students specifically identified with LD who experience difficulties in mathematical word problem solving. From here forth, in the spirit of parsimony, we use the term LD to refer to students who (a) have a documented MD or (b) are diagnosed with LD and experience difficulty in the area of mathematical problem solving. In this study, we defined SBI to have the following features: explicit instruction, a focus on the underlying problem structure, and the use of schematic diagrams (Jitendra, Dupuis, et al., 2016). By narrowing the scope of this review to only focus on the use of SBI to teach students with LD how to solve word problems, we can more clearly determine the quality of the evidence base of this particular instructional strategy for a specific group of students. We included both group and single-case design studies and evaluated the studies using the CEC's (2014) QIs and standards.

Method

Literature Search and Selection Procedures

We referred to the Preferred Reporting Items for Systematic Reviews and Meta-Analyses (PRISMA; Moher, Liberati, Tetzlaff, & Altman, 2009) to search SBI literature and identify studies that met final inclusion criteria. Specifically, we used three steps to identify SBI studies included in our evidence-based review: initial database search, screening of titles and abstracts, and evaluation of articles for inclusion.

Initial database search and screening

We conducted our search using two search engines: PsycINFO and EBSCO host. Using EBSCOhost, we searched the following databases: Academic Search Complete, Education Research Complete, Education Source, and Education Resources Information Center (ERIC). Because SBI encompasses a number of possible strategies (e.g., graphic organizers, number lines, diagrams), we used three phases for our initial screening. First, we conducted a general search to identify studies that targeted word problem-solving strategies for students with LD. Second, we conducted a more focused search using terms specifically related to SBI. Finally, we reviewed the references from literature reviews identified in the first two phases.

Phase 1: General search. We used the following terms to identify studies that targeted word problem-solving strategies for students with LD: "word problem," "learning dis*," and "math." This initial search yielded 302 articles; after duplicates were removed, 91 studies remained. We reviewed the titles and abstracts of the 91 studies to retain any studies that indicated a type of SBI strategy was used to improve word problem solving for students with LD. At this stage, we included any SBI intervention study that mentioned targeting students with LD in the abstract. Given that this review targets the effectiveness of SBI as a singular intervention, studies that used SBI studies with other components (e.g., self-monitoring) were excluded (e.g., Kingsdorf & Krawec, 2016). Although practitioner articles and concept papers were removed, we retained any reviews (i.e., meta-analyses, quality reviews, syntheses of literature) of mathematical strategies for students with LD. From this search, we identified 11 intervention studies and 7 reviews of research.

Phase 2: SBI search. Next, we searched more directly for SBI intervention studies that we did not locate using general search terms. We used the following combinations of terms: (a) (learning disab*) AND (schema) AND (math*); (b) (learning disab*) AND (schema* based) AND (math*); (c) (SBI) AND (learning disab*) AND (math*); (d) (math* disab*) AND (schema*) AND (math*); (e) (math* disab*) AND (schema* based) AND (math*); (f) (SBI) AND (math* disab*) AND (math*); and (g) (learning* disab*) AND(wordproblems solving) AND (schema*); and (h) (math* disab*) AND (word problem solving) AND (schema*). This search resulted in an additional 230 studies. After removing duplicates and studies obtained in the previous step, two studies and two reviews were added.

Phase 3: Reference review. As a final step in the screening process, we reviewed the references of the nine reviews found in Phase 1 and Phase 2 to identify any additional studies relevant to our review. This resulted in 10 additional studies. By combining these additional 10 studies with the 13 studies from the electronic search (i.e., Phases 1 and 2), we identified a total of 23 studies to be evaluated for inclusion.

Evaluation for inclusion

We evaluated each study for inclusion based on the following predetermined criteria: (a) published in a peer reviewed journal; (b) used group experimental, quasi-experimental, or single-case design; (c) defined SBI as the only independent variable; (d) targeted mathematics word problem solving as a dependent variable; (e) implemented the study in school settings for grades K–12; and (f) included students identified with LD. The recommendations for applying the CEC QIs and standards suggest that results should only be analyzed for students in the target population (B. G. Cook et al., 2015); therefore, we only included studies that had (a) participants without disabilities or (b) participants with disabilities other than LD if the results of students with LD were disaggregated. Studies that included multicomponent interventions (e.g., self-monitoring) were excluded. Out of the 32 studies evaluated, a total of 10 studies met inclusion criteria (i.e., eight single-case design and two group design studies).

Coding Procedures for CEC QIs

To classify the evidence base of SBI, the authors of this review followed CEC (2014) guidelines to (a) identify methodologically sound studies, (b) determine the effects of methodologically sound studies, and (c) classify the evidence base of SBI. To evaluate the methodological rigor of the 10 included studies, we used CEC (2014) QIs for single-case and group design studies (see Table 1). CEC (2014) outlines a total of 28 QIs; 18 QIs are applicable to both single-case and group design studies. Six QIs are applicable only to group design studies, and four QIs apply only to single-case design studies. Per CEC (2014) guidelines, only studies that met all applicable QIs (i.e., 24 QIs for group design, 22 QIs for single-case design) were considered methodologically sound and included in the next steps of this review (i.e., determining the effects of a study, classifying the evidence base of SBI).

The CEC (2014) QIs and standards are intended to be used in such a way that two researchers, familiar with applying the QIs, should be able to independently code articles with acceptable reliability (B. G. Cook et al., 2015). Prior to coding, authors discussed the application of QIs as they pertained to the specifics of this review (e.g., disability status of participants). A coding sheet developed by the first author and used in previous evidence-based reviews (e.g., Cook et al., 2017; Sweigart et

QIs	Jitendra and Hoff (1996)	Jitendra, Hoff, and Beck (1999)	Jitendra, DiPipi, and Perron-Jones (2002)	Jitendra et al. (2007)	Morin, Watson, Hester, and Raver (2017)	Sharp and Dennis (2017)	van Garderen (2007)	Walker and Poteet (1990)	Xin (2008)	Xin, Jitendra, and Deadline-Buchman (2005)
1.1. Critical features	Yes	Yes	Yes	Yes	Yes	Yes	Yes	Yes	Yes	Yes
2.1. Participant description	Yes	Yes	Yes	Yes	Yes	Yes	Yes	Yes	Yes	Yes
2.2. Participant demographics	Yes	Yes	Yes	No	Yes	Yes	Yes	Yes	Yes	Yes
3.1. Role of intervention agent	Yes	Yes	Yes	Yes	Yes	Yes	Yes	Yes	Yes	Yes
3.2. Training/qualifications	Yes	Yes	Yes	Yes	Yes	Yes	Yes	Yes	Yes	Yes
4.1. Description of intervention	Yes	Yes	Yes	Yes	Yes	Yes	Yes	Yes	Yes	Yes
4.2. Description of materials	Yes	Yes	Yes	Yes	Yes	Yes	Yes	Yes	Yes	Yes
5.1. Adherence	Yes	Yes	Yes	Yes	Yes	Yes	No	No	Yes	Yes
5.2. Dosage	Yes	Yes	Yes	Yes	Yes	Yes	Yes	Yes	Yes	Yes
5.3. Frequency of	Yes	Yes	Yes	Yes	Yes	Yes	Yes	Yes	Yes	Yes
6.1. Researcher control	Yes	Yes	Yes	Yes	Yes	Yes	Yes	Yes	Yes	Yes
6.2. Baseline described	Yes	Yes	Yes	Yes	Yes	Yes	Yes	Yes	Yes	Yes
6.3. No treatment during baseline	Yes	Yes	Yes	Yes	Yes	Yes	Yes	Yes	Yes	Yes
6.4. Description of group assignment	N/A	N/A	N/A	Yes	Yes	N/A	N/A	Yes	N/A	Yes
6.5. Three effects	Yes	Yes	Yes	N/A	N/A	Yes	Yes	N/A	Yes	N/A
6.6. Three baseline data points	No	Yes	Yes	N/A	N/A	Yes	Yes	N/A	Yes	N/A
6.7. Single-case research design	Yes	Yes	Yes	N/A	N/A	Yes	Yes	N/A	Yes	N/A
6.8. Low overall attrition	N/A	N/A	N/A	Yes	N/A	N/A	N/A	Yes	N/A	Yes
6.9. Low differential attrition	N/A	N/A	N/A	Yes	N/A	N/A	N/A	Yes	N/A	Yes
7.1. Socially important	Yes	Yes	Yes	Yes	Yes	Yes	Yes	Yes	Yes	Yes
7.2. Definition and measurement of DV defined	Yes	Yes	Yes	Yes	Yes	Yes	Yes	Yes	Yes	Yes
7.3. Outcomes reported	Yes	Yes	Yes	Yes	Yes	Yes	Yes	Yes	Yes	Yes
7.4. Frequency of measures	Yes	Yes	Yes	Yes	Yes	Yes	Yes	Yes	Yes	Yes
7.5. Reliability	Yes	Yes	Yes	Yes	Yes	Yes	Yes	Yes	Yes	Yes
7.6. Evidence of validity	N/A	N/A	N/A	Yes	Yes	N/A	N/A	Yes	N/A	Yes
8.1. Appropriate data analysis	N/A	N/A	N/A	Yes	N/A	N/A	N/A	Yes	N/A	Yes
8.2. Single-case graph	Yes	Yes	Yes	N/A	Yes	Yes	Yes	N/A	Yes	N/A
8.3. Effect size	N/A	N/A	N/A	Yes	N/A	N/A	N/A	Yes	N/A	Yes
Number of QIs met	21/22	22/22	22/22	23/24	22/22	22/22	21/22	23/24	22/22	24/24

Note. QI = quality indicators. DV = dependent variable.

Table 1. Coding Results for QIs

al., 2016) was used to rate each QI. All studies were double coded by the first and second author (both of whom have experience in conducting evidence-based reviews) with an overall, interrater agreement of 97.3% (range: 90.9%–100%). Discrepancies were resolved through a consensus meeting.

Classifying the Evidence Base of SBI

After determining the methodological rigor of the 10 included SBI studies, the next step in the evidence-based review was to determine the effects of methodologically sound studies. CEC (2014) provides criteria for classifying methodologically sound studies as having positive, neutral, or mixed effects.

To classify the effects of group design studies, CEC (2014) suggests review teams establish their own effect size criteria for methodologically sound group design studies (i.e., meet all applicable QIs). Although Cohen (1988) established criteria for small (0.2), medium (0.5), and large (0.8) effect sizes, Lipsey et al. (2012) suggested that these effect size classifications are ". . . not tailored to the effects of intervention studies in education, much less any specific domain of education interventions, outcomes, and samples" (p.4). Alternatively,

Lipsey et al. (2012) suggested comparing intervention effects to effects of similar interventions with similar participants and outcome measures. We considered two sources and took a conservative approach by utilizing the higher score to determine effect size interpretations for this review. First, we considered the What Works Clearinghouse (WWC; 2014) criteria for classifying an evidence based as having positive effects (effect size = 0.25). Second, we examined results of Lipsey et al.'s (2012) report of achievement effect sizes from randomized studies, in which researchers found a mean effect of 0.36 ($SD = 0.50$) for instructional components or skill training interventions. In that the mean found by Lipsey and colleagues (2012) was higher than the criteria established by the WWC, we used ≥0.36 to establish the cutoff for positive effects of SBI instruction, which can be considered a type of skill training (see Lipsey et al., 2012).

Single-case design studies are considered to have positive effects when "a functional relationship is established between the independent and dependent variables, resulting in a meaningful, therapeutic change in the targeted dependent variable for at least three fourths (75%) of the cases (depicted by tiers on a graph) in a study" (CEC, 2014, p. 7). In addition, there must be a total of three cases, and no cases should demonstrate an effect in the negative direction (CEC, 2014). Single-case design studies are considered to have negative effects when a nontherapeutic change occurs in three fourths of the cases (CEC, 2014). CEC (2014) suggests studies that do not meet criteria for either positive or negative effects are classified as having neutral/mixed effects.

Single-case design studies are considered to have positive effects when "a functional relationship is established between the independent and dependent variables, resulting in a meaningful, therapeutic change in the targeted dependent variable for at least three fourths (75%) of the cases (depicted by tiers on a graph) in a study" (CEC, 2014, p. 7). In addition, there must be a total of three cases, and no cases should demonstrate an effect in the negative direction (CEC, 2014). Single-case design studies are considered to have negative effects when a nontherapeutic change occurs in three fourths of the cases (CEC, 2014). CEC (2014) suggests studies that do not meet criteria for either positive or negative effects are classified as having neutral/mixed effects.

CEC (2014) recommends the use of visual analysis for classifying the effects of methodologically sound single-case research, and although visual analysis is the traditional and most commonly used approach for evaluating the effects of single-case studies (Gast, 2010), scholars have more recently suggested using methods that combine non-overlapping data trends within phases to calculate the effect size for single-case studies (i.e., Tau-U; Parker, Vannest, Davis, & Sauber, 2011). However, the use of alternative analysis for the effects of single-case research is relatively new and, in some cases, "benchmarks are not as useful as direct interpretations of the change in relationship" (Vannest & Ninci, 2015, pp. 408–409). Thus, we did not set benchmarks for single-case effect sizes, but rather considered the results of both visual analysis and Tau-U calculations to classify the effects of methodologically sound single-case studies. Once effects of individual studies were classified, we classified the overall evidence-base of SBI using CEC's (2014) five levels of classification: evidence-based, potentially evidence-based, mixed evidence, insufficient evidence, and negative effects.

Results

Description of Included Studies

Across the 10 studies that met inclusion criteria, 106 participants were identified with LD and one student was identified with a specific MD; grade level for participants ranged from third to eighth grade. Five single-case design studies (i.e., Jitendra et al., 2002; Jitendra & Hoff, 1996; Jitendra, Hoff, & Beck, 1999; Sharp & Dennis, 2017; van Garderen, 2007) and one group design (Walker & Poteet, 1990) included only participants with LD. The other four studies included other student populations (e.g., students without disabilities identified with mathematics difficulty, students classified with other disabilities), but results were disaggregated for students with LD.

Whereas the dependent variable in all studies included mathematical word problem solving, four studies targeted addition and subtraction computation (Jitendra et al., 2007; Jitendra & Hoff, 1996; Jitendra et al., 1999; Walker & Poteet, 1990); two studies targeted multiplication and division (Jitendra et al., 2002; Xin et al., 2005); two studies targeted all four computations (Morin et al., 2017; van Garderen, 2007); one study targeted algebraic expression of mathematical relations (Xin, 2008); and one study targeted comparing and ordering fractions (Sharp & Dennis, 2017). In six of the studies, the researcher served as the interventionist (i.e., Jitendra & Hoff, 1996; Jitendra et al., 1999; Morin et al., 2017; Sharp & Dennis, 2017; van Garderen, 2007; Xin, 2008). Classroom teachers provided the intervention in three studies (i.e., Jitendra et al., 2002; Jitendra et al., 2007; Walker & Poteet, 1990), and researchers (i.e., doctoral students) and classroom teachers jointly served as interventionists in one study (Xin et al., 2005).

Seven studies included in this review used single-case design. Five of these studies used a multiple probe across participants design (i.e.,

Study	Students with LD	Interventionist	Setting	Design	Type of word problem
Jitendra and Hoff (1996)	n = 3; 3rd and 4th grade	Researcher	Outside of classroom	Multiple probe	Addition and subtraction
Jitendra, Hoff, and Beck (1999)	n = 4; 6th and 7th grade	Researcher	Outside of classroom	Multiple baseline	Addition and subtraction
Jitendra, DiPipi, and Perron-Jones (2002)	n = 4; 8th grade	Teacher	Resource room	Multiple probe	Multiplication and division
Jitendra et al. (2007)	n = 4; 3 LD, 1 MD; 3rd grade	Teachers	General education	Group design with random assignment	Addition and subtraction
Morin, Watson, Hester, and Raver (2017)	n = 1; 3rd grade	Researcher	After school, conference room	Multiple baseline	Addition, subtraction, and multiplication
Sharp and Dennis (2017)	n = 3; 4th grade	Researcher	Outside of classroom	Multiple probe	Comparing and ordering fractions
van Garderen (2007)	n = 3; 8th grade	Researcher	Outside classroom	Multiple probe	Addition, subtraction, multiplication, division
Walker and Poteet (1990)	n = 70; 6th, 7th, 8th grade	Teachers	Resource room	Group design with random assignment	Addition and subtraction
Xin (2008)	n = 1; 5th grade	Researcher	After school	Multiple probe	Algebraic expression
Xin, Jitendra, and Deatline-Buchman (2005)	n = 18; 6th, 7th, 8th grade	Researcher and teacher	Resource room	Group design with random assignment	Multiplication and proportions

Note. LD = learning disability; MD = mathematics disability.

Table 2. Description of Included Studies

Jitendra et al., 2002; Jitendra & Hoff, 1996; Sharp & Dennis, 2017; van Garderen, 2007; Xin, 2008), and two studies used a multiple baseline design (Jitendra et al., 1999; Morin et al., 2017). Two studies that used a group design employed random assignment of participants to groups (i.e., Jitendra et al., 2007; Xin et al., 2005). Walker and Poteet (1990) did not randomly assign participants to conditions; the teachers were randomly assigned. See Table 2 for a description of studies included in this review.

Presence of QIs

The QI ratings for each study are presented in Table 1. All studies included in this review met 14 of the 18 QIs that were applicable to both single-case and group design studies. Five single-case design studies (Jitendra et al., 2002; Jitendra et al., 1999; Morin et al., 2017; Sharp & Dennis, 2017; Xin, 2008) met the four additional QIs that specifically evaluate single-case research. One group design study (Xin et al., 2005) met the six additional QIs that are only applicable for group design research.

The QIs that were not met across each study were related to participant demographics (QI 2.2), implementation fidelity (QI 5.1) and a sufficient collection of baseline data (QI 6.6). For the QI related to participant demographics (QI 2.2), seven single-case design studies and two of the three group design studies (i.e., Walker & Poteet, 1990; Xin et al., 2005) provided sufficient information to determine included students' eligibility for special education services for LD. For example, three studies (i.e., Jitendra et al., 2002; Jitendra et al., 1999; Walker & Poteet, 1990) stated that participants met state eligibility criteria. Participant eligibility in Jitendra and Hoff's (1996) study was inferred due to students' placement in a special education day school for students with LD. Although Xin et al. (2005) did not specifically state that students were eligible for services under state criteria for LD, achievement and IQ scores were provided and, therefore, we concluded it met QI 2.2. All studies included in this review met implementation fidelity related to dosage. For example, the seven included single-case designs met this QI by providing a single-case graph; for group design studies, authors reported the length and duration of the intervention (see B. G. Cook et al., 2015). In addition, eight of 10 studies specifically reported results of implementation fidelity related to adherence (QI 5.1).

Evidence-Based Classification of SBI

The final step in classifying the evidence base of a practice is determining the effects of methodologically sound studies (CEC, 2014). Authors followed the guidelines prescribed by CEC (2014) for analyzing the effects of group design and single-case design studies and classified the effects as positive, neutral/mixed, or negative.

Per CEC (2014) guidelines, we evaluated the effect size as reported by the authors of the one methodologically sound group design study that was included in this review (i.e., Xin et al., 2005). Xin et al. (2005) reported significant differences between the treatment group (i.e., SBI) and the control group (i.e., general strategy instruction). Specifically, the authors reported effect sizes of 1.69 (posttest), 2.53 (maintenance), 2.72 (follow-up) and 0.89 (generalization). These effect sizes well surpassed our set criteria of ≥ 0.36. Therefore, we classified the results of Xin et al. (2005) as having positive effect on word problem solving for students with LD.

Study	Phases	Tau	Var-Tau	Z	p value	CI		
						85%	90%	95%
Jitendra, DiPipi, and Perron-Jones (2002)	MC	1.0000	0.2313	4.3232	.0000	[0.6669, 1]	[0.6195, 1]	[0.5466, 1]
	Vary	0.8750	0.2887	3.0311	.0024	[0.4593, 1]	[0.4001, 1]	[0.3092, 1]
	MC + vary	0.8786	0.3146	2.7929	.0052	[0.4256, 1]	[0.3611, 1]	[0.2620, 1]
Jitendra, Hoff, and Beck (1999)	One-step	0.5954	0.2169	2.7449	.0061	[0.2831, 0.9077]	[0.2386, 0.9522]	[0.1703, 1]
	Two-step	0.7953	0.2169	3.6664	.0002	[0.4829, 1]	[0.4385, 1]	[0.3701, 1]
Morin, Watson, Hester, and Raver (2017)	Bar model drawing	1.0000	0.2270	4.4059	.0000	[0.6732, 1]	[0.6266, 1]	[0.5551, 1]
Sharp and Dennis (2017)	Model drawing	1.0000	0.1911	5.2326	.0000	[0.7248, 1]	[0.6856, 1]	[0.6254, 1]
Xin (2008)	EG + MC	1.0000	0.3162	3.1623	.0016	[0.5446, 1]	[0.4798, 1]	[0.3802, 1]

Note. CI = confidence interval, MC = multiplicative compare, EG = equal groups.

Table 3. Tau-U for Each Intervention Phase

Study	Forest plot	Tau-U (95% CI)
Sharp and Dennis (2017)		1.00 [0.62, 1.00]
Morin, Watson, Hester, and Raver (2017)		1.00 [0.55, 1.00]
Xin (2008)		1.00 [0.38, 1.00]
Jitendra, DiPipi, and Perron-Jones (2002)		0.92 [0.60, 1.00]
Jitendra, Hoff, and Beck (1999)		0.69 [0.39, 0.99]
Overall		0.87 [0.67, 1.00]

Note. CI = confidence interval.

Table 4. Forest Plot and Effect Size Data by Experiment

Using the results of our visual analysis (i.e., examining changes in level, trend, variability, and immediacy of treatment; CEC, 2014) and Tau-U calculations, we determined all five methodologically sound single-case studies were identified as having positive effects (see Table 3 for effect sizes across phases for all studies), and we calculated an overall effect size of 0.69 for this study. Effect sizes across studies ranged from 0.69 to 1.0, with an overall effect size of 0.87. These effect sizes can be interpreted as a "large change" (Vannest & Ninci, 2015, p. 408). Table 4 provides a forest plot and effect size data for each methodologically sound study.

Authors reviewed the criteria for EBP classification which require the body of research to include "one methodologically sound group comparison study with random assignment, positive effects, and at least 30 total participants, as well as three methodologically sound single-case research studies with positive effects and at least 10 total participants" (CEC, 2014, p. 8). Although the results indicate that there were sufficient number of methodologically sound group design ($n = 1$) and single-case design studies ($n = 5$) with positive effects, there were not enough participants with LD ($n = 18$ in group design studies; $n = $

13 in single-case design studies) included in the interventions for SBI to meet the classification as an "evidence-based practice." However, results of this review indicate that SBI should be classified a "potentially evidence-based practice." That is, the body of SBI research meets the following criteria: (a) one methodologically sound group study with positive effects and two methodologically sound single-case design studies with positive effects; (b) a ratio of two methodologically sound studies with positive effects to one methodologically sound study with neutral/mixed effects; and (c) no studies with negative effects on target outcomes (CEC, 2014).

Discussion

Students with LD who struggle to demonstrate academic progress in the area of mathematics often experience challenges in both procedural and conceptual understanding in addition to being poor problem solvers. More specifically, students with LD may have WM deficits that lead to difficulties in creating a plan, identifying pertinent information, and organizing information to solve a mathematical word problem. SBI addresses these difficulties by using explicit instruction to provide students with the necessary conceptual understanding to solve mathematical word problems, and as determined by this review, it is considered a potentially EBP.

Effectiveness of SBI

Although our review did yield a sufficient *number* of methodologically sound studies to deem SBI an "evidence-based practice" for students with LD, the limited number of participants included within the studies resulted in classifying SBI a "potentially evidence-based practice" (CEC, 2014) and the effectiveness of this intervention should not be diminished. Furthermore, the collective body of related research (e.g., Jitendra, Nelson, et al., 2016; NMAP, 2008), combined with the results of our systematic review, clearly provide sufficient support for the use of SBI to improve the problem-solving performance of students with LD. It is important to note that the methodologically sound studies were extremely close to meeting the criteria of an "evidence-based" practice.

Had we included studies that targeted participants with mathematics difficulties (as opposed to only including students with LD), SBI would likely be considered an EBP. However, given (a) the intention of the CEC (2014) standards to determine effective interventions for students with a clearly identified disability status and (b) the ambiguity of the term "mathematics difficulties," we maintain it is important for researchers applying the CEC (2014) standards to limit the scope of evidence-based reviews to clearly focus on a specific and clearly defined population (e.g., students with LD). Moreover, in the four studies that were not rated as "methodologically sound," these studies only missed one QI. It is important to note that all of the studies that did not meet all QIs were published before the CEC (2014) standards were disseminated. It is likely that, due to changes in reporting norms over time (e.g., page limitations, implementation fidelity), the QIs that were missed are reflective of reporting differences rather than of study quality. Despite these minor shortcomings, there is strong evidence that supports the effectiveness of SBI for improving mathematical word problem solving for students with LD.

It is critical to emphasize that teachers should not abandon the use of practices that have not *yet* met the evidence-based standard. The classification of a practice as "potentially evidence-based" indicates exactly that there is great potential that, with more time and more research, there will likely be a sufficient amount of methodologically sound empirical literature to reclassify a practice as being evidence-based. In the case of SBI for students with LD, only 10 studies met the initial inclusion criteria; however, more than half of those studies were methodologically sound. The researchers conducting these studies implemented studies adhering to the QIs at high levels and demonstrated positive impacts on student performance. We assert that the results of this review are more indicative of a paucity of research of this intervention specifically for students identified with LD, as opposed to a paucity of high-quality research.

Limitations

Despite the promising results of this evidence-base review, we acknowledge the limitations that may have affected the findings. First, although we conducted a thorough database search using two reputable, academic databases, it is possible that relevant studies were omitted due limitations of the university's library subscription. Second, we did not utilize a "blind review" process during the inclusion or evaluation stages. However, we erred on the side of inclusivity at the first stage and assessed reliability rating 100% of studies at each stage of the analysis. Finally, the purpose of this review is to establish whether SBI is an EBP for students with LD. Therefore, the scope of this review was intentionally more narrow than previous reviews (e.g., Jitendra, Nelson, et al., 2016), and this likely accounts for the difference in results.

In addition, there were two main limitations to the literature that was included in our review. First, in all but four studies, the researcher served as the interventionist, raising question about the efficacy of SBI when it is implemented by a classroom teacher or school-based personnel. Second, although we limited the scope of this review to the impact of SBI on word problems, there was variation in the types of word problems (e.g., word problems involving comparing and ordering fractions, word problems involving addition, subtraction, multiplication, and/or division) targeted across studies. Given the limited amount of research in this area, there was not a sufficient number of studies available to warrant a review of the effectiveness of SBI a specific type of word problem. Similar to other strategies that are designed to support (meta)cognition across a variety of content areas and topics (e.g., mnemonics, graphic organizers), evidence and logic support a similar transfer of the effectiveness for schema-based instruction in solving word problems. Accounting for this limitation to the extant literature, our results indicate that educators should begin or continue to use SBI for students with LD.

Implications for Research and Practice

To continue building the evidence based on SBI for students with LD, we recommend researchers replicate methodologically sound studies included in this review. As is inherent with all evidence-based reviews, the QIs used to evaluate this body of research were published several years after the studies included in the review. In fact, with the exception of two studies (Morin et al., 2017; Sharp & Dennis, 2017), the most recent study in our review was published in 2008, almost a decade before the CEC (2014) standards were released. We commend the authors of studies included in this review for designing, implementing, and reporting the research in a way that met or approached these rigorous standards. However, because of significant author overlap, we recommend the replication of methodologically sound studies by research teams who are not affiliated with the original studies. This will to help further strengthen this body of literature (Travers, Cook, Therrien, & Coyne, 2016). We encourage other groups of researchers to design, implement, and report additional SBI interventions using the CEC (2014) QIs; we believe this will (a) address the lack of current empirical investigations and (b) increase the likelihood that SBI is eventually classified as an EBP.

Researchers interested in conducting SBI intervention research may also consider replicating methodologically sound studies for students with LD in high school settings. Although this review targeted SBI interventions for students in grades K–12, only participants in Grades 3 to 8 were included in the studies meeting our review criteria. We suggest building the research of SBI for students in high school settings may provide further insight into how to support older students with LD in increasing mathematical outcomes.

We also recommend researchers continue to examine SBI in combination with other interventions that may address computational fluency for students with LD (Riccomini et al., 2016). Although participants in the included studies were identified as poor word problem solvers, the majority were identified as being able to solve basic computations (e.g., Jitendra et al., 2002; Jitendra & Hoff, 1996; Jitendra et al., 1999; Xin, 2008). For example, participants in Jitendra et al. (1999) were able to compute basic addition and subtraction problems (with regrouping) with at least 90% accuracy. Students with LD who experience difficulty in mathematical computation will likely need additional interventions to effectively use SBI. Addressing computational and conceptual domains accounts for constraints on WM, which offers great potential for students with LD and MD (see Fuchs et al., 2014; Geary et al., 2007).

As previously discussed, SBI is a potentially EBP for students with LD and, thus, seems to be an important practice to consider for teachers targeting mathematical word problems with this particular population. Interestingly, only three studies included in this review utilized classroom teachers as the interventionists. Designing future investigations to include the teacher as the interventionist will provide more information about the efficacy of training teachers to implement this practice. Moreover, all SBI interventions included in the review, including those that did employ the use of the classroom teacher as the interventionist, relied on scripts developed by the research team. This indicates a need for the development of uniformed training and materials for using SBI when teaching students with LD how to understand and efficiently solve word problems in mathematics. We encourage researchers to collaborate with practitioners to develop and pilot test sample curriculum materials and training protocols to increase the accessibility, generalizability, and fidelity of the practice.

Conclusion

The research in mathematics is underdeveloped in such a way that special educators as well as general educators must make instructional decisions based on the best evidence (NMAP, 2008) when planning instruction for students with LD. It is our judgment, based on the results of this evidence-based review, that SBI has sufficient evidence to warrant the use by teachers and is likely more effective than current problem-solving strategies common in classrooms (Riccomini et al., 2016). The results of this systematic review bring continued insight into effective methods for teaching students with LD to understand and efficiently solve word problems in mathematics. The findings of this review build and extend the findings of previous analyses on SBI and provide additional confidence in the application of SBI by those responsible for providing students with LD high-quality mathematics programs and supports.

Declaration of Conflicting Interests

The author(s) declared no potential conflicts of interest with respect to the research, authorship, and/or publication of this article.

Funding

The author(s) received no financial support for the research, authorship, and/or publication of this article.

References

Baddeley, A. (1992). Working memory: The interface between memory and cognition. *Journal of Cognitive Neuroscience, 4*, 281–288.

Cohen, J. (1988). *Statistical power analysis for the behavioral sciences* (2nd ed.). Hillsdale, NJ: Lawrence Erlbaum.

Cook, B. G., Buysse, V., Klingner, J. K., Landrum, T. J., McWilliam, R. A., Tankersley, M., & Test, D. W. (2015). CEC's standards for classifying the evidence base of practices in special education. *Remedial and Special Education, 36,* 220–234.

Cook, S. C., Cook, B. G., & Cook, L. (2017). Classifying the evidence base of classwide peer tutoring for students with high- incidence disabilities. *Exceptionality, 25,* 9–25.

Council for Exceptional Children. (2014). *Council for Exceptional Children standards for evidence-based practices in special education.* http://www.cec.sped.org/~/media/Files/Standards/Evidence%20based%20Practices%20and%20Practice/CECs%20Evidence%20Based%20 Practice%20Standards.pdf

Edens, K., & Potter, E. (2008). How students "unpack" the structure of a word problem: Graphic representations and problem solving. *School Science and Mathematics, 108,* 184–196.

Fuchs, L. S., Powell, S. R., Seethaler, P. M., Cirino, P. T., Fletcher, J. M., Fuchs, D., & Hamlett, C. L. (2010). The effects of strategic counting instruction, with and without deliberate practice, on number combination skill among students with mathematics difficulties. *Learning and Individual Differences, 20,* 89–100.

Fuchs, L. S., Schumacher, R. F., Sterba, S. K., Long, J., Namkung, J., Malone, A., . . .Changas, P. (2014). Does working memory moderate the effects of fraction intervention? An aptitude-treatment interaction. *Journal of Educational Psychology, 106,* 499–514.

Garrett, A. J., Mazzocco, M. M., & Baker, L. (2006). Development of the metacognitive skills of prediction and evaluation in children with or without math disability. *Learning Disabilities Research & Practice, 21,* 77–88.

Gast, D. L. (2010). *Single subject research methodology in behavioral sciences.* New York, NY: Routledge.

Geary, D. C., Hoard, M. K., Byrd-Craven, J., Nugent, L., & Numtee, C. (2007). Cognitive mechanisms underlying achievement deficits in children with mathematical learning disability. *Child Development, 78,* 1343–1359.

Gersten, R., Fuchs, L. S., Compton, D., Coyne, M., Greenwood, C., & Innocenti, M. S. (2005). Quality indicators for group experimental and quasi-experimental research in special education. *Exceptional Children, 71,* 149–164.

Hegarty, M., & Kozhevnikov, M. (1999). Types of visual–spatial representations and mathematical problem solving. *Journal of Educational Psychology, 91,* 684–689.

Horner, R. H., Carr, E. G., Halle, J., McGee, G., Odom, S., & Wolery, M. (2005). The use of single-subject research to identify evidence-based practice in special education. *Exceptional Children, 71* (2), 165–179.

Hua, Y., Woods-Groves, S., Kaldenberg, E. R., Lucas, K. G., & Therrien, W. J. (2015). Effects of the TIP strategy on problem solving skills of young adults with intellectual disability. *Education and Training in Autism and Developmental Disabilities, 50,* 31–42.

Hwang, J., & Riccomini, P. J. (2016). Enhancing mathematical problem solving for secondary students with or at risk of learning disabilities: A literature review. *Learning Disabilities Research & Practice, 31,* 169–181.

Jitendra, A. K., DiPipi, C. M., & Perron-Jones, N. (2002). An exploratory study of schema-based word-problem—Solving instruction for middle school students with learning disabilities: An emphasis on conceptual and procedural understanding. *The Journal of Special Education, 36,* 23–38.

Jitendra, A. K., Dupuis, D. N., Star, J. R., & Rodriguez, M. C. (2016). The effects of schema-based instruction on the proportional thinking of students with mathematics difficulties with and without reading difficulties. *Journal of Learning Disabilities, 49,* 354–367.

Jitendra, A. K., Griffin, C. C., Haria, P., Leh, J., Adams, A., & Kaduvettoor, A. (2007). A comparison of single and multiple strategy instruction on third-grade students' mathematical problem solving. *Journal of Educational Psychology, 99,* 115–127.

Jitendra, A. K., Griffin, C. C., McGoey, K., Gardill, M. C., Bhat, P., & Riley, T. (1998). Effects of mathematical word problem solving by students at risk or with mild disabilities. *The Journal of Educational Research, 91,* 345–355.

Jitendra, A. K., & Hoff, K. (1996). The effects of schema-based instruction on the mathematical word-problem-solving performance of students with learning disabilities. *Journal of Learning Disabilities, 29,* 422–431.

Jitendra, A. K., Hoff, K., & Beck, M. M. (1999). Teaching middle school students with learning disabilities to solve word problems using a schema-based approach. *Remedial and Special Education, 20,* 50–64.

Jitendra, A. K., Nelson, G., Pulles, S. M., Kiss, A. J., & Houseworth, J. (2016). Is mathematical representation of problems an evidence-based strategy for students with mathematics difficulties? *Exceptional Children, 83,* 8–25. doi:10.1177/0014402915625062

Kalyuga, S. (2006). Rapid cognitive assessment of learners' knowledge structures. *Learning and Instruction, 16,* 1–11.

Kingsdorf, S., & Krawec, J. (2016). Assessing a multi-component math intervention within a cognitive-behavioral framework on the word problem-solving responses of a diverse group of third graders. *Cogent Education, 3,* 1160638.

Li, Y., & Geary, D. C. (2013). Developmental gains in visuospatial memory predict gains in mathematics achievement. *PLoS ONE, 8*(7), e70160.

Lipsey, M. W., Puzio, K., Yun, C., Hebert, M. A., Steinka-Fry, K., Cole, M. W., . . . Busick, M. D. (2012). *Translating the statistical representation of the effects of education interventions into more readily interpretable forms* (NCSER 2013-3000). Washington, DC: National Center for Special Education Research, Institute of Education Sciences, U.S. Department of Education. https://ies.ed.gov/ncser/pubs/20133000/pdf/20133000.pdf

Moher, D., Liberati, A., Tetzlaff, J., & Altman, D. G. (2009). Preferred reporting items for systematic reviews and meta- analyses: The PRISMA statement. *PLoS Medicine, 6*(7).

Montague, M. (2008). Self-regulation strategies to improve mathematical problem solving for students with learning disabilities. *Learning Disability Quarterly, 31*, 37–44.

Morin, L. L., Watson, S. M., Hester, P., & Raver, S. (2017). The use of a bar model drawing to teach word problem solving to students with mathematics difficulties. *Learning Disability Quarterly, 40*, 91–104. doi:10.1177/0731948717690116

National Council of Teachers of Mathematics. (2014). *Principles to actions: Ensuring mathematical success for all.* Reston, VA: Author.

National Mathematics Advisory Panel. (2008). *Foundations for success: The final report of the National Mathematics Advisory Panel.* Washington, DC: U.S. Department of Education. http://www2.ed.gov/about/bdscomm/list/mathpanel/report/final-report.pdf

Palincsar, A. S., & Brown, D. A. (1987). Enhancing instructional time through attention to metacognition. *Journal of Learning Disabilities, 20*, 66–75.

Parker, R. I., Vannest, K. J., Davis, J. L., & Sauber, S. B. (2011). Combining nonoverlap and trend for single-case research: Tau-U. *Behavior Therapy, 42*, 284–299.

Powell, S. R. (2011). Solving word problems using schemas: A review of the literature. *Learning Disabilities Research & Practice, 26*, 94–108.

Powell, S. R., Fuchs, L. S., Fuchs, D., Cirino, P. T., & Fletcher, J. M. (2009). Effects of fact retrieval tutoring on third-grade students with math difficulties with and without reading difficulties. *Learning Disabilities Research & Practice, 24*, 1–11.

Riccomini, P. J., Hwang, J., & Morano, S. (2016). Developing mathematical problem solving through strategic instruction: Much more than a keyword. In B. G. Cook, M. Tankersley, & T.J. Landrum (Eds.), *Advances in learning and behavioral disabilities: Instructional practices with and without empirical validity* (Vol. 29, pp. 39–60). West Yorkshire, England: Emerald Group Publishing Limited.

Rosenzweig, C., Krawec, J., & Montague, M. (2011). Metacognitive strategy use of eighth-grade students with and without learning disabilities during mathematical problem solving: A think-aloud analysis. *Journal of Learning Disabilities, 44*, 508–520.

Sharp, E., & Dennis, M. S. (2017). Model drawing strategy for fraction word problem solving of fourth-grade students with learning disabilities. *Remedial and Special Education, 38*, 181–192.

Steele, D. F., & Johanning, D. I. (2004). A schematic–theoretic view of problem solving and development of algebraic thinking. *Educational Studies in Mathematics, 57*, 65–90.

Swanson, H. L. (2012). Cognitive profile of adolescents with math disabilities: Are the profiles different from those with reading disabilities? *Child Neuropsychology, 18*, 125–143.

Swanson, H. L., Jerman, O., & Zheng, X. (2009). Math disabilities and reading disabilities: Can they be separated? *Journal of Psychoeducational Assessment, 27*, 175–196.

Swanson, H. L., Lussier, C., & Orosco, M. (2013). Effects of cognitive strategy interventions and cognitive moderators on word problem solving in children at risk for problem solving difficulties. *Learning Disabilities Research & Practice, 28*, 170–183.

Swanson, H. L., Orosco, M. J., & Lussier, C. M. (2014). The effects of mathematics strategy instruction for children with serious problem-solving difficulties. *Exceptional Children, 80*, 149–168.

Sweigart, C. A., Collins, L. W., Evanovich, L. L., & Cook, S. C. (2016). An evaluation of the evidence base for performance feedback to improve teacher praise using CEC's quality indicators. *Education and Treatment of Children, 39*, 419–444.

Travers, J. C., Cook, B. G., Therrien, W. J., & Coyne, M. D. (2016). Replication research and special education. *Remedial and Special Education, 37*, 195–204.

U.S. Department of Education, Institute of Education Sciences, National Center for Education Statistics. (2018). *National assessment of educational progress: Mathematics assessment*. Washington, DC. https://nces.ed.gov/nationsreportcard/mathematics/

van Garderen, D. (2007). Teaching students with LD to use diagrams to solve mathematical word problems. *Journal of Learning Disabilities, 40*, 540–553. doi:10.1177/002221940

van Garderen, D., & Montague, M. (2003). Visual-spatial representation, mathematical problem solving, and students of varying abilities. *Learning Disabilities Research & Practice, 18*, 246–254.

Vannest, K. J., & Ninci, J. (2015). Evaluating intervention effects in single-case research designs. *Journal of Counseling & Development, 93*, 403–411.

Vukovic, R. K., & Siegel, L. S. (2010). Academic and cognitive characteristics of persistent mathematics difficulty from first through fourth grade. *Learning Disabilities Research & Practice, 25*, 25–38.

Walker, D. W., & Poteet, J. A. (1990). A comparison of two methods of teaching mathematics story problem-solving with learning disabled students. *National Forum of Special Education Journal, 1*, 44–51.

Watson, S. M., & Gable, R. A. (2010). Using knowledge of student cognition to differentiate instruction. In *Reaching every learner: Differentiating instruction in theory and practice.* Learn NC. http://www.learnnc.org/lp/editions/every-learner/6693

Watson, S. M., & Gable, R. A. (2013). Unraveling the complex nature of mathematics learning disability: Implications for research and practice. *Learning Disability Quarterly, 36,* 178–187.

What Works Clearinghouse. (2014). *Procedures and standards handbook* (Version 3.0). Institute of Education Sciences. https://ies.ed.gov/ncee/wwc/Docs/referencere-sources/wwc_procedures_v3_0_standards_handbook.pdf

Xin, Y. P. (2008). The effect of schema-based instruction in solving mathematics word problems: An emphasis on prealgebraic conceptualization of multiplicative relations. *Journal for Research in Mathematics Education, 39,* 526–551.

Xin, Y. P., Jitendra, A. K., & Deatline-Buchman, A. (2005). Effects of mathematical word problem—Solving instruction on middle school students with learning problems. *The Journal of Special Education, 39,* 181–192.

Guiding Questions

1. On a scale of 1 to 10, what is your confidence in the reliability of the journal Ms. Jackson's article is published in? Provide evidence for your rating.
2. Based on the article title and abstract, is this a useful article given Ms. Jackson's problems and context? Explain why.
3. Does the introduction provide a rationale for the purpose of the literature review? What is that rationale? Provide a summary of the introduction in your own words.
4. Are research questions explicitly stated? If not, should they be and why?
5. On a scale of 1 to 10, how rigorous would you rate the method section of Ms. Jackson's article? Provide evidence for your rating.
6. Are the results of the article presented clearly and in an objective manner? Explain your answer. Summarize the results section in your own words, including data.
7. On a scale of 1 to 10, how well does the discussion section answer the "so what?" question? In other words, does the authors explain why the results matter? Provide evidence for your rating.
8. On a scale of 1 to 10, how confident are you in the overall believability, reliability, and validity of Ms. Jackson's article? Provide evidence for your rating.
9. What criticisms do you have of Ms. Jackson's article? What are some limitations of the article that the authors did not identify?

10. Given your answers for the previous nine questions, what conclusions can Ms. Jackson draw about schema-based instruction?

Use Professional Judgment to Implement Researched Strategies Across Individual Contexts

After reading the literature review on SBI, Ms. Jackson is convinced that the practice is valid and could improve her math teaching instruction. She now needs to learn more about how to effectively implement SBI with her students. Some more poking around on the internet leads Ms. Jackson to a website called Pirate Math Equation Quest. It is a free program for educators to assist in math word problem instruction using SBI. Ms. Jackson recognizes that the creators of the program are prominent researchers in special education and mathematics. Between that and her recent reading of the SBI literature review, she is confident in the validity of the program (see Chapter 10 for additional details on product and curricula reviews).

Ms. Jackson is pleased to see extensive resources provided with the Pirate Math Equation Quest program, including teacher materials, student materials, and instructional videos. She knows it will take planning time to look through the materials and figure out how best to integrate them into her instruction. Ms. Jackson also wants to offer this supplemental instruction as a small-group intervention or remediation tool for any student whom she encounters, not just those on her caseload. Thankfully, the program offers resources for both individual and small-group instruction. Ms. Jackson is excited to have a new intervention that can assist her students in becoming more successful in mathematics.

WHERE CAN I FIND MORE INFORMATION ABOUT MATH INSTRUCTION?

IRIS Module: The IRIS Center provides a wide variety of resources and services to suit a diverse set of instructional needs and circumstances. This module explores high-quality mathematics instruction: https://iris.peabody.vanderbilt.edu/module/math/#content.

Pirate Math Equation Quest: With Pirate Math Equation Quest, students receive explicit instruction on reading, interpreting, setting up, and solving word problems with a focus on schemas. This free, evidence-based program provides teacher and student resources for individual and small-group instruction of students experiencing mathematics difficulty. Visit and download materials at https://www.piratemathequationquest.com/index.html.

The Science of Math: The Science of Math website provides resources related to effective math instruction. Its goal is to ensure that all students, regardless of background or status, have equitable access to high-quality math instruction. To guide the Science of Math, the creators rely on well-researched instructional strategies and research about how students learn. Explore more at https://www.thescienceofmath.com/.

SRSD Math: SRSD Math is a collection of research-based strategies grounded in the self-regulated strategy development (SRSD) framework. This website provides information and resources for teachers to implement SRSD strategies. It can be found at https://www.teachsrsdmath.com/.

DISCUSSION QUESTIONS

1. What are some common barriers to math instruction and learning?
2. Explain the differences between procedural and conceptual knowledge? Why are both important?
3. Research and explain some other best practices in mathematics instruction besides those listed in the chapter.
4. Explain your experience reading the provided literature review. What did you learn from the experience? What questions do you have?
5. What could you do differently if you were in Ms. Jackson's position?

KEY TERMS

conceptual knowledge: Multifaceted construct that includes knowledge of categories, relationships, principles, and representations.

concrete–representation–abstract: A three-stage learning process where students learn through physical manipulation, pictorial representation, and abstract notation.

explicit instruction: A systematic, direct, engaging, and success-oriented method of teaching.

mathematics literacy: The ability to problem-solve, reason, and analyze information.

procedural knowledge: Refers to the step-by-step algorithms needed to solve math problems.

scaffolded instruction: Instructional technique in which teachers offer support for students learning new skills by systematically building on their experiences and knowledge.

schema: A framework, outline, or plan for solving a problem.

schema-based instruction: A word problem–solving strategy that teaches students to identify problem types by focusing on the underlying structure of the mathematical situation.

self-regulated strategy development: The use of goal setting, self-monitoring, self-talk, and self-reinforcement to monitor and manage behaviors for success.

working memory: The small amount of temporary information that can be held in mind and used in the execution of a cognitive task.

REFERENCES

Archer, A. L., & Hughes, C. A. (2010). *Explicit instruction: Effective and efficient teaching.* Guilford.

Baddeley, A. (1992). Working memory: The interface between memory and cognition. *Journal of Cognitive Neuroscience, 4*, 281–288. https://doi.org/10.1162/jocn.1992.4.3.281

Bouck, E. C., Satsangi, R., & Park, J. (2018). The concrete–representational–abstract approach for students with learning disabilities: An evidence-based practice synthesis. *Remedial and Special Education, 39*(4), 211–228. https://doi.org/10.1177/0741932517721712

Bruner, J. S., & Kenney, H. J. (1965). Representation and mathematics learning. *Monographs of Society for Research in Child Development, 30*(1), 50–59. https://www.jstor.org/stable/1165708

Fuchs, L. S., Schumacher, R. F., Sterba, S. K., Long, J., Namkung, J., Malone, A., Hamlett, C. L., Jordan, N. C., Gersten, R., Siegler, R. S., & Changas, P. (2014). Does working memory moderate the effects of fraction intervention? An aptitude treatment interaction. *Journal of Educational Psychology, 106*, 499–514. https://psycnet.apa.org/doi/10.1037/a0034341

Gersten, R., Chard, D. J., Jayanthi, M., Baker, S. K., Morphy, P., & Flojo, J. (2009). Mathematics instruction for students with learning disabilities: A meta-analysis of instructional components. *Review of Educational Research, 79*, 1202–1242. https://doi.org/10.3102/0034654309334431

Hott, B. L., Peltier, C., Heiniger, S., Palacios, M., Le, M. T., & Chen, M. (2021). Using schema-based instruction to improve the mathematical problem solving skills of a rural student with EBD. *Learning Disabilities: A Contemporary Journal, 19*(2), 127–142. https://files.eric.ed.gov/fulltext/EJ1314840.pdf

IRIS Center. (n.d.). *SRSD: Using learning strategies to enhance student learning.* https://iris.peabody.vanderbilt.edu/module/srs/#content

Jitendra, A. K., Dupuis, D. N., Star, J. R., & Rodriquez, M. C. (2016). The effects of schema-based instruction on the proportional thinking of students with mathematics difficulties with and without reading difficulties. *Journal of Learning Disabilities, 49*(4), 354–367. https://psycnet.apa.org/doi/10.1177/0022219414554228

Li, Y., & Geary, D. C. (2013). Developmental gains in visuospatial memory predict gains in mathematics achievement. *PLoS ONE, 8*(7), e70160. https://doi.org/10.1371/journal.pone.0070160

Miller, S. P., Stringfellow, J. L., Kaffar, B. J., Ferreira, D., & Mancl, D. B. (2011). Developing computation competence among students who struggle with mathematics. *Teaching Exceptional Children, 44*(2), 38–44. https://doi.org/10.1177/004005991104400204

National Association for Educational Progress. (2022). *NAEP report card: 2022 NAEP mathematics assessment*. The Nations Report Card. https://www.nationsreportcard.gov/highlights/mathematics/2022/

Swanson, H. L. (2012). Cognitive profile of adolescents with math disabilities: Are the profiles different from those with reading disabilities? *Child Neuropsychology, 18*, 125–143. https://doi.org/10.1080/09297049.2011.589377

Swanson, H. L., Orosco, M. J., & Lussier, C. M. (2014). The effects of mathematics strategy instruction for children with serious problem-solving difficulties. *Exceptional Children, 80*, 149–168. https://doi.org/10.1177/001440291408000202

Vukovic, R. K., & Siegel, L. S. (2010). Academic and cognitive characteristics of persistent mathematics difficulty from first through fourth grade. *Learning Disabilities Research & Practice, 25*, 25–38. https://doi.org/10.1111/j.1540-5826.2009.00298.x

Zacharopoulos, G., Sella, F., & Cohen Kadosh, R. (2021). The impact of a lack of mathematical education on brain development and future attainment. *Proceedings of the National Academy of Sciences, 118*(24), e2013155118. https://doi.org/10.1073/pnas.2013155118

Chapter 10

Product and Curriculum Reviews

Hopefully, the case has been made that special education teachers are better educators with experience in accessing and judiciously consuming research to inform practice. Chapters 8 and 9 examined how a teacher identified a problem and used research literature to find a solution. However, sometimes solutions to problems are presented to us before we know there is a problem. Commercials are designed to make consumers realize they need a product and then to purchase it. The field of education is no different. Billions of dollars are spent every year on educational resources, such as textbooks, curriculum materials, and technology. It is a massive market for companies to innovate within and profit from, and there have been many valuable educational programs and tools created for the benefit of teachers and students with disabilities. Yet it can be challenging for teachers to differentiate between educational products that are legitimate versus those that are not. A company may have a large marketing budget, and their product may look like it will solve every problem. But will it really? How can special educators sift through the plethora of educational products and curricula to identify what might be worth pursuing as a new tool and what to quickly move on from?

Evidence-based practices (EBPs), as identified in research, typically do not require a monetary purchase. As the term "practice" implies, they are behaviors or procedures that teachers can do to affect student outcomes. Sure, a variety of resources might be needed to perform the practice, such as data collection sheets to monitor behavior, a recording device for video reflection, or tangibles to hand out for reinforcement, but generally, there are no up-front purchases. Educational products and curricula are different. These are designed by companies to solve a problem—or relieve a pain, as the industry says—and are sold to consumers to make a profit. There have been many educational products and curricula supported by research to positively affect student outcomes. There have also been many unproven products that might look flashy but have not been empirically validated. As pedagogical understanding deepens within educational research and technology advances, there are many opportunities for private companies to develop truly beneficial educational products and curricula. It is up to the consumer (e.g., special education teacher) to explore which ones are valid and worth considering for adoption.

In this final chapter, we will discuss how special education teachers can critically examine educational products and curricula to assess their quality and advocate for their adoption if deemed valuable. We will answer these essential questions:

1. What are some of the issues concerning product and curriculum reviews?
2. How do I assess the validity of products and curricula?
3. How do I advocate for the adoption of a product or curriculum in my school?
4. Where can I find more information about product and curriculum reviews?

WHAT ARE SOME OF THE ISSUES CONCERNING PRODUCT AND CURRICULUM REVIEWS?

The U.S. economy is driven by the consumer. In fact, nearly 70% of economic activity is contributed to by consumer spending (Bureau of Economic Analysis, 2018). Whether it is through television commercials, pop-up internet ads, or billboards along the highway, nearly everywhere we look, advertisements are trying to sell us a product or service. Although many advertisements may seem redundant and irrelevant, marketing a product and getting it "in front of consumers" is the most proactive way to ensure a purchase—and the success of the product. This is true for trivial products, such as a new cereal type with a catchy cartoon character, or more consequential innovations, such as a new diabetes drug. Decades of research have gone into marketing strategies and how best to find consumers, present a product, and secure a purchase. The internet opened a whole new world to advertisers and reaching consumers with websites, search engines, and social media.

A vast majority of people (90%) have aversive perceptions of advertisements (An, 2020). There are varying degrees of annoyance depending on the medium, such as online pop-up ads (73% dislike), TV ads (36% dislike), and magazine/print ads (18% dislike; An, 2020). Nevertheless, advertisements are a necessary component to the economy. Any business owner recognizes the importance of promoting their product or service. Sometimes that requires paid advertising, but other times, it is through happy customers telling other potential customers.

One important aspect of business is understanding **market size**. Market size is simply the number of people who could become customers. In education, that is a lot of people! Given compulsory education laws in every state (Markelz & Bateman, 2021), every child must attend school, whether public, private, or homeschooled. In the fall of 2021, 49.4 million children attended public elementary and secondary schools, and there were 3.2 million full-time teachers employed (National Center for Education Statistics, 2023). Apart from slight macro trends with enrollment, the education market remains stable with new students entering education every year. It is only natural that entrepreneurs will want to enter the education market to innovate new ideas and sell products.

Types of Products and Curricula

Gone are *Little House on the Prairie* days where school buildings consisted of one classroom for children of all ages. A chalkboard at the front of the room was the teacher's main resource, and students used paper and pencils. Today, educational products and technology are infused throughout all aspects of education. Although this is not an exhaustive list, we can organize the types of products and curricula into general buckets for understanding.

Physical Products

From a business perspective, a new product is successful if it continues to sell. From a consumer perspective, a new product is successful if it does what it is supposed to do. The array of physical educational products on the market today is vast, especially in the early childhood developmental years. In fact, there is a blurring of lines between toys and educational products because a child's using their imagination to play with a Lego set is both fun and educational. In special education, there are educational products designed for specific purposes, for example, a rubber mold that fits on a pencil to assist with a student's grip, a visual timer that sits on a student's desk to help with time management, math manipulatives, noise-canceling headphones, and so much more. The list of physical educational products designed to solve a problem or support a skill is extensive. Although some of these products might be small, cheap, and ordinary (e.g., stickers for doing a good job), others might be larger, more expensive, and integral to a student's success (e.g., an electric wheelchair).

Texts and Curricula

Textbooks, novels, and curricula are central in the education of students. Textbooks and curricula might be synonymous sometimes, but a curriculum does not have to include a textbook. A curriculum might be a series of worksheets, projects, or individualized goals. Textbooks and novels often support a curriculum. A curriculum can be defined as a course of study that includes learning objectives, content of instruction, teaching methods, and evaluation or assessment of student performance. School districts adopt subject-specific and grade level–appropriate curricula to guide the progression of student learning. Apart from curricula often thought of, such as math and reading, shorter and more targeted curricula are developed for a variety of knowledge and skills as well, for example, a three-week curriculum on cyberbullying prevention.

As we discussed in Chapter 1, curriculum debates have been going on for decades about what should or should not be included in the education of students. These debates often take place at state levels given the individuality of state education systems (Markelz et al., 2023). National conversations have shaped curricula through movements, such as the **Common Core Standards** (Gewertz, 2015), but individual states maintain authority to decide what standards their children should obtain. Larger curricula designed for grade-level subjects (e.g., social studies) are big business. Private companies, often in collaboration with researchers from universities and state/district educational leaders, are involved in the designing, testing, adoption, and implementation of curricula.

Hardware and Software

In the past 30-plus years, technology has flooded into our lives and schools. Physical textbooks and workbooks are quickly being replaced with e-books and online programs. Many schools now have a tablet or laptop device for each student to use throughout the day and at home to complete academic content. The assortment of educational games, apps, and programs is overwhelming. **Learning management systems** (LMSs) are necessary online programs to organize courses, modules, assignments, instruction, and communication. Similar to physical products, there are inconsequential items, such as a free app that allows a student to practice fact fluency, all the way to extensive intervention programs with significant subscription fees and everything in between. Believe it or not, special education teachers used to write individualized education programs with paper and pencil! Now, software systems facilitate the entry of information and collection of data. We will not even begin to predict where technology will take education with the development of artificial intelligence (AI), but we know it will undoubtedly happen.

HOW DO I ASSESS THE VALIDITY OF PRODUCTS AND CURRICULA?

With so many products, texts, and curricula and so much technology on the market, it can be difficult and overwhelming to decide if something would benefit your instruction and students. Commercial marketing will always be present through TV and pop-up ads, sponsored search results, mailers, and more; however, social media has added a new aspect to marketing with professional influencers pushing products or colleagues and their Pinterest pages. Websites such as Teachers Pay Teachers have online marketplaces where educators can purchase downloadable resources created by other educators.

Smaller product purchases may seem trivial in the overall effect on student behaviors and outcomes, but teachers should be careful not to gravitate toward false narratives about trending fads. Take fidget spinners for example. With increasing numbers of children diagnosed with attention deficit hyperactivity disorder (ADHD), many parents are searching for help, making them vulnerable to targeted—and potentially false—marketing (Davis, 2017). Research evidence does not support the use of fidget toys in classroom for students with ADHD (Kriescher et al., 2023), but that does not stop many parents or teachers from "believing" they help. In fact, the field of special education is filled with products promising parents a quick fix or solution to a behavior their child may be demonstrating. Of course, this type of **predatory advertising** is not isolated to parents and educators of children with disabilities. The health industry is also filled with revolutionary discoveries to lose weight and live forever with the simple purchase of a pill (sarcasm implied). There are, however, many well-intentioned inventors and companies hoping to solve a problem and make people's lives better. How can you tell the difference?

Understanding the **validity** of a product is about ensuring the product will do what it is supposed to do. Let's say a company is marketing a new chair that will help kids focus and stay on task. That is a pretty big claim! Should schools rush out and buy thousands of new chairs, or should they first check the validity of the chairs before spending thousands of dollars? The next section of this chapter will lay out general steps teachers can take to investigate and assess the validity of products and curricula (Figure 10.1).

Step 1: Conduct a Search

Usinga search engine, such as Google, is a great first step to explore whether others have assessed the validity of a product or curriculum. News or magazine articles may have been written to discuss the evidence for or against

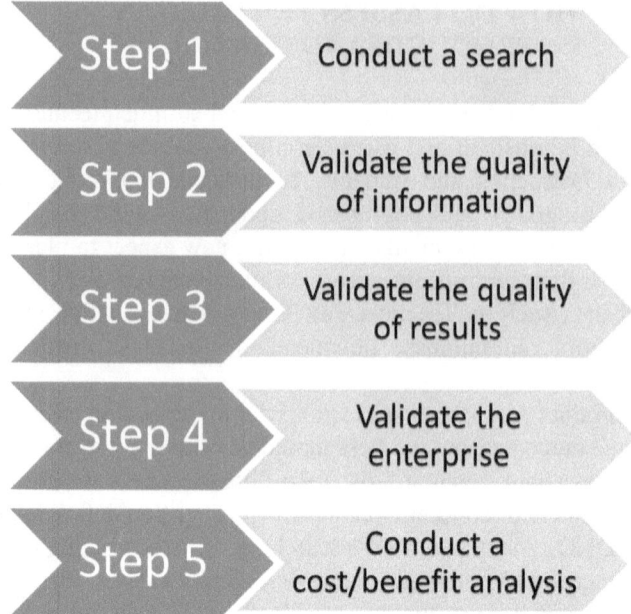

Figure 10.1 Steps to Assessing the Validity of a Product or Curriculum

something. Peer-reviewed research will appear at the top of a general Google search, but Google Scholar can be used to examine additional research articles. Colleagues can be asked about whether they have heard about or used a particular product or curriculum. Curricula and more extensive products will likely have corresponding websites dedicated to informing potential consumers about the product or curriculum. Some of these websites might have a tab that lists previous research supporting the validity of the product or curriculum.

Step 2: Validate the Quality of the Information

After conducting a wide search to gather information on the product or curriculum you are interested in adopting, the next step is to validate the quality of that information. Remember that just because a product does not have information about it, does not immediately mean it is invalid and not worth exploring further. Any new product takes time for teachers to adopt it and for scholars to research it. However, teachers should approach new products without evidence of their validity with skepticism. Using one's professional judgment is also needed to determine if a product is supported by well-known pedagogical practices. Take, for example, a new student-centered self-monitoring app that students can have on their tablet at their desk while completing independent work. Although an initial search found no information about this particular app, self-monitoring as a strategy for behavior change has ample empirical support (Bruhn et al., 2015). A teacher can have more confidence in a product if it is grounded in more universally known best educational practices. At the same time, products that are grounded in unsupported practices should be dismissed from consideration, for example, the pervasive educational myth of **learning styles**. The myth is that designing lessons to appeal to a student's learning style (i.e., visual, auditory, or kinesthetic) accelerates student learning. This educational theory has consistently been debunked (Furey, 2020), yet its intuitive appeal is so strong that many educators and preparation programs continue to promote it as a valid practice.

If information about the product or curriculum is located, assessing the quality of that information is important. Is the information published from a **credible** online newspaper, magazine, or education-focused website? An article examining the claims of a new product published by *Education Week* (https://www.edweek.org/) should hold more credibility than an individual's blog post with 17 views. If empirical research has been conducted on the product, then the quality of the publishing journal should be assessed. Chapter 2 provided information about various academic journals, but questions to ask are (a) Does the journal publish peer-reviewed research? (b) Does the journal have an impact factor? (c) If the journal is open access, do authors have to pay an article processing charge (APC; "pay to publish")? and (d) Do the authors of the article have an established track record for rigorous empirical research in this area?

Step 3: Validate the Quality of the Results

Part II of this book examined various methodologies in special education research. We discussed how scientific practitioners can read and interpret results sections based on experimental design (e.g., single case, quantitative, or qualitative). If a product or curriculum has had empirical research conducted to test its validity and effect on student or teacher outcomes, then examining those results is an important step. It is not sufficient, for example, to simply see that a website lists a few research articles and believe the product does what the company claims. Teachers should also be careful not to conflate two commonly used phrases when discussing educational curricula and programs. **Research-based** programs are developed or informed by scientific theories or research findings. The program, however, does not have its own evidence to support its effectiveness. An **evidence-based** program has undergone empirical testing and systematic evaluation to determine its effectiveness. As an example, an educational researcher may develop a reading fluency intervention based on research from educational theories and published studies. The researcher can describe their program as being research based because the intervention is grounded in previously studied theories and practices. The intervention, however, does not have its own evidence of effectiveness. If the researcher then conducts a study to test how well the intervention works, the results demonstrate positive effects, and the study is peer reviewed, then the intervention is approaching the category of evidence based.

Step 4: Validate the Enterprise

An additional step to validating a product or curriculum is to scrutinize the selling company, organization, or individuals. For more extensive products or curricula, there will likely be a corresponding website with valuable information. Many websites will have an "about" tab that describes the company or organization structure, leadership team, and mission. Identifying whether the company is for profit or nonprofit suggests motivations for selling the product or curriculum. **For-profit** companies seek to provide a product or service to consumers for financial gain. Ensuring the product sells for more than it costs to produce is essential to for-profit companies. Continuously increasing the quantity of products sold also contributes to a for-profit company's sustainability. **Nonprofit** organizations seek to provide a product or service to the community with no intention of earning a profit. There may be costs associated with the product or service, but those costs are to maintain the community benefit, not to gain financially.

One may initially think nonprofit organizations are superior to for-profit companies regarding educational products because they are not seeking financial gain; however, there are many complexities to this comparison. Entrepreneurship is essential to the growth of the U.S. economy, and it is the American dream for many to solve problems by innovating and creating. Financial incentives have—and will continue—to drive revolutionary innovations that advance society in many great ways. The same is true for educational products and curricula. Knowing whether a product or curriculum is being sold by a for-profit company or nonprofit organization is only one data point in validity assessment.

Step 5: Conduct a Cost-Benefit Analysis

The final step to assessing the validity of a product or curriculum is to conduct a cost-benefit analysis. There are several aspects to consider when determining whether the purchase and adoption of a product or curricula is worth it (see Figure 10.2). First, does it solve a problem? Throughout this book, we claim special education teachers are called to be scientific practitioners. That

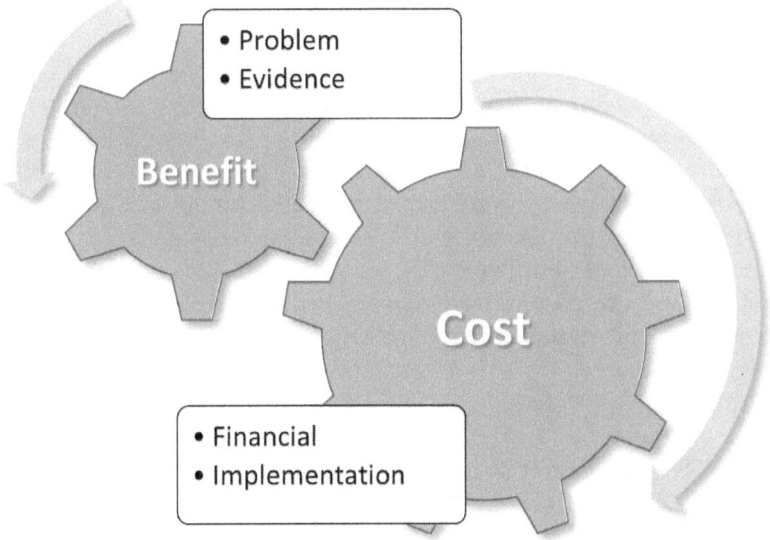

Figure 10.2 Cost-Benefit Calculations

means one must be able to (1) identify and understand a problem in the classroom, (2) know where to look for potential researched solutions, (3) read and understand a variety of research articles to gather information and (4) use professional judgment to implement researched strategies across individual contexts. All of these components of a scientific practitioner will help a teacher assess whether a product or curriculum is likely to solve their problem.

The second aspect to consider is whether the product or curriculum has evidence of effectiveness. Based on the steps to assessing a curriculum's validity, there may be ample evidence suggesting the curriculum expedites student academic performance and that teachers and students highly rate the program. Or there may be minimal evidence because a product is new and has not been studied by scholars yet. Or there may be no evidence because the product is a marketing fad with no empirical support. Most likely, a product or curriculum will fall somewhere within the spectrum of strong evidence-based support and no information. Using one's professional judgment is needed.

The third aspect to consider is the monetary cost of the product or curriculum. For cheaper items, monetary cost may factor little into the decision-making process. More expensive products or curricula will be a major factor of consideration within the cost-benefit analysis. Not only will an up-front cost be necessary, but there might also be ongoing costs associated, such as subscription fees.

Finally, one should consider implementation costs. These costs may be unforeseen monetary costs, such as additional trainings to support teachers, but also other implementation costs, such as personnel time, resistance to adoption, and sustainability. How long will it take those using the new product or curriculum to become fluent with it? Do those who will be using it want to use it? Will there be resistance to adopting the product or curriculum? What supports are needed to ensure the product or curriculum is used and does not end up in a closet somewhere? All of these questions are related to whether a product or curriculum is implemented with the fidelity required to be successful. Purchasing an evidence-based curriculum but not implementing it as intended will likely affect the effectiveness of that curriculum. **Implementation fidelity** is a critical aspect to consider in a cost-benefit analysis.

HOW DO I ADVOCATE FOR THE ADOPTION OF A PRODUCT OR CURRICULUM IN MY SCHOOL?

Ms. Flores is a fifth-grade special education teacher and has been teaching for six years. She provides services to students on her caseload in the general education setting. She co-teaches with general educators during reading and math time. Depending on the classroom, Ms. Flores will have around five students with individualized education programs (IEPs). Most of the students on her caseload have intellectual disabilities and are several grade levels behind their peers in reading and math. She often provides small-group instruction during her time in the classroom or moves around for individual (one-on-one) support. Ms. Flores would like to co-plan with her co-teachers more regularly to establish a team-teaching model so that she can provide some direct instruction to the entire class, but her planning time does not align with the other fifth-grade teachers' schedules.

Ms. Flores has noticed that her co-teachers rarely engage the students with IEPs. In fact, she is quite sure that her co-teachers see them as "her students" and that it is her responsibility to provide instruction for them. She remembers learning during her preparation training that special education teachers who push in to general education classrooms often get relegated to the "teacher assistant" role. They enter classrooms not knowing what the topic of instruction is and have not prepared any material. As a result, they walk around the room, provide individual support, and keep students on task but are not regarded as an equal co-teacher. Furthermore, students with individualized goals are often excluded from assessment accountability in the general education curriculum, so general educators do not engage them in their instruction. Even though the students are technically "included" in the general education classroom, they are only physically included, not academically, and often, not socially. Ms. Flores would like to find a way to meaningfully include students with IEPs in their classrooms. She would like her co-teachers to engage with these students more frequently to foster a truly inclusive classroom environment.

As a scientific practitioner, Ms. Flores knows that she must identify and understand the problem first. She has identified that her co-teachers overlook students with IEPs in the general education classrooms and do not view them as part of the class. She understands that this is a common phenomenon pertaining to included students with disabilities in general education classrooms, especially for students with more intensive support needs. Ms. Flores understands that general education teachers have 25 students in their classrooms and many responsibilities and that they naturally refer instruction and responsibility to her because she is the special education teacher in charge of the students' IEPs. The students on her caseload also have very few behavioral challenges; therefore, they quietly sit in the classroom while the general education teacher deals with other students' disruptive behaviors.

The second component of being a scientific practitioner is knowing where to look for potentially researched solutions. Ms. Flores regularly attends the annual Council for Exceptional Children (CEC) conference. At the conference, there is an educational exhibit hall, which is always filled with hundreds of exhibitors showing new educational products and curricula. This year, as Ms. Flores is walking the aisles in the exhibit hall, she sees a booth for a new program called With-It Teachers. The tagline reads "engaging students with disabilities in the general education classroom." This sounds like a potential solution! Ms. Flores begins speaking with the person at the booth for more information.

With-It Teachers is a program that consists of recorded webinar trainings, data collection sheets, and online software to track progress. The mission of the program is to provide teachers with the knowledge and skills to meaningfully engage all students in the educational process. Ms. Flores is excited that this might be a useful tool for her school, but she knows that being a scientific practitioner involves understanding a variety of research articles to assess the validity of a product or curriculum. That means, she has some homework to do.

The With-It Teachers program has a website with a lot of information. There is a tab that says, "research resources." Upon examination, the With-It Teachers program is not evidence based but rather, research based. The program promotes active supervision (Haydon et al., 2019), behavior-specific praise (Ennis et al., 2018), and teacher self-monitoring for sustained behavior change (Rispoli et al., 2017). Ms. Flores is aware that these three classroom management practices have strong empirical support. The website lists several empirical studies under each practice. She downloads a few articles and immediately notices that they have been published in high-quality special education journals. A variety of methodologies have been used (e.g., single case, mixed methods, and literature reviews), and the results of the studies suggest evidence-based practices. She is confident that the With-It Teachers program is grounded in strong evidence.

Ms. Flores then investigates the company selling the program. It is a for-profit company led by previous educators. The leadership team has several years of experience in special education and business. The cost of the program is $500 for access to the online trainings, data collection sheets, and progress monitoring software. After the first year, an annual teacher subscription fee costs $50 per user.

The final step in assessing the With-It Teachers program is to conduct a cost-benefit analysis. Ms. Flores is convinced that advocating for students with IEPs to be more meaningfully included in general education classes is worth it. The With-It Teachers program seems like a perfect solution to this problem. She also knows that the $500 initial cost is going to be a barrier but not insurmountable. Convincing her co-teachers to use the program may also prove challenging, but she knows them well enough that they are not excluding students with IEPs on purpose; it is just a natural phenomenon that has occurred. Ms. Flores believes that if they were presented with a proactive method for engaging the students, they would genuinely try. Ms. Flores commits to advocating for the adoption of the With-It Teachers program in her school.

Advocacy in Action

When Ms. Flores was in graduate school earning her master's degree, she was assigned a textbook titled *The Essentials of Special Education Advocacy* (Markelz et al., 2023). She remembers that advocacy involves three important steps. First, an advocate must identify and understand the problem. Because this is the first step to being a scientific practitioner, she already has examined the reasoning behind why her co-teachers are not including students with IEPs. She understands that if one cannot understand the "why" behind a problem, it is challenging to find a solution.

The next step to being an advocate is inviting key stakeholders to the discussion (Markelz et al., 2023). Knowing whom to advocate to is just as important as knowing what to advocate for. Ms. Flores invites her fifth-grade co-teachers and principal to a meeting to discuss the problem and her proposal to implement the With-It Teachers program. She comes prepared to the meeting with lots of information, but she also knows that the adoption of the program will require a team effort. Rather than demanding the school and co-teachers do something, she wants to build consensus that this program will help the co-teachers and students with IEPs.

The third step in advocacy is finding a solution (Markelz et al., 2023). Ms. Flores's co-teachers are in favor of using the With-It Teachers program, yet as predicted, the $500 initial cost has her principal reluctant. Ms. Flores came prepared for this pushback and offers to lead a campaign through Donors Choose (https://www.donorschoose.org/), an online fundraising platform for classrooms. The principal agrees that if she can fundraise the cost of the program, the fifth-grade team will be given time during regularly scheduled professional development seminars to watch the online trainings and begin implementing the program.

Bringing It All Together

The previous scenario involved a fictional teacher who assessed and validated a made-up program; however, the problem Ms. Flores attempted to solve is real (Kurth et al., 2015). In fact, there is no shortage of problems that special education teachers encounter every day. There is also no shortage of potential solutions available. As we have considered in this chapter, educational products and curricula have been growing at an exponential rate. The proliferation of technology has and will continue to introduce innovative—and potentially revolutionary—products for special education teachers and students with disabilities. Therefore, it is essential that special education teachers can critically examine educational products and curricula to assess their quality and advocate for their adoption.

WHERE CAN I FIND MORE INFORMATION ABOUT PRODUCT AND CURRICULUM REVIEWS?

Common Sense Education: Common Sense Education is the nation's leading nonprofit organization dedicated to improving the lives of all kids and families by providing the trustworthy information, education, and independent voice they need to thrive in the 21st century. Common Sense Education has a variety of resources and EdTech reviews to prepare students for success in a connected world. Explore Common Sense Education at https://www.commonsense.org/education.

EdReports: EdReports is an independent nonprofit designed to improve K–12 education. EdReports increases the capacity of teachers, administrators, and leaders to seek, identify, and demand the highest-quality instructional materials. Drawing upon expert educators, its reviews of instructional materials and support of smart adoption processes equip teachers with excellent materials nationwide. Learn more about EdReports at http://www.edreports.org/.

What Works Clearinghouse (WWC): WWC has been a central and trusted source of scientific evidence on education programs, products, practices, and policies. WWC reviews the research, determines which studies meet rigorous standards, and summarizes the findings. It focuses on high-quality research to answer the question "What works in education?" Visit WWC at https://ies.ed.gov/ncee/wwc/.

Zombie Ideas in Education: Some bad ideas never seem to die despite research showing they do not actually work. In this article by ASCD author Goodwin (2021), six commonly held (false) beliefs about educational practices are examined. Read the article at https://www.ascd.org/el/articles/zombie-ideas-in-education.

DISCUSSION QUESTIONS

1. What are some current products or curricula trends/fads? Predict where the educational industry will go regarding educational products and curricula.
2. What would you do if you were in Ms. Flores's position? How would you advocate for change?
3. If you could invent a solution to an educational problem, what would it be?
4. Are you in favor of or against the marketization of educational products and curricula?
5. Why are the steps to assessing the validity of products and curricula important?

KEY TERMS

Common Core Standards: An educational initiative from 2010 that details what K–12 students throughout the United States should know in English language arts and mathematics at the conclusion of each school grade.

credible: Something that is believable or convincing.

evidence based: Supported by a comprehensive body of high-quality empirical evidence.

for profit: Selling a product or service to consumers to make a financial gain.

implementation fidelity: The degree to which an intervention or program is implemented as intended.

learning management system: Software application for the administration, documentation, tracking, reporting, automation, and delivery of educational courses, training programs, materials, or learning and development programs.

learning styles: The debunked educational myth that students/people have preferred methods of learning information (i.e., visual, auditory, or kinesthetic).

market size: The number of people who could potentially become customers.

nonprofit: Providing a product or service to benefit the community with no intention of financial gain.

predatory advertising: The practice of manipulating vulnerable people into purchasing a product or service through exploitation of these vulnerabilities.

research based: Informed by scientific theories and research findings.

validity: The extent to which a concept, conclusion, or measurement is well founded and corresponds accurately to the real world.

REFERENCES

An, M. (2020, January 14). *Why people block ads (and what it means for marketers and advertisers)*. HubSpot. https://blog.hubspot.com/marketing/why-people-block-ads-and-what-it-means-for-marketers-and-advertisers

Bruhn, A., McDaniel, S., & Kreigh, C. (2015). Self-monitoring interventions for students with behavior problems: A systematic review of current research. *Behavioral Disorders*, *40*(2), 102–121. https://doi.org/10.17988/BD-13-45.1

Bureau of Economic Analysis. (2018, September 6). *Consumer spending*. https://www.bea.gov/resources/learning-center/what-to-know-consumer-spending

Davis, W. (2017, May 14). *Whirring, purring fidget spinners provide entertainment, not ADHD help*. NPR. https://www.npr.org/2017/05/14/527988954/whirring-purring-fidget-spinners-provide-entertainment-not-adhd-help

Ennis, R. P., Royer, D. J., Lane, K. L., Menzies, H. M., Oakes, W. P., & Schellman, L. E. (2018). Behavior-specific praise: An effective, efficient, low-intensity strategy to support student success. *Beyond Behavior*, *27*(3), 134–139. https://doi.org/10.1177/1074295618798587

Furey, W. (2020). The stubborn myth of "learning styles": State teacher-license prep materials peddle a debunked theory. *Education Next*, *20*(3), 8–12. https://www.educationnext.org/wp-content/uploads/2022/01/ednext_XX_3_furey.pdf

Gewertz, C. (2015, September 30). *The common core explained*. Education Week. https://www.edweek.org/teaching-learning/the-common-core-explained/2015/09

Goodwin, B. (2021). Zombie ideas in education. *Educational Leadership, 78*(8), 44–49. https://www.ascd.org/el/articles/zombie-ideas-in-education

Haydon, T., Hunter, W., & Scott, T. M. (2019). Active supervision: Preventing behavioral problems before they occur. *Beyond Behavior, 28*(1), 29–35. https://doi.org/10.1177/1074295619835190

Kriescher, S. L., Hulac, D. M., Ryan, A. M., & King, B. L. (2023). Evaluating the evidence for fidget toys in the classroom. *Intervention in School and Clinic, 59*(1), 66–69. https://doi.org/10.1177/10534512221130070

Kurth, J. A., Lyon, K. J., & Shogren, K. A. (2015). Supporting students with severe disabilities in inclusive schools: A descriptive account from schools implementing inclusive practices. *Research and Practice for Persons with Severe Disabilities, 40*(4), 261–274. https://doi.org/10.1177/1540796915594160

Markelz, A. M., & Bateman, D. F. (2021). *The essentials of special education law.* Rowman & Littlefield.

Markelz, A. M., Nagro, S. A., Monnin, K., & Bateman, D. F. (2023). *The essentials of special education advocacy.* Rowman & Littlefield.

National Center for Education Statistics. (2023). *Fast facts: Back-to-school statistics.* https://nces.ed.gov/fastfacts/display.asp?id=372

Rispoli, M., Zaini, S., Mason, R., Brodhead, M., Burke, M. D., & Gregori, E. (2017). A systematic review of teacher self-monitoring on implementation of behavioral practices. *Teaching and Teacher Education, 63*, 58–72. https://doi.org/10.1016/j.tate.2016.12.007

Index

ABA. *See* applied behavioral analysis
ABC contingency, of antecedent, behavior, and consequence, 24
abstract: CRA, 195; in educational research article, 34–35; in group research design, 71; in "Schema-Based Instruction for Mathematical Word Problem Solving," 198; in systematic literature review, 48; in "Using a Daily Report Card to Reduce Off-Task Behaviors for a Student with Autism Spectrum Disorder," 160
academic publications, peer-review process for, 26–27, 47, 231–32
Academic Search Complete, 204
Accessing Open Peer-Reviewed Research (Cook, B.), 37–38
action research, 23
additional research methods: case study, *131*, 132–34; Colorado State University on, 141; Delphi research, *131*, 139–40; factors for appropriate methodology use in, 129–30; information on, 141; *Journal of Teacher Action Research* on, 141; mixed-methods research, 13, *14*, 130–32, *131*; NIH on, 141; program evaluation, *131*, 140–41;

QuestionPro on, 141; SDA, *131*, 136–37; survey research, *131*, 134–36, *135*; teacher action research, *131*, 137–39, 141; Westat tool kit on, 141
additive schema, 195
ADHD. *See* attention deficit hyperactivity disorder
advocacy, for adoption of product and curriculum reviews, 236–39
AERA. *See* American Educational Research Association
AI. *See* artificial intelligence
alternating treatments design, SCRD and, 90, *92*
American Educational Research Association (AERA), 6, 16
analysis of variance (ANOVA), 61, *65*, 68
ANCOVA, *65*, 68
ANOVA. *See* analysis of variance
antecedent, in ABC contingency, 24
antecedent-based strategies: prompting, 152, *153*; visual schedules, 152, *154*
applied behavioral analysis (ABA): as autism intervention, 8–9, 16; ethics and punishment procedures of, 9
artificial intelligence (AI), 230
ASD. *See* autism spectrum disorder
The Assayer (Galileo), 3

243

assessment domain, in HLPS, 14, *15*
attention deficit hyperactivity disorder (ADHD), 162, 231; classroom behaviors of, 161
attention subcategory, of social function, 150, *151*
Autism journal, 28
autism spectrum disorder (ASD): ABA treatment for, 8–9, 16; problem behaviors of, 161. *See also* "Using a Daily Report Card to Reduce Off-Task Behaviors for a Student with Autism Spectrum Disorder"
automatic behaviors. *See* sensory behaviors

Banks, Joy, 117, *118*
baseline logic, 87, 88
behavior: in ABC contingency, 24; ASD problem, 161; operant and respondent, 8; self-monitoring for change in, 233. *See also* classroom behaviors; function of behavior; human behavior
behaviorism, 8–9; of Watson, 147–48
behavior-specific praise (BSP), 94–95
believability, 72–73
bell curve, 73
between-group design, 62
bi- and multivariate inferential statistical tests: ANCOVA, *65*, 68; ANOVA, 61, *65*, 68; Chi square, *65*, 67; MANCOVA, *65*, 69; MANOVA, *65*, 68; *t*-Test, *65*, 67
bias: coding study characteristics of error and, 54–55; nonresponse, 134; publication, 27, 54; systematic literature reviews error and, 52
Black special education teachers (BSETs), 111–12
Boolean operators, in Google Search, 32
Boston University Medical School, 58
bots, 136
bounded context, in case study, 133

BSETs. *See* Black special education teachers
BSP. *See* behavior-specific praise

case study, *131*, 132; bounded context in, 133; epistemological underpinnings, 133; focus groups, 111; grounded theory procedures, 111–12; limitations of, 133–34; as qualitative research design type, *111*, 111–12; reactivity limitation, 134
causation, correlation compared to, 69
cause-and effect relations, 102
CCD. *See* changing criterion design
CEC. *See* Council for Exceptional Children
changing criterion design (CCD), 166
child-based goals, 6
Chi square, *65*, 67
Christensen, L, 16
classical conditioning, of Pavlov, 147
classroom behaviors, 24; functions of, 149, 150; of LD, EBD, and ADHD students, 161; positive and proactive approach to, 148; school-wide initiatives, 149, 161; student-centered approaches to, 149, 161; teacher-centered tactics for, 149, 161; teacher-student relationship focus for, 149, 161
classroom management, 147; CEC on, 187; competing pathways model example, *157*; information on, 187–88; Intervention Central on, 187; IRIS Module on, 187; issues concerning, 148–49; potential research solutions for, 158–59; problem identification and understanding, 157–58; research articles for, 159; research to address, 156–87; WestEd on, 187
classroom management EBPs: antecedent-based strategies, 152, *153*, *154*; consequence-based strategies, 153–54; function of

behaviors and, 149, 150; group contingencies, 155; MTSS for, 155–56; rules and routines importance, 149, 150, 152, 161; token economies, 155
Cochrane Qualitative and Implementation Methods Group, 123
coding study characteristics, 51–52; error and bias in, 54–55; flawed conclusions detection error, 55; inaccurate coding, 54–55; lack of objective reporting error, 55
collaboration domain, in HLPs, 14, *15*
Colorado State University, 141
combination designs, SCRD and, 94, *95*
Committee on Training in Clinical Psychology, scientific practitioners term of, 22–23
Common Core Standards, 230
Common Sense Education, 239
competing pathways model example, *157*
component analysis, SCRD and, 92–94, *93*
compulsory education laws, special education exclusion from, 5
conceptual knowledge, for mathematics literacy, 193, 194, 199, 201
concrete-representation-abstract (CRA), 195
confirmability, 115, 120
confounding variables, 79
consequence, in ABC contingency, 24
consequence-based strategies, 153–54
contexts, 23–24, 26, 52, 57, 71, 109, 113
control, in SCRD, 86
Cook, B. G., 37–38
Cook, Sara Cothren, 197, 198–221
Cooperative Research Act (1954), 7
correlation, *65*, 69; causation compared to, *69*
cost-benefit analysis, in product and curriculum validity assessment, *231*, 234–36, *235*

Council for Exceptional Children (CEC), 39, 75, 80, 237; on classroom management, 187; Essential Quality Indicators of SCRD, 98, *98–99*, 103; group research design standards, 77–78, *78*; HLPs identified by, 14; QIs and standards for SBI, 198, 203, *206*, *207*; on qualitative research designs, 123; on research quality indicators, 117; Standards for Evidence-Based Practices in Special Education, 103
CRA. *See* concrete-representation-abstract
credibility, 27, 29, 116, 117, 119, 120; information quality validation and, 233
credible, 25, 31, 72
Cult of Pedagogy, 38
curriculum. *See* product and curriculum reviews

daily behavior report cards (DBRCs), 155; FAST instrument and, 163, 169, 178, 179; necessary components of, 162; parent reinforcement involvement, 163; positive impact on classroom behaviors, 161; social validity for, 173, 178–79
data analyses, "Using a Daily Report Card to Reduce Off-Task Behaviors for a Student with Autism Spectrum Disorder," 171; reliability, fidelity, and validity, 172–73; Tau-U statistical analysis, 172
database searches, for SBI, 204–5
data collection, in experimental procedures, 169–70
DBRCs. *See* daily behavior report cards
default setup, for educational research, 11
Delphi research, *131*; limitations of, 139–40
democratic equality approach, 6–7
dependability, 115, 120

dependent variable (DV), 35–36, 166; in SCRD, 86–92, 96–97; in within-subject design, 62
differential reinforcement, 149, 161
disability categories, of IDEA, 11; implication section in, 52
discussion: contexts in, 52; in educational research article, 36–37; in group research designs, 75; in systematic literature reviews, 52; in "Using a Daily Report Card to Reduce Off-Task Behaviors for a Student with Autism Spectrum Disorder," 177–81
discussion, in "Schema-Based Instruction for Mathematical Word Problem Solving": limitations and, 214–15; research and practice implications, 215–16; SBI effectiveness, 213–14
disproportionality, in special education, 16
DV. *See* dependent variable

EAHCA. *See* Education for All Handicapped Children Act
EBD. *See* emotional behavioral disorders
EBPs. *See* evidence-based practices
EBSCO host database, 204
Edanz research support services, 58
EdReports, 239–40
educational research: brief history of, 5–9; on child-based growth goals compared to society-centered goals, 6; Cooperative Research Act, 7; default set up for, 11; EAHCA and, 8; Elementary and Secondary Education Act, 7; ethics importance in conducting, 9–10, *10*; Ford Foundation philanthropic funding for, 7; GI Bill and, 7; hard science rejection of, 6; medical research compared to, 22; as soft science, 5; Thorndike concept of reinforcement, 6, 46; Truman Commission on High Education, 7
Educational Research (Johnson and Christensen), 16
educational research articles: emailing research authors, 34; finding and reading, 21–39; keywords identification process, *30*, 30–31; reasons for, 22–24; reliable information in, 25; research-to-practice gap, 22, 23, 27–28; university institutional access, 32, 34. *See also* Google Scholar
educational research articles, reading of, *38*; abstract in, 34–35; discussion in, 36–37; introduction in, 35; methods in, 36; research question in, 35–36; results in, 36; title in, 34
educational research types: mixed-methods approach, 13, *14*, 130–32, *131*; qualitative approach, 12–13, *14*; quantitative approach, 12, *14*, 61
Education for All Handicapped Children Act (EAHCA) (1973), 8
Education Research Complete database, 204
Education Resources Information Center (ERIC), 204
Education Source database, 204
Education Week, 233
"Effect Size in Single-Case Research" (Parker), 103
effect sizes, 64, 74; analysis, 176; interpretation of, 79–80; in SCRD, 103, *104*
Elementary and Secondary Education Act (1965), 7–8
emotional behavioral disorders (EBD), classroom behaviors of, 161
empirical studies, 27; systematic literature reviews and, 46
Endrew F. v. Douglas County School (2017), 13
enterprise validation, *231*, 234

Index   247

epistemological underpinnings, in case study, 133
ERIC. *See* Education Resources Information Center
escape/avoidance subcategory, of social function, 150, *151*
essential questions, in qualitative research design, 118–19, *119*
The Essentials of Special Education Advocacy (Markelz), 238
ethics: ABA punishment procedures and, 9; educational research importance, 9–10, *10*; social validity and, 9–10
ethnography, *111*, 112
evaluation: checklist for systematic literature reviews, 55, *56*; program evaluation research, *131*, 140, 141; "Schema-Based Instruction for Mathematical Word Problem Solving" study, 205–6
evidence-based practices (EBPs), 233–34; for classroom behaviors, 149–56; for product and curriculum reviews, 227–28; in research journals, 29; SBI as, 198, 211–13, *212*; in "Schema-Based Instruction for Mathematical Word Problem Solving," 198, 202–3, 207–9, 211–13, *212*; in special education, 13. *See also* classroom management EBPs; math instruction EBPs
exclusion criteria, in methods, 73
experimental design, 61; in "Using a Daily Report Card to Reduce Off-Task Behaviors for a Student with Autism Spectrum Disorder," 166
experimental procedures: data collection, 169–70; intervention phase changes, 170–71; maintenance, 171
explicit instruction, for math instruction, 194
explicit systematic instruction, 201
extant data, 136

external validity, 46, 96–97; SDA and, 137

FAST. *See* function assessment screening tool
FBA. *See* functional behavior assessment
Fechner, Gustav, 147
fidelity, 22, 172; DBRC implementation, 173, 176–77, 236
Fisher, R. A., 61
focus groups, 111
Ford Foundation, education research philanthropic funding by, 7
for-profit companies, 234
functional behavior assessment (FBA), 156
functional relation, in visual analysis, 102
function assessment screening tool (FAST), 163, 169, 178, 179
function of behavior, 152, 156; nonsocial and social function, 150, *151*; scientific practitioners and, 24

Galileo, 3
generalizability of outcomes, as SCRD limitation, 96
generalizations, 12; in systematic literature reviews, 46
germane information, for qualitative research design, 110
GI Bill (1944), 7
Glass, G. V., 46
Google Scholar, 31, *33*, 47, 57, 197, 231–32; Boolean operators in, 32; for DBRCs, 158; keywords for, 45
grey literature, 54
grounded theory, *111*, 113; case study and procedures of, 111–12
group contingencies, 155
group membership, logistics regression and, *65*, 70
group research design components, 70; discussion, 75; introduction, 71–72;

method, 72–74; results, 74–75; title and abstract, 71
group research design limitations: mitigating, 76–77, 76–78, *78*; WWC standards, 75, 76, 76–77
group research designs: between-group design, 62; CEC standards for, 77–78, *78*; confounding variables in, 79; on DBRCs, 162; defined, 62–70; effect sizes in, 64; Fisher and, 61; information on, 80–81; interpretation of, 79–80; quantitative statistics, 63; RCT, 63; for SBI, 207–8; within-subject design, 62

hard science, 5; education research rejection by, 6
high-leverage practices (HLPs), 14, *15*
Horner, R. H., 96–97
human behavior: function of brain and, 147; Pavlov classical conditioning and, 147; Skinner operant conditioning and, 148; Watson behaviorism on, 147–48
hypothesis, 12, 46, 49, 72

IDEA. *See* Individuals with Disabilities Education Act
IEP. *See* individualized education program
IES. *See* Institute of Education Sciences
immediacy of effect, in visual analysis, 100–101
impact factor, in research journals, 29, 159
implementation fidelity, 173, 176–77, 236
implications section, in discussion, 52
improvement rate difference (IRD), 103, *104*
inclusion criteria, in methods, 73
independent variable (IV), 35–36, 165–66; in between-group design, 62; in SCRD, 86–92, 96–97

individualized education program (IEP), in special education, 13, 196, 236–37
Individuals with Disabilities Education Act (IDEA) (2004), 10; disability categories of, 11, 52; specially designed instruction in, 13
induction, 3
inefficient lag, in peer-review process, 26–27
inference, 3
information, 233; additional research methods, 141; classroom management, 187–88; educational research articles reliable, 25; group research designs, 80–81; math instruction, 223; product and curriculum reviews, 239–40; qualitative research design, 110, 123; SCRD, 103–5; systematic literature reviews, 58
information quality validation, *231*, 232–33
Institute of Education Sciences (IES), 37, 80
instruction domain, in HLPS, 14, *15*
interfering behaviors, 149
internal validity, 46, 96–97
internet, nonacademic publications and, 25
interobserver agreement (IOA), 97
interpretation: of effect sizes, 79–80; of group research designs, 79–80; of qualitative research design, 121–23, *122*; of SCRD, 99–103; of systematic literature reviews, 55–58
intervention: phase changes in experimental procedures, 170–71; in "Using a Daily Report Card to Reduce Off-Task Behaviors for a Student with Autism Spectrum Disorder," 177, 180
Intervention Central, on classroom management, 187
interventionist training, in pre-experimental procedures, 167

introduction: in educational research article, 35; group research design, 71–72; in "Schema-Based Instruction for Mathematical Word Problem Solving," 199–204; in systematic literature review, 48; in "Using a Daily Report Card to Reduce Off-Task Behaviors for a Student with Autism Spectrum Disorder," 161–64

Introduction to Educational Research YouTube video, 17

IOA. *See* interobserver agreement

IRD. *See* improvement rate difference

IRIS Module: on classroom management, 187; on math instruction, 223

iterative steps, of scientific method, 3–4, *4*

IV. *See* independent variable

JARS. *See* Journal Article Reporting Standards

JOBE. *See Journal of Behavioral Education*

John Hopkins University, as first research university, 5

Johnson, R. B., 16

Journal Article Reporting Standards (JARS), 70

Journal of Behavioral Education (JOBE*)*, 159

The Journal of Special Education, 28

Journal of Teacher Action Research, 141

keywords, 196–97; for Google Scholar, 45; identification process with, *30*, 30–31; for "Schema-Based Instruction for Mathematical Word Problem Solving," 198; in "Using a Daily Report Card to Reduce Off-Task Behaviors for a Student with Autism Spectrum Disorder," 160

law of effect, of Thorndike, 8, 148

learning disabilities (LD): classroom behaviors of, 161; SBI and, 199–204

learning management systems (LMSs), 230

learning styles: myth of, 233; nonacademic publications and, 25–26

legislation: Cooperative Research Act, 7; EAHCA, 8; Elementary and Secondary Education Act, 7; GI Bill, 7; IDEA, 10, 11, 13, 52

level, in visual analysis, 99, *100*

limitations: of case study, 133–34; of Delphi research, 139–40; generalizability of outcomes as SCRD, 96; of group research design, 75–78, *76–77*, *78*; of mixed-methods research, 132; of program evaluation research, 141; of qualitative research design, 118–23, *119*; in "Schema-Based Instruction for Mathematical Word Problem Solving," 214–15; of SCRDs, 96–98, *98–99*, 103; of SDA, 137; of survey research, 134, 136; of systematic literature reviews, 52–55; of teacher action research, 139

LMSs. *See* learning management systems

logistics regression, *65*, 70

magnitude of effects, systematic literature review understanding of, 57–58

maintenance, in experimental procedures, 171

MANCOVA, *65*, 69

MANOVA, *65*, 68

Markelz, A. M., 238

market size, 229

mathematics disability (MD), SBI and, 199–204

mathematics literacy: characteristics influencing, *192*; conceptual knowledge for, 193; procedural knowledge for, 193

math instruction, 191; information on, 223; IRIS Module, 223; issues concerning, 192–93; Pirate Math Equation Quest, 222–23; potential research solutions for, 197; problem identification and understanding, 196–97; research articles for, 198; research to address, 196–221; "Schema-Based Instruction for Mathematical Word Problem Solving," 198–221; Science of Math website on, 223; SRSD Math on, 223; working memory and, 192
math instruction EBPs, 193; CRA, 195; explicit instruction, 194; SBI, 195, 197; scaffolded instruction, 194; SRSD, 194–95, 223
maturation, 96
MD. *See* mathematics disability
mean, *64*, 66
median, *64*, 66
medical research, educational research compared to, 22
member checking, 116
meta-analysis, Glass introduction of, 46
methodology use, in additional research methods, 129–30
methods: coding study characteristics, 50–51; in educational research article, 36; exclusion criteria in, 73; in group research design, 72–74; inclusion criteria in, 73; PRISMA procedures, 50–51, *51*, *58*; in "Schema-Based Instruction for Mathematical Word Problem Solving," 204–9; in systematic literature review, 50–52; in "Using a Daily Report Card to Reduce Off-Task Behaviors for a Student with Autism Spectrum Disorder," 164–73
mixed-methods research, 13, 130–31, *131*; limitations of, 132; perspectives of, *14*
mode, *64*, 66–67

MSWO. *See* multiple stimulus without replacement
mulitiered system of supports (MTSS): DBRCs for, 156; FBA for, 156; PBIS, 155; RtI, 155
multiple baseline design, SCRD and, 88–89, *90*
multiple probe design, SCRD and, 89–90, *90*, *91*
multiple regression, *65*, 70
multiple stimulus without replacement (MSWO), 169, 178
multiplicative schema, 195
myth, of learning styles, 233

NAEP. *See* National Association for Educational Progress
NAP. *See* nonoverlap of all pairs
narrative inquiry, *111*, 113
National Association for Educational Progress (NAEP), on mathematics assessments, 192
National Institutes of Health (NIH), 141
National Society of College Teachers of Education, 6
NIH. *See* National Institutes of Health
NMAP, on mathematical word problem solving, 201
nonacademic publications: internet and, 25; learning styles and, 25–26; validity problem for, 25
nonoverlap of all pairs (NAP), 103, *104*
nonprofit organizations, 234
nonresponse bias, 134
nonsocial function of behavior, sensory behaviors and, 150, *151*
null hypothesis, 72

open science reforms, for peer-review process, 27
operant behaviors, 8
operant conditioning, of Skinner, 148
overlap, 102

PAND. *See* Percentage of all nonoverlapping data
parent: DBRC reinforcement involvement by, 163; training in pre-experimental procedures, 167
Parker, R. I., 103
participatory research, *111*, 114
path analysis, *65*, 70
Pavlov, Ivan, 147
PBIS. *See* positive behavior intervention support
peer-review process, for academic publications, 231–32; inefficient lag in, 26–27; open science reforms for, 27; publication bias in, 27, 54; systematic literature reviews and, 47
Percentage of all nonoverlapping data (PAND), 103, *104*
Percentage of nonoverlapping data (PND), 103, *104*
phenomena, qualitative research design and, 110
phenomenology, *111*, 114
physical products, 229
pictorial representations, 201
Pirate Math Equation Quest program, 222–23
PND. *See* Percentage of nonoverlapping data
positionality, 121
positive and proactive approach, to classroom behaviors, 148
positive behavior intervention support (PBIS), 155
practical significance, 74
practitioner journals: empirical studies and, 27; research-to-practice gap and, 27–28; *TEACHING Exceptional Children* as, 27–28, 32, 39
pre-baseline observation and interviews, in pre-experimental procedures, 168
predatory advertising, 231
predatory journals, 29
prediction, 87

pre-experimental procedures, in "Using a Daily Report Card to Reduce Off-Task Behaviors for a Student with Autism Spectrum Disorder": FAST, 163, 169, 178, 179; interventionist training, 167; MSWO, 169; parent training, 167; pre-baseline observation and interviews, 168; student training, 168; training, 167
Preferred Reporting Items for Systematic Reviews and Meta-Analysis (PRISMA) procedures, 50–51, *51*, 58; for SBI literature search, 204
primary data, 136
PRISMA. *See* Preferred Reporting Items for Systematic Reviews and Meta-Analysis
procedural knowledge, for math literacy, 193, 200
product and curriculum reviews: advocacy for adoption of, 236–39; Common Sense Education, 240; EBPs for, 227–28; EdReports and, 239–40; hardware and software, 230; information on, 239–40; issues concerning, 228–30; physical products, 229; WWC and, 239; Zombie Ideas in Education, 239
product and curriculum validity assessment: cost-benefit analysis in, *231*, 234–36, *235*; enterprise validation, *231*, 234; information quality validation, *231*, 232–33; results quality validation, *231*, 233–34; search conducted in, *231*, 231–32
professional judgment, on systematic literature review use, 57
program evaluation research, *131*, 140; limitations of, 141
prompting, as antecedent-based strategy, 152, *153*
psychology, Fechner origination of, 147
"Psychology as the Behaviorist Views It" (Watson), 147–48

PsycINFO database, 204
publication bias: grey literature and, 54; open science reforms for, 27; in peer-review process, 27; during search procedures, 54
Publication Manual of the American Psychological Association, Seventh Edition, 70, 80
publication types: academic publications, 26–27; nonacademic publications, 25–26; practitioner journals, 27–28, 39; research journals, 28–29
punishment: ethics on ABA procedures of, 9; Skinner on, 8, 148
Pustejovsky, James, 103

QIs. *See* Quality Indicators
qualitative approach, 12; perspectives of, *14*; socially constructed reality and, 13
qualitative research design, 109; CEC on, 123; Cochrane Qualitative and Implementation Methods Group on, 123; defined, 110; germane information for, 110; goals of, 110; information on, 123; interpretation of, 121–23, *122*; phenomena and, 110; QIs for, 117–18, *118*, 120–21; QualPage on, 123; QuestionPro on, 123; University of North Carolina and, 123
qualitative research design components, 117; confirmability, 115; member checking, 116; respondent validation, 115–16; triangulation, 115, *116*; trustworthiness, 116
qualitative research design limitations, 122–23; credibility, 27, 29, 116, 117, 119, 120, 233; dependability, 120; essential questions and, 118–19, *119*; mitigating, 120–21; positionality, 121; transferability, 120, 133, 134; trustworthiness, 120

qualitative research design types: case studies, *111*, 111–12; ethnography, *111*, 112; grounded theory, *111*, 112–13; narrative inquiry, *111*, 113; participatory research, *111*, 114; phenomenology, *111*, 114
Quality Indicators (QIs), in qualitative research, 118; Banks on, 117, *118*; CEC on, 117; reflexivity and, 117, 120–21
Quality Indicators (QIs) and standards, of CEC for SBI, 198, 203; coding procedures for, 206, *207*
QualPage, 123
quantitative approach: generalizations and, 12, 61; hypothesis in, 12; perspectives of, *14*. *See also* group research designs
quantitative statistics, 63
QuestionPro: on additional research methods, 141; on qualitative research design, 123

randomization, 61, 63
randomized controlled trial (RCT), 63
reactivity, case studies limitation of, 134
reflexivity, 117, 120–21
reinforcement: DBRCs and parent involvement with, 163; differential, 149, 161; Skinner on, 8, 148; Thorndike concept of, 6, 46
reliability, in "Using a Daily Report Card to Reduce Off-Task Behaviors for a Student with Autism Spectrum Disorder," 172
reliable information, in educational research articles, 25
replicability, 72–73
replication, 87–89, 96, 134, 215
reproductibility, 72–73
research: to address classroom management, 156–87; emailing authors for, 34; reading variety of articles for, 159; special education, 8–9, 13–16

research, history of, 3–18; *Autism* journal, 28; educational research history, 5–9; John Hopkins University as first research university, 5
research-based programs, 233
research journals: EBP in, 29; impact factors in, 29, 159; *The Journal of Special Education*, 28; for potential research solutions, 158–59; predatory journals, 29. *See also specific journal*
research question: in educational research article, 35–36; hypothesis in, 49; IV and DV in, 35–36; in systematic literature review, 47–49
research-to-practice gap, 22, 23; practitioner journals and, 27–28
respondent behaviors, 8
respondent validation, 115–16
response to intervention (RtI), 155
results: in educational research article, 36; in group research designs, 74–75; in systematic literature review, 52
results, in "Schema-Based Instruction for Mathematical Word Problem Solving": EBP classification in, 211–13, *212*; included studies description, 209–10, *210*; QIs presence in, 210–11
results, in "Using a Daily Report Card to Reduce Off-Task Behaviors for a Student with Autism Spectrum Disorder": effect size analysis, 176; visual analysis, 173–76, *174*
results quality validation, *231*, 233–34
reversal design, SCRD and, 88
The Review of Educational Research journal, 47
rewards, Skinner on, 148
Riden, Benjamin S., 159
routines, 149, 150, 152, 161
RtI. *See* response to intervention
Ruiz, Sal, 159
rules, 149, 150, 152, 161

Sage publishing company, 197
sample size, 63, 71, 73, 74
SBI. *See* schema-based instruction
scaffolded instruction, for math instruction, 194
schema, additive and multiplicative, 195
schema-based instruction (SBI): as EBP, 198, 211–13, *212*; group research designs for, 207–8; for math instruction, 195, 197; SCRD for, 208; visual analysis for, 208–9
"Schema-Based Instruction for Mathematical Word Problem Solving" (Cook, S.), 197, 217–21; abstract in, 198; CEC QIs and standards, 198, 203, *206*, *207*; conclusion, 216; database search for, 204–5; discussion, 213–16; group research designs and, 207–8; introduction, 199–204; keywords, 198; on MD, LD, and WM, 199–204; method in, 204–9; NMAP on explicit systematic instruction, 201; pictorial and schema representations, 201; PRISMA literature search, 204; results, 209–13; SBI EBP exploration, 202–3, 207–9; SCRD and, 208; study evaluation for inclusion in, 205–6; visual analysis and, 208–9
schema representations, 201
schemas: additive, 195; multiplicative, 195
school-wide initiatives, for classroom behavior, 149, 161
science, defined, 3
Science of Math website, 223
scientific knowledge, cumulative, 46
scientific method, iterative steps of, 3–4, *4*
scientific practitioners, *23*; ABC contingency and, 24; Committee on Training in Clinical Psychology term of, 22–23; function of behavior and, 24; problem understanding

and identification of, 24–25; special education teachers a, 22–23. *See also* practitioner journals
SCRD. *See* single-case research design
secondary data analysis (SDA), *131*; extant data and, 136; external validity and, 137; limitations of, 137; primary data and, 136
self-monitoring, for behavior change, 233
self-regulated strategy development (SRSD), for math instruction, 194–95, 223
sensory behaviors, of nonsocial function, 150, *151*
sequence conditions, in SCRD, 87
Single-Case Design Technical Documentation, of WWC, 103
Single-Case Effect Size Calculator, 104
single-case research design (SCRD): on DBRCs, 162; effect sizes in, 103, *104*; information on, 103–5; interpretation of, 99–103; IRD statistics, 103, *104*; IVs and DVs in, 86–92, 96–97; NAP statistics, 103, *104*; PAND, 103, *104*; PND statistics, 103, *104*; for SBI, 208; statistics applied to, 102–3; Tau-U, 103, *104*, 162, 172; visual analysis for, 99–103, *100*, *101*
single-case research design components, 85; AB design in, 87–88, *89*; alternating treatments design, 90, *92*; baseline logic, 87, 88; CCD, 90–92, *92*; component analysis, 92–94, *93*; control in, 86; multiple baseline design, 88–89, *90*; multiple probe design, 89–90, *90*, *91*; prediction, 87; replication, 87–89; reversal design, 88, *89*; sequence conditions in, 87; steady state responding, 87; verification, 87
single-case research design limitations: CEC Essential Quality Indicators of, 98, *98–99*, 103; generalizability of outcomes and, 96; Horner standards for, 96–97; IOA and, 97; maturation and, 96; mitigating, 96–97, *98–99*
skew, 54
Skinner, Burrhus Frederick "B. F.": on functional relation and cause-and-effect relations, 102; operant conditioning and, 148; on reinforcement and punishment, 8, 148
social desirability, 136
social efficiency approach, 6, 7
social/emotional/behavioral domain, in HLPs, 14, *15*
social function of behavior, 150, *151*
socially constructed reality, 13
social mobility approach, 6, 7
social validity, 96–97, 110; for DBRC, 173, 178–79; ethics in educational research and, 9–10, *10*
society-centered goals, 6
soft science, educational research as, 5
special education: compulsory education laws exclusion for, 5; disproportionality in, 16; EBPs in, 13; HLPs for, 14, *15*; IEP in, 13, 196, 236–37; operant and respondent behaviors, 8; research influence on, 10–16; specially designed instruction in, 13
special education research: behaviorism and, 8–9; benefits of, 13–16
special education teachers, as scientific practitioners, 22–23
specially designed instruction, in special education, 13
Spurious Correlations, 104
SRSD. *See* self-regulated strategy development
SRSD Math, on math instruction, 223
standard deviation, *64*, 67
Standards for Evidence-Based Practices in Special Education, of CEC, 103
statistical analysis, 58

statistical inference, 61
Statistical Methods for Research Workers (Fisher), 61
statistical relationships: correlation, *65*, 69, *69*; multiple regression, *65*, 70; path analysis, *65*, 70
statistical significance, 74
statistical testing essentials: mean, *64*, 66; median, *64*, 66; mode, *64*, 66–67; standard deviation, *64*, 67; variance, *64*, 67
statistics: application of, 61; Fisher as father of, 61; SCRD application of, 102–3. *See also* bi- and multivariate inferential statistical tests
steady state responding, 87
stimulus: association of Pavlov, 147; function and, 150; MSWO, 169, 178. *See also* classical conditioning
student-centered approaches, to classroom behaviors: differential reinforcement, 149, 161; time-out, 149, 161
student training, in pre-experimental procedures, 168
survey research, *131*, *135*; bots and, 136; limitations of, 134, 136; nonresponse bias and, 134; social desirability limitation, 136
systematic literature review components: description, 47; discussion in, 52; explanation of procedures, 47; introduction, 48; methods, 50–52; objective reporting of findings, 47; research questions, 47–49; results in, 52; steps in, *50*; study characteristics, 47; title and abstract, 48
systematic literature reviews, 197; checklist for evaluation of, 55, *56*; defined, 46–47; drawing conclusions, 55; empirical studies and, 46; error and bias in, 52; external validity and, 36; generalizations in, 46; information on, 58; internal validity and, 46; interpretations of, 55–58; limitations of, 52–55; magnitude of effects understanding, 57–58; peer-review process and, 47; professional judgment on use of, 57; searching and selecting, 54; skew in, 54; summary of articles in, *53*; validity of, 54–55

tangible subcategory, of social function, 150, *151*
Tau-U, 103, *104*, 162, 172
Taylor, Jontè C., 159
teacher action research, *131*, 137–38, 141; limitations of, 139
teacher-centered tactics, of routines and rules, 149, 150, 152, 161
teachers: BSETs, 111–12; interfering behaviors impact on, 149; special education as scientific practitioners, 22–23
teacher-student relationship, for classroom behaviors, 149
TEACHING Exceptional Children, 27–28, 32, 39
Thorndike, Edward: concept of reinforcement, 6, 46; law of effect of, 8, 148
time-out, 149, 161
title: in educational research article, 34; in group research design, 71; in systematic literature review, 48
token economies, 155
training, in pre-experimental procedures, 167
transferability, 120, 133, 134
trend, in visual analysis, 100, *101*
triangulation, 115, *116*
Truman Commission on Higher Education (1947), 7
trustworthiness, 116, 120
t-Test, *65*, 67

university institutional access, for educational research articles, 32, 34

University of North Carolina, 123
unsystematic literature reviews, systematic literature reviews compared to, 46, 47
"The Use of Single-Subject Research to Identify Evidence-Based Practice in Special Education" (Horner), 96–97
"Using a Daily Report Card to Reduce Off-Task Behaviors for a Student with Autism Spectrum Disorder" (Riden, Taylor, Ruiz), in *JOBE*, 159; abstract in, 160; data analyses in, 171–73; discussion, 177–81; DVs, 166; experimental design, 166; experimental procedures, 169–71; intervention acceptability, 177; intervention elements, 180; introduction in, 161–64; IVs, 165–66; keywords in, 160; methods in, 164–73; participants and setting for, 164–65; pre-experimental procedures, 167–69; results, 173–77; in secondary schools, 163, 165

validation: enterprise, *231*, 234; information quality, *231*, 232–33; respondent, 115–16; results quality, *231*, 233–34
validity, 231; DBRC social, 173; external, 46, 96–97, 137; internal, 46, 96–97; nonacademic publications problems with, 25; social, 9–10, 96–97, 110, 173, 178–79; of systematic literature reviews, 54–55. *See also* product and curriculum validity assessment
variability, in visual analysis, 100, *101*
variance, *64*, 67
verification, 87, 96, 115
visual analysis, 173–76, *174*; for SBI, 208–9
visual analysis, of SCRD, 103; functional relation and, 102; immediacy of effect in, 100–101; level in, 99, *100*; overlap and, 102; trend in, 100, *101*; variability in, 100, *101*
visual schedules, as antecedent-based strategy, 152, *154*

Watson, John B., 147–48
Westat tool kit, 141
WestEd, on classroom management, 187
What Works Clearinghouse (WWC), 17, 80–81; group research design standards of, 75, 76, *76–77*; product and curriculum reviews and, 240; SBI and, 208; Single-Case Design Technical Documentation, 103
Wikipedia, 58
within-subject design, DV in, 62
With-It Teachers program, 237–39
working memory (WM), 192; SBI and, 199–204
WWC. *See* What Works Clearinghouse

YouTube, 39

Zombie Ideas in Education, 240

www.ingramcontent.com/pod-product-compliance
Lightning Source LLC
Chambersburg PA
CBHW021853230426
43671CB00006B/371